The Puzzle of Judicial Behavior

Analytical Perspectives on Politics

ADVISORY EDITORS:

John Aldrich, Duke University
Bruce Bueno de Mesquita, Hoover Institution and New York University
Robert Jackman, University of California, Davis
David Rohde, Michigan State University

Political Science is developing rapidly and changing markedly. Keeping in touch with new ideas across the discipline is a challenge for political scientists and for their students.

To help meet this challenge, the series Analytical Perspectives on Politics presents creative and sophisticated syntheses of major areas of research in the fields of political science. In each book, a high-caliber author provides a clear and discriminating description of the current state of the art and a strong-minded prescription and structure for future work in the field.

These distinctive books provide a compact review for political scientists, a helpful introduction for graduate students, and central reading for advanced undergraduate courses.

Robert W. Jackman, *Power without Force: The Political Capacity of Nation-States*

Linda L. Fowler, *Candidates, Congress, and the American Democracy*

Scott Gates and Brian D. Humes, *Games, Information, and Politics: Applying Game Theoretic Models to Political Science*

Lawrence Baum, *The Puzzle of Judicial Behavior*

Barbara Geddes, *Paradigms and Sand Castles: Theory Building and Research Design in Comparative Politics*

Rose McDermott, *Political Psychology in International Relations*

Ole R. Holsti, *Public Opinion and American Foreign Policy, Revised Edition*

The Puzzle of Judicial Behavior

LAWRENCE BAUM

Ann Arbor

THE UNIVERSITY OF MICHIGAN PRESS

Copyright © by the University of Michigan 1997
All rights reserved
Published in the United States of America by
The University of Michigan Press
Manufactured in the United States of America
♾ Printed on acid-free paper

2005   2004   6   5   4

No part of this publication may be reproduced, stored in a retrieval system, or transmitted in any form or by any means, electronic, mechanical, or otherwise, without the written permission of the publisher.

A CIP catalog record for this book is available from the British Library.

Library of Congress Cataloging-in-Publication Data

Baum, Lawrence.
    The puzzle of judicial behavior / Lawrence Baum.
        p.   cm. — (Analytical perspectives on politics)
    Includes bibliographical references and index.
    ISBN 0-472-08335-X (pbk. : acid-free paper). — ISBN 0-472-10670-8
(cloth : acid-free paper)
    1. Judicial process—United States.   2. Judicial power and
political questions—United States.   3. Judicial process—Social
aspects.   4. Judicial process—Psychological aspects.   I. Title.
II. Series.
KF8775.B38   1997
347.73'12—dc21   97-4870
                                                          CIP

To Carol

Contents

Preface

On June 29, 1992, I finally realized how little I understood about judicial behavior.

That realization had been a long time in coming. As a young student of the courts in the early 1970s, I thought I had a very good explanation of judicial behavior—or at least of Supreme Court behavior. Presidents appointed justices on the basis of their policy preferences, those justices then voted on cases in accord with their preferences, and the Court's decisions and doctrinal positions reflected the collective preferences of its members.

Events over the next two decades began to erode my confidence about understanding judicial behavior. One thing I knew in the early 1970s was that President Nixon's four appointments to the Supreme Court had produced a conservative Court. Had I been told that no Democratic president would appoint a new justice until 1993, I would have predicted a very sharp turn to the right. The Court did become more conservative, but its turn to the right was not nearly as decisive as I had expected. And the Court's unexpected path suggested the need for a more complicated explanation than the one I had maintained over the years.

In the Supreme Court shaped by Richard Nixon's appointments, one of the rulings that surprised me most was the 1973 decision in *Roe v. Wade.* But subsequent decisions on abortion were consistent with my understanding of the Court: as new Republican appointees came onto the Court, there was a decline in the number of justices who supported *Roe v. Wade.* By 1992, as the Court considered a case involving Pennsylvania's restrictions on abortion, the only question for me was whether the Court would overturn *Roe* in its decision or only weaken it further and leave the overturning for later.

On June 29, of course, the Court did neither. Rather, in *Planned Parenthood v. Casey,* it gave renewed support to most of what it had ruled in 1973. At that point I had no choice but to reconsider the way I thought about explanation of the Supreme

Court's behavior. And if I understood the Court so poorly, what about other courts for which I had never developed so simple an explanation? I was required to revisit old questions and try to think them through in new ways, a process that has continued since then.

By a happy coincidence, my quest had hardly begun when a new wave of scholarship on judicial behavior started to appear. In 1993 Jeffrey Segal and Harold Spaeth published *The Supreme Court and the Attitudinal Model,* a book that laid out one important explanation of judicial behavior more fully and more clearly than ever before. Reactions to that book helped to renew a long-standing debate over the relative importance of law and policy in judicial decisions. At about the same time, students of judicial behavior started to look more closely at strategic behavior by judges from a rational choice perspective, thereby initiating a debate over the extent to which judges act strategically.

Since then, scholars with a variety of perspectives and interests have been producing innovative research. Month after month, new papers and publications challenge existing conceptions of judicial behavior and offer new ways of thinking about that behavior. Even if the courts themselves had not jolted me out of my complacency, this new wave of scholarship would have done so. And it has provided me with a great deal of assistance in my effort to think through explanations of judicial behavior.

Even with all that assistance, I am still some distance from formulating a satisfactory theory of judicial behavior. I remain uncertain how to explain the Supreme Court's decision in *Casey,* let alone judges' decisions in general. But I have gained a clearer sense of the state of knowledge about judicial behavior, and that is the subject of this book: my goal is to assess what the relevant scholarship tells us about explanations for judicial behavior.

I use a framework centered on judges' goals as a way to think about the explanation of judicial behavior. Within that framework the book focuses on three major issues: the relative importance of judges' concern with the content of legal policy and other goals such as limited work loads and continued tenure in office; the balance between judges' interest in good law and their interest in good policy; and the extent to which judges act strategically to carry out their policy goals. These issues encompass the preponderance of the research on judicial behavior and the major controversies in the field today. On each issue I consider the theoretical questions involved and examine the stock of empirical evidence, discussing its implications for the validity of competing explanations.

One theme of the book, perhaps the central theme, is that we are a long way from achieving explanations of judicial behavior that are fully satisfactory. My standard for good explanations is high, but I think that most other standards would lead to a similar conclusion. In any case, if progress toward good explanations of judicial behavior has been limited, the primary reason is not scholarly deficiencies. Whatever those deficiencies may be, they are far less important in limiting knowledge than is the inherent difficulty of explaining human behavior. Students of judicial behavior are hardly unique in their lack of fully satisfying explanations of the phenomena they study.

Within the unavoidable limits on success in explanation, it is possible for scholars to advance the state of knowledge a great deal. The new wave of scholarship on judicial behavior has brought about very substantial advances, in part because of its diversity. In the book I argue that diversity facilitates progress toward good explanations of judicial behavior and that the field needs to maintain and enhance that diversity. I give particular emphasis to diversity in theoretical approaches: scholars can profit by using both economic and psychological perspectives to analyze judicial behavior.

It is a little presumptuous for anyone to assess the state of knowledge in a field of inquiry, because all scholars hold assumptions and biases that narrow their fields of vision. What I can offer is one person's perception of what we know and do not know about judicial behavior. My hope is that presentation of this perception will contribute to the process of moving toward better explanations.

Acknowledgments

In writing this book I accumulated more than the usual number of debts to professional colleagues. First of all, a number of scholars provided very useful ideas and suggestions that helped me in the project. I appreciate the comments on draft chapters of the book and on related papers and presentations by James Brudney, Daniel Chow, John Geer, David Goldberger, Timothy Hagle, Roger Handberg, Wayne McIntosh, Deborah Merritt, Thomas Nelson, Joseph Sanders, Donald Sylvan, Herbert Weisberg, and Lawrence Wrightsman. I learned important things about relevant bodies of social science theory from conversations with Margaret Hermann, Dean Lacy, and Huib Pellikaan. Elliot Slotnick read several chapters of a draft of the book and gave me very helpful comments. And the book reflects what I have learned over the years from Elliot and Greg Caldeira, my Ohio State colleagues in judicial politics.

Lee Epstein and Jeffrey Segal gave me very good advice on drafts of chapters, as did Saul Brenner and Harold Spaeth on a full draft of the book. But I have benefited just as much from my conversations and correspondence with these four colleagues over the years about the issues discussed in the book. And in considerable part, the book is a response to the innovative and thought-provoking research that each of these scholars has done.

The book's completion would have come much later without the year's leave of absence that I was granted by Ohio State University. I appreciate the assistance of Paul Beck, the political science chair, and Randall Ripley, former chair and now dean of the College of Social and Behavioral Sciences, in making that leave possible. I also appreciate the good working environment that they have helped to create over the years. The Center for Socio-Legal Studies at the Ohio State College of Law provided me with an office during the leave year, thus facilitating both my research and my writing for the book. I am grateful to Dean Gregory Williams and Professor Barbara Snyder, director of the Center, for that assistance.

Karen Swenson assisted me in an important way early in the writing process by collecting and analyzing relevant scholarship on judicial behavior. I appreciate that help.

The good work of the staff at University of Michigan Press benefited me a great deal. I am particularly grateful to Malcolm Litchfield, who encouraged me to develop this project and helped to shape it into a book, and to Charles Myers, who did much to facilitate the book's improvement and completion.

I owe the greatest debts to two people. Over the last several years, discussions with David Klein have sharpened my thinking about difficult issues in judicial behavior. Dave also gave me careful and insightful comments on two drafts of the book. Those discussions and comments have made a great deal of difference for the book.

Carol Mock offered very helpful comments on drafts of the book. More important, she did a great deal to help me recognize and think through theoretical and methodological issues that are discussed in the book. It would have been very difficult to take on this project without that help.

It is more important than usual to absolve all these people of responsibility for remaining limitations in the book. In addressing a subject of this broad scope, it is impossible to take all the relevant scholarship fully and properly into account or to address adequately all facets of the issues that are considered. Whatever may be the book's deficiencies, however, they are far more limited than they would have been without the extraordinary assistance that I have received. I am very grateful for that assistance.

CHAPTER 1

General Perspectives

Harold Baer, a federal district judge in New York City, ruled that the cocaine seized from a car was inadmissible as evidence against a criminal defendant. The decision and Baer himself were attacked by everyone from editorial writers to the president. Though he was protected by a life term, Baer retreated and reversed his decision (Goshko and Reckler 1996). James Heiple, a justice on the Illinois Supreme Court, wrote his court's opinion in a child custody dispute. The decision aroused strong opposition: a Chicago newspaper columnist attacked Heiple and the court in a number of columns, and the state legislature and governor tried to undo the decision. Potentially vulnerable to defeat in a retention election, Heiple nonetheless adhered to his position in the case after a rehearing and wrote an opinion lashing out at his critics (*Petition of Doe* 1994).

Felix Frankfurter and William O. Douglas were among the most brilliant people to sit on the Supreme Court, yet neither had great influence on his colleagues. Frankfurter expected to be a leader of the Court, but instead he alienated several other justices (Hirsch 1981). Douglas seemed to be ambivalent about trying to win support from his colleagues, and he ultimately occupied a peripheral position on the Court (J. Simon 1990). William Brennan did not have a reputation for brilliance, but he achieved an extraordinary degree of influence over the Court's collective choices (Eisler 1993).

Judges dislike reversal of their decisions by higher courts, and they often exert considerable effort to avoid reversal. But a federal district judge in Alabama virtually demanded reversal by declaring that the Supreme Court was wrong in its constitutional position on school religious observances (*Jaffree v. Board of School Commissioners* 1983). And over several years, the federal court of appeals for the Ninth Circuit on the West Coast suffered an unusual number of reversals because its judges adopted doctrinal positions that conflicted with the Supreme Court's conservative leanings (Maher 1985; Bishop 1992).

Political scientists who study courts examine the behavior of people in many roles. Among the subjects of their research are individuals who consider whether to file lawsuits and administrators who respond to court decisions. But the primary concern of their work is judges, and the issue that they study the most is explanation of judicial behavior.

In part, this intense interest in judicial behavior simply reflects the importance of judges. Another reason for this interest is that questions about judicial behavior are both difficult and intriguing; for instance, when do judges yield to outside pressures, what determines their influence within a court, under what conditions do they work hardest to avoid appellate reversal? Judicial behavior presents a complex puzzle, and generations of scholars have found it satisfying to work on that puzzle.

This book is an assessment of progress toward explanation of judicial behavior. I think this is a particularly good time for such an assessment. We are now in a period of great achievement in research on judicial behavior, one in which scholars are doing much to illuminate major issues. Both the findings that result from this new wave of research and its innovative approaches to the analysis of judicial behavior merit careful consideration.

At the outset, I should be explicit about the behavior to be explained. The book deals solely with judges in the United States. That restriction reflects the concentration of scholarship on the United States as well as a need to keep the book's scope manageable. In other respects its scope is broad, encompassing all judges who serve in the judicial branch and thus all courts.

The term *judicial behavior* refers to what judges do as judges, leaving aside other activities such as speech making and presidential advising. Antonin Scalia's off-the-bench statements about his religious views may provide insights on the sources of some of his doctrinal positions (Biskupic 1996), and Abe Fortas's consultation with President Johnson may have affected what he did on the Court (Kalman 1990), so both should be taken into account. But I am not concerned with explanation of these types of "nonjudicial" behavior in themselves.

The most consequential forms of judicial behavior typically consist of decisions or contributions to decisions. Decisional behavior can be defined broadly to include preliminary actions such as setting bail and determining whether to hold oral argument in a case. In final decisions it includes both the determination of outcomes for the litigants and the pronouncement of legal doctrine. Some kinds of behavior that might not be considered decision making, such as presiding over trials and interacting with colleagues, also constitute judicial behavior.

Four themes are central to the book. First, I begin with the premise that full explanation goes well beyond successful prediction, that it reaches fundamental sources of behavior. Thus I think that it is necessary to set a high standard for explanation of judicial behavior.

Second, I conclude that even by a more lenient standard, our progress toward explanation of judicial behavior has been limited: what we do not know stands out more than what we do know. Research has told us a good deal about the sources of judicial behavior, but the major issues in the field remain unresolved. That lack of resolution is obvious on issues that are the subject of active debate among scholars. It is less obvious but also true of issues on which there is a degree of consensus.

Third, I believe that this limited progress results only in small part from weaknesses of research in the field and that its primary source is inherent difficulties of explanation. Certainly there are theoretical and methodological shortcomings in the scholarship on judicial behavior, and those shortcomings have an impact on the state of knowledge. But that impact is overshadowed by the fundamental problems involved in explaining the behavior of any set of people, problems that bedevil scholars in every field.

Largely because of this belief about the difficulty of explanation, the book is written as an assessment of the state of knowledge about judicial behavior rather than as a critique of the scholarly research on that behavior. Certainly such critiques are useful, but even research that met the highest standards would still confront the difficulty of explaining judges' choices. For that reason, it is less useful for my purposes to measure scholars' work against those standards than to consider more broadly what it does and does not establish.

Finally, I argue that progress toward greater knowledge will come most quickly if research is diverse—in theory, in method of inquiry, and in subject matter. Like other scholarly pursuits, the study of judicial behavior has always had participants who believe that all research should follow a particular mode. Such beliefs are understandable, but I think they are mistaken: the difficulties of explanation can be attacked most successfully by research that takes differing approaches and forms.

Consistent with this last theme, the book does not advocate a particular theory of judicial behavior or a particular approach to its analysis. If there is a single best way of studying judicial behavior, I do not know what it is. Even if I thought I knew that way, I would hesitate to champion it, because I think that the field profits from a lack of consensus about what to study and how to study it. Thus I limit myself to suggesting some directions for research that I see as useful.

The five chapters of the book fall into three parts. First, this chapter addresses some introductory matters. I begin by discussing my perspective on explanation, taking up the book's first theme on the requisites of full explanation. The following section discusses the task of assessing the state of knowledge on a matter such as judicial behavior. The final section lays out a framework for consideration of the issues in the field, one centered on the goals that judges hold and seek to advance.

The next three chapters use this framework to consider three major issues in the explanation of judicial behavior. In these chapters I bring out the book's second theme, our limited progress in explanation. The issue for chapter 2 is the relative importance of judges' concern with the content of legal policy[1] and of other kinds of goals such as maintaining their positions or minimizing their work loads. Insofar as judges are concerned with the content of legal policy, the most contentious issue in the field has been the balance between their interest in good law and their interest in good policy. That issue is the subject of chapter 3. In chapter 4 I turn to the question of how judges seek to advance their goals, specifically to another issue that has become increasingly important: to what extent do policy-oriented judges act strategically[2] to achieve good policy?

Chapter 5 pulls together the implications of the analyses in chapters 2 through 4. I begin by summarizing what I see as the field's limited progress in explanation. I then turn to the third theme, the inherent difficulties of explaining political behavior. The remainder of the chapter focuses on the final theme, the one

---

1. As I use them, the terms *content of legal policy* and *legal policy* refer to the substance of a court's decisions and, in some contexts, the decisions that other institutions make on the same issues. As discussed later in the chapter, a judge who is motivated by an interest in legal policy cares about the substance of decisions for their own sake, whether as law or as public policy.

2. The meaning of strategic behavior is discussed in chapter 4. In general terms, following the definition used in that chapter, strategic judges do not simply take positions consistent with their preferences. Rather, in voting and other contexts they act in ways intended to bring about collective results that advance their preferred positions.

with the most direct implications for future research: the value of diversity in the study of judicial behavior.

A Perspective on Explanation

Richard Braithwaite (1953, 348–49) wrote that "an explanation . . . is an answer to a 'Why?' question which gives some intellectual satisfaction." I agree with that definition, one that allows for the whole range of scholarly approaches to explanation (E. Nagel 1961; C. Taylor 1964; Elster 1983a; Salmon 1990).

The book's first theme does indicate an important preference: I believe that full explanation goes beyond successful prediction to identify the fundamental sources of behavior. That belief is not universal. One important body of thought closely equates explanation and prediction (Hempel and Oppenheim 1948). That equation is widely accepted among economists and other social scientists whose scholarship reflects an economic perspective (M. Friedman 1953). In the study of courts, as in other fields of political science, it is common for scholars implicitly to treat predictive success as equivalent to good explanation. That position was made explicit in work by two leading students of judicial behavior (Schubert 1963b; Spaeth 1979, 140).

I disagree with the equation of explanation and prediction on two grounds (see Elster 1989, 8–10). First, I do not think that predictive accuracy is a requisite to good explanation. In Braithwaite's terms, not all satisfying answers to "why" questions take a form suitable for successful prediction. Stephen Jay Gould (1989) argued in his account of the evolution of species that even with a full comprehension of the laws that drive the world, we may not be able to predict the course of events in the long term. The source of the inability to predict, in his view, is contingencies in the operation of those laws.

I find Gould convincing on this point. To take an example of slightly lesser import than the existence of our species, scholars who fully understood the forces driving Supreme Court policy could not necessarily have predicted the emergence of the Warren Court (Baum 1992). Yet an understanding of those forces would provide the basis for a very good explanation of the Court's collective behavior.

Second, explanations that produce high predictive accuracy in the short term or in a limited sense are not always satisfying (Kavka 1991, 381). For one thing, such explanations may be incomplete. In his book *Judicial Behavior* (1964a), as elsewhere, Glendon Schubert argued for the centrality of prediction to science (4). But he also pointed out that "even if we could complete a perfect description *and prediction* of judicial decision-making on the basis of individual judicial attitudes, we still would be left with the question: what explains judicial attitudes?" (446; emphasis in original). We would also be left with a second question: what accounts for the dominance of judicial attitudes as the basis for judicial behavior?

Another reason not to be fully satisfied with predictive accuracy is the theoretical ambiguity of behavior. One student of Congress (Ferejohn 1995, ix) noted that "[v]ery different theories of legislatures can have quite similar observational consequences in a wide range of settings." In doing so he pointed to a broader truth: patterns of behavior in a particular setting often are basically consistent with many different explanations. To accept an explanation on the basis of predictive success and thus to terminate the search for other explanations may be myopic.

The book reflects my views about criteria for good explanation in two ways. First, I look for alternative explanations even when a particular explanation seems to account for a pattern of behavior fairly well. One result is that in chapters 2 through 4, I emphasize readings of empirical evidence that depart from the most widely accepted interpretations of that evidence. Second, I favor explanations that get as close as possible to the fundamental sources of behavior. If the policies of a particular court track trends in public opinion, does that relationship reflect judges' interest in following public opinion rather than some other mechanism? And if judges seek to follow public opinion, why?

Two other issues concerning explanation should be considered. One is the trade-off between comprehensiveness and coherence. The question is whether scholars should prefer explanations that account for more behavior at the cost of greater complexity.

My general preference is for coherence. Relatively simple models that account for a large share of the behavior in question have one of the qualities that make explanations satisfying, that give them "beauty" (Lave and March 1975, 61–64). Their beauty lies largely in their clarity.

Clarity is a hallmark of a widely accepted explanation of judicial behavior, the "attitudinal" model in which the behavior of Supreme Court justices in some contexts directly reflects their attitudes toward policy issues. The same quality characterizes the increasingly prominent rational choice models of judging, models that posit strategic behavior by judges on behalf of their policy goals or other ends. Largely because of their coherence, both types of explanation have proved valuable in the understanding of judicial behavior.

Despite my preference for coherence, the book gives greater emphasis to comprehensiveness. If knowledge is to grow further, it is important to identify the gaps in existing explanations. One benefit of the clarity in attitudinal and rational choice models of judicial behavior is that it helps in identifying their limitations and thus assists in further development of explanations; I want to take advantage of that benefit. This aspect of my approach, like my interest in probing alternative and deeper explanations, exacts a cost from readers: the discussions of various issues will be more complicated than they might be. I think, however, that this cost is justified.

A final issue in explanation concerns the level of analysis. Judges make their choices within groups. Even trial judges, who usually decide cases as individuals, interact with attorneys and other people in courtroom "workgroups" (Eisenstein and Jacob 1977) or "courthouse communities" (Nardulli, Eisenstein, and Flemming 1988). Of course, appellate judges typically reach collective decisions within groups of three or more.

In such situations, analysis could focus either on the individual or on the group. Psychologists and economists typically prefer individual-level analysis, while sociologists give emphasis to groups as well as individuals (Alexander, Giesen, Münch, and Smelser 1987). Students of judicial behavior generally focus on individual judges, building explanations of collective choices from the individual level.

My own appraisal of issues in the field is primarily at the individual level. In part, this choice simply reflects the orientation of research in the field. It also stems from the relative ease of analyzing behavior at the individual level, though this advantage should not be exaggerated (Mock 1988).

But group elements of behavior cannot be ignored, because the choices of individual judges are affected by their membership in larger decision-making groups. Explanations of Supreme Court behavior that treat the justices basically as isolated individuals can be quite useful. But no complete explanation of the justices' behavior could leave aside their interactions with colleagues on the Court.

Also important is the aggregation of individual choices into group decisions. Scholars with an economic perspective have told us a good deal about this aggregation process in general (Sen 1970; T. Schwartz 1987) and, increasingly, about its impact on court decisions (Rogers 1990–91; Kornhauser and Sager 1993). Because my concern is with judges' behavior rather than with court decisions, the book considers these processes only to the extent that judges themselves take them into account. An example is the Supreme Court's requirement of four positive votes to accept a case for decision on the merits (see B. Palmer 1995). The "rule of four" helps determine which cases the Court accepts, and in itself that effect is beyond the scope of the book's concerns. However, a justice may take this effect into account in voting whether to hear a case, and *that* consequence of the rule must be considered.

Assessing What We Know

Scholars often undertake "reviews of the literature" with little explicit consideration of methods for weighing and aggregating empirical findings. But some scholars have thought systematically about how to assess the state of knowledge on an issue (Light and Pillemer 1984), and they have underlined the need to consider methods of assessment. Their work and other scholarship also point to characteristics of published research that complicate the task of assessment.

One relevant characteristic of research is obvious: it is imperfect. In quantitative analysis, models are underspecified, indicators measure variables only in part, and statistical methods do not fully match analytic tasks.[3] While the extent of these imperfections may differ from one field of research to another, the critical point is that no field is immune to them.

A second characteristic is the role of interpretation in the research process. Kritzer (1996) showed with particular clarity that interpretation is as integral to quantitative analysis as it is to qualitative research (see also Leamer 1978). Data do not announce their own implications; rather, what scholars infer from their data is based on their own management and reading of those data.

Readers of research reports may have great difficulty in discerning imperfections in research and ambiguities of interpretation. For one thing, the authors of studies often are unaware of

---

3. In this section I focus on quantitative research, but analogous processes and problems exist in qualitative research (Kirk and Miller 1986; G. King, Keohane, and Verba 1994).

them (see Mock and Weisberg 1992). Just as important, the requisites of publication reduce the likelihood that imperfections and ambiguities will be disclosed. Of course, authors prefer to highlight the strengths of their work and to minimize or even ignore its shortcomings; articles that dwell on the weakness of their methods or the fragility of their findings are not abundant. Similarly, to describe the complicated process of interpretation that preceded the analysis presented in a paper would detract from the crispness of presentation and might raise doubts about the robustness of findings. Further, the preference of editors and reviewers for statistically significant findings leads to the "file-drawer problem" in which nonsignificant results tend to remain in researchers' offices and the results actually reported in published studies of an issue are unrepresentative (R. Rosenthal 1979; M. Smith 1980; Dickersin et al. 1987).[4]

How should a reviewer take into account the imperfections and ambiguities of empirical research, particularly those that cannot readily be discerned? One possible stance is general suspicion of empirical research: "Hardly anyone takes data analyses seriously. Or perhaps more accurately, hardly anyone takes anyone else's data analyses seriously" (Leamer 1983, 37).[5] A variant is the position of skeptical Bayesians, who give little weight to findings that diverge from their prior expectations (see Bergmann 1987, 192). But blanket suspicion seems unjustified, and skeptical Bayesians may cling to their own prior beliefs more than is appropriate (Nisbett and Ross 1980).

An alternative approach is simply to accept the validity of empirical findings, on the assumption that they are more accurate than inaccurate and with the hope that one study of an issue will correct for the weaknesses of another. This is a common approach in practice, but it underestimates the impact of the imperfections and ambiguities I have discussed. Further, it probably assumes a greater degree of self-correction in scholarly fields than actually

---

4. On this preference, see Greenwald 1975 and Coursol and Wagner 1986. One scholar (Feige 1975) actually estimated the monetary payoff in lifetime salary of producing statistically significant results in a journal submission. On the impact of this preference on research, see Selvin and Stuart 1966; Mayer 1975; David Freedman 1983; and Mock and Weisberg 1992.

5. This quotation is from an article entitled "Let's Take the Con out of Econometrics." The article is part of a small body of provocative literature on problems in the research and publication processes. Other titles in this literature include "Data Mining" (Lovell 1983), "Are All Economic Hypotheses False?" (De Long and Lang 1992), and "Econometrics—Alchemy or Science?" (Hendry 1980) (see also Leamer 1974; Bergmann 1987). As the titles indicate, economists have contributed heavily and enthusiastically to this literature.

exists—at least in fields such as judicial politics, where research is scattered across a large domain. The difficulty of the reviewer's task is compounded by the need to aggregate the findings of different studies. How should contradictory findings be reconciled, and how should one's varying degrees of confidence in differing studies be taken into account? Scholars have developed techniques for combining and analyzing findings on an issue under the rubric of *meta-analysis* (Hedges and Olkin 1985; R. Rosenthal 1991). In the process, judgments about the differential quality of studies can be taken into account. It is even possible to take into account the bias favoring statistical significance, allowing the reviewer to estimate the magnitude of the file-drawer problem and to correct for its impact (Iyengar and Greenhouse 1988).

I can describe my own stance in light of this background. I think there is good reason for a degree of skepticism in reading the findings of published studies. But this hardly means that empirical findings should be dismissed altogether. Nor does it mean that all studies should be given equal weight. If it is impossible to assess any study with complete confidence, there is often good reason to accord more weight to one than to another.

The more studies of an issue, the better. No single study, no matter how skillfully it is carried out, should be regarded as the definitive treatment of a question. Similar findings from multiple studies can be accorded more confidence. However, studies based on the same theoretical orientations, types of data, and analytic strategies tend to share the same limitations. Where studies differ in these respects, they are far more likely to compensate for each other's limitations.

In considering the empirical evidence on various issues, I do not use the formal techniques of meta-analysis. One reason is that in the explanation of judicial behavior, there usually is too small a body of findings on a particular question to make those techniques applicable. Further, findings often are presented in forms that are not amenable to meta-analysis.

More important, my primary concern is not with empirical findings in themselves but with their broader theoretical implications, a quite different matter that is beyond the scope of meta-analysis (R. Rosenthal 1991, 13).[6] Of course, this is an enterprise

---

6. Like any other reviewer, of course, I need to consider the findings of single and multiple studies in their own terms. In this task, the insights of scholars concerned with reviewing research, including those who undertake meta-analysis, are helpful.

that necessarily involves a good deal of subjectivity. I am confident that readers will bring to my assessments the skepticism that is appropriate for anyone with the temerity to assess the results of a large body of scholarly research.[7]

A Framework for Analysis

Assessment of a body of knowledge is facilitated by an explicit framework of analysis. The framework that I use in this book is built around the concept of goals, the ends that people seek to realize (Pervin 1983, 10).[8]

I chose a goal-based framework for two reasons. First, it encompasses rather well the major issues in the scholarship on judicial behavior. Research on judicial behavior most often is framed as an effort to identify the determinants of judges' choices (see Gibson 1983). But underlying the specific determinants that scholars consider are questions—usually implicit—about what judges seek to achieve and how they go about trying to achieve it. If caseload pressures affect actions by trial judges, if the Supreme Court responds favorably to the federal government as a litigant, that behavior can be traced back to judges' goals. Moreover, some of the most significant research on judicial behavior has begun with explicit premises about the identity of judges' goals and then examined the relationship between goals and decisional behavior (W. Murphy 1964; Rohde and Spaeth 1976; Segal and Spaeth 1993). Indeed, the link between goals and action is central to rational choice analysis of judicial behavior.

The second reason for use of a goal-based framework is its analytic value. Such a framework requires systematic consideration of what people are trying to accomplish and directs attention to the processes that determine their goal orientations. Further, it leads to examination of the ways that goals are put into action and

---

7. In any case, readers have available to them other assessments of the state of knowledge about judicial behavior. Gibson 1983 provided an extensive and insightful analysis of the judicial behavior research. More recently, Jacob 1991 and Gibson 1991 analyzed the research on judicial behavior in trial and appellate courts, respectively. For broader analyses of scholarship on judicial politics, see Pritchett 1968, 1969; Grossman and Tanenhaus 1969; Murphy and Tanenhaus 1972; Sheldon 1974; Baum 1983; Gibson 1986; Slotnick 1991; Gates and Johnson 1991; Shapiro 1993; and Hensley and Kuersten 1995.

8. Goals are related to motives and incentives (Loomis 1994, 343–44). I think that the concept of goals is particularly useful for purposes of the book, but that is not a strong preference, and I sometimes use the terms *motives* and *motivations* as synonyms for goals.

thus of the processes through which people make choices. Because of these virtues, explanations of behavior based on the goals of legislators have proved quite useful (Fenno 1973; Mayhew 1974; J. Hansen 1991; Parker 1992; see Rieselbach 1992; Loomis 1994; Shepsle and Weingast 1995). The same is true of goal-based analyses of judges (W. Murphy 1964; Rohde and Spaeth 1976; Toma 1991; Mark Cohen 1992; Ferejohn and Weingast 1992b; Segal and Spaeth 1993).

A framework that begins with individual goals represents a particular approach to explanation (see E. Nagel 1961; Boden 1972). Explanations built on goals carry with them the assumption that the behavior in question is goal-oriented to at least a significant degree. Some scholars have expressed doubts about the centrality of goals to human behavior, either in certain contexts or more generally (Michael Cohen, March, and Olsen, 1972; Eckstein 1991; Johnston 1991; see Rowland and Carp 1996, 158).

The doubts that these scholars express are quite important. But it should be underlined how little a goal-based framework requires in assumptions about human behavior. Such a framework can be used so long as we assume that people do have goals and that they make efforts to advance those goals.[9] Those assumptions would be accepted by at least some scholars who question the centrality of goals to behavior. Their concerns are largely about people's capacities to act in ways that advance their goals, questions that can be addressed within a goal-based framework. Thus most psychologists doubt that individuals can consistently identify the actions that would maximize achievement of their goals, but psychologists often treat goals as important or even central to behavior (Graham, Argyle, and Furnham 1980; Ajzen 1985; Frese and Sabini 1985; Pervin 1989; Fiske 1993). Indeed, psychologists have contributed much to an understanding of the complexities of goal-based behavior (e.g., Pervin 1983).

---

9. There is disagreement about whether goal-directed behavior must be conscious or intentional (G. Becker 1976, 7; Posner 1986, 3–4; Lewis 1990; Bargh 1990; Bohman 1992, 216–17). I think it makes sense to treat as goal-directed not only those actions that are quite consciously aimed at particular goals but also actions taken "semiconsciously" in furtherance of such goals. Much of what judges do to enhance their standing with people who are important to them can be considered semiconscious. Judges may do various things to win the favor of legal scholars, for instance, without fully recognizing that this is what they are trying to accomplish. The same might be said of judges' efforts to advance their policy goals. It is likely that some judges act on their policy preferences without fully recognizing that basis for their choices; this is one implication of the theory of motivated reasoning, discussed in chapter 3 (see Rowland and Carp 1996, 164–69). It would be unduly restrictive, I think, not to treat such behavior as goal-directed.

In any case, I do not argue that goals are the only lens through which judicial behavior can be analyzed effectively. Such an argument would run contrary to both my view that behavior can be explained in many ways and my emphasis on the value of diversity in research. And the goal-based framework used in this book is sufficiently open that readers who prefer different frameworks or perspectives should find it easy to put the book's discussions of judicial behavior research in those other terms.

One other proviso is appropriate. Although most research on judicial behavior fits comfortably within the book's framework, by no means is all that research directly concerned with identification of judges' goals and their impact on judicial behavior. It would be pointless to evaluate a body of scholarship on the basis of what it tells us about judges' goals when much of that scholarship has a quite different purpose. Rather, the task is to assess the state of knowledge on judicial behavior from the vantage point of goals.

The Framework

Figure 1.1 depicts the book's general framework. The first column reflects the truism that individuals have sets of goals that they would like to achieve, what may be called *inherent* goals. Different people have different inherent goal orientations: sets of goals and priorities among them. In turn, these orientations reflect all the influences that shape individuals.[10]

Recruitment processes bring a sample of the general population to courts and smaller samples to specific levels and types of courts. Thus the set of judges who serve on all courts and those subsets who sit on particular courts have their own mixes of goal orientations. While those orientations might be representative of the population as a whole, recruitment processes almost certainly are selective in this respect (as they are in others). Judges as a single group are unrepresentative of the general population, and subsets of judges may differ from each other. We would not necessarily

10. Scholars disagree about the need to investigate the sources of people's goals and the processes that determine them (H. Simon 1983, 14; Schwarz and Thompson 1990, 49–51; Bohman 1991, 69). I think that a full comprehension of people's behavior requires an understanding of these sources and processes. However, I address this set of issues only in some limited ways. One reason is theoretical: if there is a wide range of goal orientations in the general population, the determinants of this range of orientations are less important than the processes that bring one mix of orientations to the courts rather than another. The other reason is that this is a matter that the scholarship on judicial behavior barely touches.

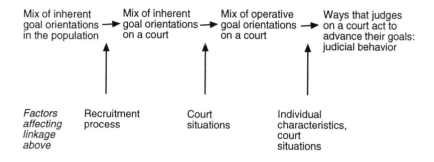

Fig. 1.1. A framework for analysis of judicial behavior. (Terminology is explained in the text.)

expect those judges who sit on municipal courts and those on federal courts of appeals to have the same mixes of goal orientations.

Of the various inherent goals that individual judges hold, some may be irrelevant to their work as judges. Further, the relative importance of those that are relevant may differ between the judicial arena and a judge's life as a whole. The sets of goals that actually affect the judicial behavior of judges can be termed *operative,* and judges' operative goal orientations are based on that set of goals and their relative importance to judges in the judicial arena.

The translation of inherent into operative goal orientations is a product of the court situations in which judges work. By *situation* I mean both the institutional arrangements emphasized by rational choice theorists (e.g., Shepsle 1979; Krehbiel 1987) and any other characteristics of courts in general, or of particular courts, that affect the relevance of judges' goals.[11] Richard Epstein (1990) argued that characteristics of the judiciary as a whole render a wide range of self-interested motives irrelevant to the decision process. In contrast,

> Whenever judges appear at conferences, serve on committees, teach in law schools, or sit on boards, they act pretty much the way the rest of us do, because they no longer labor under the distinctive set of incentives that apply to their case work. (R. Epstein 1990, 844)

---

11. This usage of the term *situation* is common in psychological research (e.g., L. Ross and Nisbett 1991; Fiske and Taylor 1991, 5). For the most part judges' situations are exogenous, beyond their control, but judges sometimes can shape their own situations. One example is the Supreme Court's successful lobbying over time for increased control over its jurisdiction, control that transformed the Court as an institution.

Whether or not one agrees with Epstein's conclusion, it underlines the distinction between inherent and operative goals. Characteristics of courts such as length of tenure in office, extent of review by higher courts, and control over the agenda influence how inherent goal orientations translate into operative orientations.

The final linkage is from operative goals to judicial behavior. How judges act on their goals and how well their actions serve those goals depend in part on their characteristics as individuals. For instance, the effort that judges devote to persuasion of colleagues reflects their level of comfort with that kind of personal interaction, and the success of such efforts depends in part on judges' ability to identify and carry out effective means of persuasion.

Characteristics of court situations also affect this linkage. Supreme Court chief justice John Marshall (1801–35) had an excellent opportunity to use his persuasive skills on colleagues with whom he lived during court sittings (Beveridge 1919, 86–88), and this opportunity undoubtedly encouraged him to employ those skills on behalf of his policy goals. He would have been in a far weaker position as chief judge of a court whose members come together occasionally and in constantly shifting panels, like some current federal courts of appeals. Other characteristics of a court such as the volume and composition of its agenda may also affect the ways that judges act on their goals.

A judge's goals and means of carrying them out might change over time. While some scholars argue that individual goals are highly stable (Stigler and Becker 1977), others emphasize the possibility of change (von Weizsäcker 1971; R. Frank 1987; R. Smith 1988). Even change in the specific content of judges' goals, such as their policy preferences, may have considerable effect on their choices (see S. Ulmer 1973a; Segal 1985; L. Epstein et al. 1995). A judge's experience in the job or modification of a judge's situation may bring about change of a more fundamental sort, in the relative importance of different goals (see Alpert, Atkins, and Ziller 1979). A trial judge who struggles with a flood of cases may come to care less about interpreting the law well and more about coping with the work load.[12] Similarly, judges might change the ways in which they put their goals in practice. Learning from colleagues, an appellate judge may become increasingly strategic in acting on a set of policy goals. Even if stability of goals and means is the general rule, change cannot be ignored.

---

12. Dodd's (1986) discussion of congressional careers suggests the possibility that judges' goal orientations might evolve in a systematic way during their careers on the bench.

The Goals

But what are the goals that judges might hold and act on? Goals may be conceptualized at different levels of abstraction and proximity to judges' choices. We might conceive of goals in terms of the fundamental needs and motives identified by psychologists and other scholars (Murray 1938; J. Atkinson 1958; Maslow 1970; Winter 1973). Some typologies of such needs and motives have been applied in useful ways to public officials (Barber 1965; Payne and Woshinsky 1972; Payne et al. 1984; Hermann 1988), including judges (Caldeira 1977; Sarat 1977; Aliotta 1988). In contrast, scholars often identify quite concrete goals for public officials, goals that are fairly proximate to the specific choices they face (W. Murphy 1964; Mayhew 1974; Niskanen 1994).

For analysis of behavior within a goal-based framework, it is useful to focus primarily on goals that are at least moderately concrete and proximate.[13] Table 1.1 presents a typology of such goals that might be operative in judges' behavior as judges. The typology is neither comprehensive nor theoretically coherent. Rather, it is intended to set out a broad range of goals to consider in thinking about judicial behavior. The labels for specific goals and categories of goals in the table generally are used in the chapters that follow.

The various goals listed in the table are not entirely distinct from each other. For judges, as for other people, different goals often are linked as ends and means (see Boden 1972, 158–89). For instance, a judge may seek popularity in the community as a means to maximize the chances of re-election. In turn, interest in re-election may stem from an interest in maintaining the income of a judgeship. It would not be difficult to construct a variety of similar chains among goals listed in the table. These chains may extend to very distal and nonconcrete goals such as self-esteem (see Beach 1985, 124). (I use the term *distal* to mean nonproximate.)

The existence of these chains complicates analysis of judges' goal orientations. Most students of judicial behavior have minimized these complications by focusing on the goals that are most directly connected with judges' behavior and ignoring those that underlie these proximate goals. This approach is a reasonable one, because the most proximate goals often provide a quite sufficient

---

13. As discussed later in this section, however, more abstract and distal goals sometimes should be taken into account. The role of such goals in law- and policy-oriented behavior is considered in chapters 3 and 4.

TABLE 1.1.   A Partial Typology of Possible Goals for Judges

I. *Content of Legal Policy*
    Accurate interpretation of the law ("legal accuracy")
    Clear and consistent interpretation of the law ("legal clarity")
    Good policy as gauged by the judge's policy preferences ("good policy")

II. *Personal Standing with Court Audiences*
    Popularity and respect in the legal community
    Popularity and respect in the community as a whole
    Power outside the court

III. *Career*
    Continued tenure in the current judicial position
    Promotion to a higher court
    Securing attractive nonjudicial positions

IV. *Life on the Court*
    Good relations with other judges and with participants in the courts who have
        other positions
    Power within the court
    Limited work loads
    Court resources

V. *Standard of Living*
    Personal income
    Personal comfort

basis for analysis.[14] We may learn what we want to know about a trial judge by determining that the judge's highest priority is popularity in the community without identifying the deeper motivational bases for this priority.

Yet more distal goals may be critical to judges' behavior. The judge who seeks popularity in order to win re-election and ultimately to maintain a good income may behave in a way that is most consistent with the last goal. If a four-year term is converted into a life term, the judge's decisions might no longer reflect public opinion. If the judge perceives a good opportunity to achieve a higher-paying position in corporate law, the judge's decisions might now be aimed at pleasing the business community rather than the general public. In such circumstances, analysis that focused only on the interest in community approval would be incomplete. To take a different kind of example, whether judges act on their policy goals sincerely or strategically may depend on

14. Focusing on proximate goals also avoids the prospect of what Riker (1995, 40) called "infinite regress."

the more fundamental motivations that underlie the policy goals. For that reason, analysis of goal-oriented behavior sometimes must extend to such motivations.

Links between goals can go in multiple directions. If judges care solely about good policy, and if they act strategically to achieve it, other goals that may appear to be proximate to judges' choices (such as popularity in the community and good relations with colleagues) are actually means to advance policy goals (see W. Murphy 1964). This example also highlights the difficulty of identifying judicial motivations through empirical analysis: what one observer perceives as an interest in harmony with fellow judges for its own sake looks to another like a means to advance a policy agenda.

The list of goals in table 1.1 underlines a distinction between the framework sketched in this section and some other goal-based formulations. Gibson (1983, 9) suggested that "judges' decisions are a function of what they prefer to do, tempered by what they think they ought to do, but constrained by what they perceive is feasible to do." Knight and Epstein (1996a, 1021) viewed precedent "as a constraint on justices acting on their policy preferences." These formulations make a distinction between goals and constraints.[15] Further, they explicitly or implicitly treat as constraints a large share of the goals in the table, such as legal coherence and respect in the community.

These formulations provide useful ways of thinking about judicial behavior. But it is more useful for the purposes of this book to analyze all the forces on judges' behavior in terms of goals. After all, constraints would not be constraints if they did not have a basis in judges' goals. Judges who take public opinion into account when they decide cases do so either because they care about public approval for its own sake or because attention to public opinion assists them in achieving another goal. Thinking about the various elements in a judge's calculus in terms of their goals helps in understanding how those elements interrelate in shaping judges' behavior.

Moreover, the Gibson and Knight–Epstein formulations assume the primacy of policy goals: judges would simply follow their vision of good policy if they were not faced with constraints.

---

15. Gibson (1983, 17) refers to role conceptions ("what they think they ought to do") as institutional constraints.

That assumption may be accurate, but what we know about judicial behavior is most effectively assessed if judges' goal orientations are treated as an open question. Until evidence establishes otherwise, we should not dismiss the possibility that judges seek legal coherence for its own sake or that respect in the legal community outweighs policy goals for some judges.

Identifying Goals

Central to the analytic scheme in figure 1.1, and important for the understanding of judicial behavior from most perspectives, is the content of judges' operative goal orientations. Two general methods have been used to identify the goals of judges and other public officials. The first is to draw data from expressions by those officials. Caldeira (1977) and Sarat (1977) used interviews to gather information about the incentives of trial judges, and many other scholars have interviewed or surveyed judges to help understand their behavior (e.g., Glick 1971; Ryan et al. 1980; Howard 1981; Perry 1991). Psychologists who study political leaders often seek to identify their motivations by analyzing expressions in the public record (e.g., Winter and Carlson 1988). Aliotta (1988) took this approach, employing the testimony of Supreme Court nominees before the Senate Judiciary Committee.

Of course, it is quite common to utilize judges' nonpublic writing, such as diaries and correspondence, as a source of information about the reasons for their behavior. This is standard procedure in biographies (e.g., Hirsch 1981; Yarbrough 1992). Such writing was also an important data source for Walter Murphy's (1964) pioneering analysis of policy goals as foundations of Supreme Court behavior.

Judges' expressions can tell us a great deal (see Rowland and Carp 1996, 146–47), but they need to be interpreted with care (see Marvell 1978, 9–13, 106–16). Judges usually speak and write with audiences in mind, and they ordinarily present themselves in a way that they think will be received favorably. Further, they do not always understand their goals fully, and they may mislead themselves as well as their audiences. For both reasons, to take one important example, scholars have been appropriately skeptical about statements by Supreme Court justices that their only goal is to interpret the law accurately (Spaeth 1995, 305). This problem is reduced in psychological research that focuses on underlying themes in judges' expressions, themes that may not be affected very much by judges' concern with audiences or by their self-knowledge. But such themes are likely to reflect judges' inherent priorities rather than their operative goals as judges.

The preponderance of research on judicial behavior uses a different source of data, inferring goals and motives from judicial behavior rather than expressions.[16] At most court levels, scholars study primarily the behavior recorded in votes and opinions. In studies of state trial courts, many scholars use direct observation of judges' behavior on the bench. At least implicitly, much of this research involves a search for revealed preferences, "preferences manifested in the pattern of the agent's choices" (Bohman 1991, 69).

Two kinds of difficulties can arise in inferring judges' operative goals from their behavior. The first lies in the theoretical ambiguity of behavior: patterns of behavior often are consistent with multiple goal orientations. As discussed earlier, this ambiguity raises questions about equating good explanation with successful prediction. Empirical analysis may seem to support a particular conception of judges' goals when it would provide as much support for another conception.

Second, working backward from behavior to goals is most straightforward when behavior is consistent with the best means to achieve one or more goals. When the link between behavior and goals is weaker or more complex, inferences from one to the other can be inaccurate (see Boden 1972, 31; Marini 1992, 29). Given sufficient ineptitude, a judge whose aim is to win support from colleagues for a set of policy goals may look like a judge who seeks to alienate those colleagues.[17]

These difficulties certainly do not preclude the use of judges' behavior as a source of information about judges' goals and motives. Research that takes this approach has taught us a great deal and will continue to do so. But scholars who infer goals and motives from judges' behavior should be sensitive to complexities and open to alternative interpretations. The same is true of those who assess research that is based on this inference.

---

16. On data sources in judicial behavior research, see Tate 1983 and Johnson 1990.

17. I am alluding to the case of Justice Felix Frankfurter, mentioned at the beginning of the chapter. This issue is discussed more extensively in chapter 4.

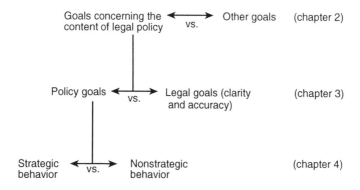

Fig. 1.2. Issues to be analyzed in chapters 2 through 4

Format of Analysis

Within the broad framework presented in figure 1.1, the next three chapters examine three major issues in the explanation of judicial behavior. As shown in figure 1.2, these issues are nested hierarchically.

Chapters 2 and 3 deal with the identities of judges' operative goal orientations and with the recruitment processes and court situations that determine them. The central issue in chapter 2 is the extent to which judges act on the basis of goals related to the content of legal policy rather than the array of other possible goals. Scholars have depicted state trial judges as people who hold and act on a wide range of goals and who differ among themselves in their goal orientations. In contrast, Supreme Court justices usually are depicted as people concerned only with legal policy. This difference in portrayals suggests the metaphor of a pyramid, in which operative goal orientations become narrower and more homogeneous at higher levels in the judiciary. Chapter 2 considers how accurately that metaphor captures reality, particularly the reality of the Supreme Court.

In part because of their concentration on the Supreme Court, scholars emphasize the content of legal policy as a motivation for judges. But those who share this emphasis disagree sharply about the mix of content-related goals. Some argue that in practice judges act almost solely on the basis of policy goals, while others believe that legal accuracy and clarity also are important to judges. Chapter 3 addresses those differing points of view.

The final issue concerns the links between goals and behavior. Because of the emphasis on judges' policy goals, students of judicial behavior have concerned themselves primarily with one specific link: the extent to which judges act strategically on behalf of their policy goals. Chapter 4 examines strategic behavior by policy-oriented judges.

On each of these three issues, one point of view occupies something of a favored position. That is especially true of the belief that Supreme Court justices are concerned solely with the content of legal policy. In contrast, the relative importance of law and policy for judges is a matter of considerable dispute. But in scholarship on the Supreme Court—the primary focus of judicial behavior research—the view that policy considerations are dominant over legal considerations has been taken by the most prominent work. The conception that judges act strategically has been strongly disputed, but it has already become quite influential, and the strong position of the rational choice approach in political science guarantees that its influence on analysis of judicial behavior will grow further.

In my analyses of these three issues, I take something of a skeptical stance toward the point of view that has the favored position. In chapter 3, for instance, I emphasize ways in which the empirical evidence on Supreme Court decision making may be consistent with law-oriented behavior. I do so not because I necessarily disagree with the favored positions—indeed, I think there is considerable basis for each of those positions—but because a skeptical stance assists in thinking carefully about theoretical issues and empirical evidence. Moreover, progress toward a better understanding of these and other issues is facilitated by a full recognition of the uncertainties in our current understanding.

CHAPTER 2

Legal Policy and Other Goals

According to James March (1956, 534), "it is probably true to say that judges correspond with, more than they differ from, people."[1] If so, most judges want a great many things, from high income to popularity to short working hours. But people give higher priorities to some goals than to others, and they differ in their priorities. Further, the relevance of people's goals to their choices depends on the situations in which they act, and situations vary a good deal. Thus the goals on which judges act depend on both their inherent goal orientations and the situations that translate them into operative goal orientations—those configurations of goals that actually affect judicial behavior.

This chapter considers the breadth of judges' operative goal orientations. Its central issue is the balance between two types of goals: those related to the content of legal policy—legal and policy goals—and the diverse array of goals that fall into other categories.

Students of judicial behavior seldom compare the goal orientations of judges who sit on different courts. But their separate depictions of various courts suggest the metaphor of a pyramid: at increasingly higher levels of the judiciary, the range of operative goals narrows and variation among judges diminishes. At the lowest levels, in this metaphor, interest in the content of legal policy is one of many motivations for judges' behavior, motivations whose importance differs from judge to judge. At the highest level, in the Supreme Court, only an interest in the content of legal policy influences the behavior of any justice.

In the first section of the chapter, I describe the pyramid metaphor as it emerges from scholarly work on judicial behavior. The second section considers differences among courts in theoretical terms. The final section focuses on the Supreme Court, surveying empirical evidence to assess the conception that only legal and policy goals motivate the justices.

---

1. This observation was quoted in Schubert 1965, 37. Thomas Jefferson expressed a similar view (quoted in Haar 1996, 156).

The Pyramid Metaphor

Some research on state trial courts focuses on judicial decision making, generally in sentencing (e.g., Uhlman 1978; Gibson 1978b, 1980; Kuklinski and Stanga 1979; Pruet and Glick 1986; Welch, Combs, and Gruhl 1988; M. Myers 1988; Tillman and Pontell 1992; J. Ulmer and Kramer 1996). But most of the trial court research has a broader scope (see Jacob 1991; Mather 1995). Largely for this reason, studies of these courts provide only limited evidence on judges' goals (see M. Myers and Talarico 1987, 1–15). Moreover, the evidence they do provide is not entirely consistent. Still, two images emerge from this research, each involving a form of complexity.

The first image is one of diversity: judges differ in their hierarchies of operative goals. A number of studies depict state trial judges as a heterogeneous group, with wide variation in what they seek to achieve (Dolbeare 1967, 65–66; Galanter, Palen, and Thomas 1979; Wice 1985, 99–103; Conley and O'Barr 1990, 85–106; see Gibson 1978b, 1980). Some research points directly to variation in goal orientations. Caldeira's (1977) study of New Jersey judges and Sarat's (1977) study of Wisconsin judges both found that judges ranged widely in their primary incentives. In a study of a single urban trial court, Smith and Blumberg (A. Smith and Blumberg 1967; Blumberg 1967, 137–42) placed judges in such categories as "intellectual-scholar" and "judicial pensioner," categories that reflect different goals.

The second image is one of multiple motivations: individual judges act on the basis of many goals (Mileski 1971; Buckle and Buckle 1977; Cook 1979; Flemming 1982; Flemming, Nardulli, and Eisenstein 1992; McCoy 1993; J. Ulmer and Kramer 1996). For instance, Eisenstein and Jacob (1977, 24–28) cited four kinds of goals pursued by judges and other members of courtroom workgroups: doing justice, maintaining cohesion, disposing of caseload, and reducing uncertainty. One recurrent theme in the trial court research is that judges' support for plea bargaining reflects multiple goals. Heumann (1978, 144–48) described three benefits to plea bargaining: it saves time and effort and makes the judge's job easier, it reduces the chances of reversal on appeal, and it helps to satisfy administrative demands for disposition of cases (see also Neubauer 1974, 93–96; Alschuler 1976; Langbein 1979; Ryan and Alfini 1979; McCoy 1993).

Some studies support the first image more than the second,

describing different types of judges who each have a single dominant goal (e.g., Caldeira 1977, 5–6). Taken as a whole, however,
research on state trial courts presents a picture that combines the
two images: judges' behavior reflects a multiplicity of goals, and
judges differ in their priorities among those goals.[2] In deciding
whether to accept a plea bargain, in imposing a criminal sentence,
in instructing the jury in a personal injury case, a trial judge acts on
several motivations. And another judge down the hall who faces
the same choices may act on a different set of motivations, or at
least give different weights to the same ones.

That picture is not very startling. Rather, it comports with the
way that most people think about human behavior. But the dominant picture of the Supreme Court in political science research is
quite different.

As depicted in most of that research, Supreme Court justices
are motivated by goals of a single type, those connected with the
content of legal policy. In the terms introduced in chapter 1, their
behavior as justices reflects only their interest in good policy, legal
accuracy, and legal clarity. Of the whole range of motives that
human beings hold, then, the great majority are inoperative. And
because only one type of goal motivates justices, there is little room
for variation among them. Felix Frankfurter and William O.
Douglas, Warren Burger and Thurgood Marshall: in this important sense, they are all the same.

The image of justices as single-minded comes through clearly
in research based on the attitudinal model of decision making, a
model that interprets decisional behavior on the Supreme Court as
a reflection of the justices' policy preferences (Schubert 1965, 1974;
Rohde and Spaeth 1976; Segal and Spaeth 1993). The attitudinal
model in its various versions has been the most influential conception of judicial behavior in political science. Proponents of the
model in its purest form take strong positions on each of the three
issues discussed in chapters 2 through 4: justices act only on their
interest in the content of legal policy, they seek to achieve good
policy rather than good law, and their votes on case outcomes are
direct expressions of their preferences rather than deviating from
those preferences for strategic reasons.[3]

A similar image can be found in other bodies of research on

---

2. The same picture emerges from journalistic accounts of trial judges (e.g., Donald Dale Jackson 1977).

3. The role of strategy in the attitudinal model is discussed more extensively in
chapter 4.

Supreme Court decision making. Most studies of the impact of justices' personal attributes or social background characteristics rest on the premise that these characteristics shape policy preferences, which in turn determine justices' positions in cases (Schmidhauser 1961; S. Ulmer 1973b, 1986; Tate 1981; Tate and Handberg 1991).[4] Most studies that posit strategic behavior by justices assume that this behavior is aimed at advancing policy goals (Murphy 1964; Rohde 1972b, 1972c; E. Schwartz, Spiller, and Urbiztondo 1994; L. Epstein and Walker 1995).

These bodies of work accord primacy or even exclusivity to justices' policy goals. In contrast, some scholars argue that justices seek legal accuracy or clarity as well as good policy (e.g., Brigham 1978; Perry 1991; Gillman 1993; Kahn 1994; Brenner and Stier 1995). But the long-standing and sometimes heated debate between these two camps obscures their agreement on one fundamental matter: justices care overwhelmingly, or even solely, about the content of legal policy.[5]

The image of Supreme Court justices as like-minded also comes through clearly in political science scholarship. While empirical research emphasizes differences among justices, the differences are in their policy positions. In contrast with state trial courts, typologies of Supreme Court justices are based on variation in their conceptions of good policy rather than in their hierarchies of goals (e.g., Spaeth 1979, 135). Some scholars argue that justices differ in the relative importance that they accord to legal and policy considerations (e.g., Mendelson 1991). But even this variation is within a quite narrow range, compared with the variation that has been ascribed to state trial judges.[6]

Some significant bodies of writing on Supreme Court behavior depart from these images. Historical and biographical studies often suggest a range of motivations that extend beyond the content of legal policy, such as obtaining respect in the legal community and minimizing work loads (e.g., B. Schwartz 1990; Lamb and

---

4. However, a few studies analyze the relationship between background characteristics and the propensity to dissent (S. Ulmer 1970; Aliotta 1988) or to overrule precedents (Schmidhauser 1962).

5. Research on the relationship between the Court and external forces such as public opinion and interest groups suggests the possibility that goals other than legal policy motivate the justices. But explicitly or implicitly, much of the research on links between the Court and its environment treats the influence of external forces as a consequence of the justices' policy goals. This subject is discussed in the final section of the chapter.

6. The same is true of posited variation in "activism" and "restraint" among justices. The theoretical meaning of activism and restraint is discussed in chapter 3.

Halpern 1991). The same is true of journalistic accounts of the Court (e.g., Woodward and Armstrong 1979; Savage 1992). Scholars with a rational choice perspective have pointed to a wide array of other goals that might influence Supreme Court justices (Eskridge 1988; R. Epstein 1990; Spiller and Spitzer 1992; Macey 1994). But on the whole, these bodies of writing emphasize justices' concern with legal policy. And in the most influential bodies of research in political science, that emphasis is overwhelming.

While the dominant picture of state trial judges is not very startling, the standard picture of Supreme Court justices *is* startling—or it would be if scholars were not so accustomed to it. If all the people who serve in a particular institution are motivated by the same narrow set of goals, this is a very unusual organization (see Rowland 1991, 78).[7] And it is remarkable that in this picture of the Court, its members seek only to maximize the collective goods of good policy or good law; they are unaffected by anything that looks like self-interest.[8] Political scientists who study the Supreme Court might be reluctant to accept Justice Harold Burton's description of the Court as akin to "a monastery" (Berry

---

7. It is true that some scholars posit re-election as a single dominant goal for members of Congress (Mayhew 1974; Arnold 1990; see Peltzman 1984). But if re-election is dominant, its dominance rests in part on its serving as a necessary means to other important goals (Mayhew 1974, 16; Fiorina 1989, 37). Further, even those who treat re-election as dominant recognize the impact of other goals (Mayhew 1974, 15–16), and most legislative scholars explain congressional behavior on the basis of multiple goals (Fenno 1973; Dodd 1977; Smith and Deering 1983; M. Thomas 1985; Sinclair 1989; Parker 1992; Loomis 1994; J. Clark 1996).

Niskanen (1971, 1994) has posited budget maximization as the dominant "maximand" for bureaucrats (see Blais and Dion 1991). But the possible dominance of the budget is based on its serving a variety of operative goals such as salary, power, and public reputation. Although justices' concern with the content of legal policy also could stem from several different goals, it typically is treated as flowing from a narrow concern with legal policy in itself.

On problems with a single-goal model of presidential behavior, see Sinclair 1993, 223.

8. Spiller and Gely (1992, 464) and E. Schwartz, Spiller, and Urbiztondo (1994, 57) model the Court as "a self-interested, ideologically motivated institution," but ideological motivation is not self-interested in any conventional sense. Public policy *is* a collective good. Even if a justice could have a decisive impact on some aspect of public policy, the subjects of the Court's decisions are seldom matters that affect the justices much in a direct way.

It is true that even economic analyses of behavior need not assume that people are completely self-interested (G. Becker 1993; Wildavsky 1994), but a depiction of policymakers as people whose actions do not reflect self-interest at all is nonetheless striking. In this respect most students of the Supreme Court implicitly go much further than those who argue that policymakers and other people sometimes transcend self-interest (Mansbridge 1990).

1978, 27), but the Court that most of them depict has some of the qualities that we associate with monasteries.

Between the Supreme Court and state trial courts are courts that collectively can be labeled "mid-level."[9] Social scientists have written relatively little about state intermediate appellate courts (but see Davies 1982; Scheb, Ungs, and Hayes 1989; Stow and Spaeth 1992). The scholarship on state supreme courts and lower federal courts is more substantial, but that work is diverse in approach and theme (Glick 1991; Rowland 1991; Songer 1991).

Much of the research on these courts is similar to Supreme Court scholarship in its emphasis on legal and policy goals, especially the latter. Like analogous research on the Supreme Court, studies of the relationship between judges' personal attributes or background characteristics and their decisional behavior in mid-level courts typically treat policy preferences as central to judges' behavior (S. Nagel 1961; Goldman 1966, 1975; Walker and Barrow 1985; Gryski and Main 1986; Stidham and Carp 1987; Songer, Davis, and Haire 1994; see Lloyd 1995). Some other research on decisional behavior in these courts also assumes the primacy of judges' policy goals (Jaros and Canon 1971; Atkins 1972; Rowland and Carp 1983). A number of scholars emphasize legal policy but treat both legal and policy considerations as important (Howard 1977, 1981; Kritzer 1978; Johnson 1987; Swinford 1991; Scheb, Bowen, and Anderson 1991; Emmert and Traut 1994).

In contrast with Supreme Court research, however, much of the research on mid-level courts explicitly or implicitly depicts judges as acting on a multiplicity of goals (Schick 1970; Atkins 1973; Beiser 1974; Tarr and Porter 1988; Lawler and Parle 1989; Hall and Brace 1996). In particular, work on state supreme courts and federal district courts often emphasizes judges' interest in their standing with audiences outside their courts. Several studies of elected state judges focus on tension between judges' concern with the content of legal policy and their desire to continue in office, as that tension plays out on controversial issues such as race relations (Vines 1965) and the death penalty (Hall 1987, 1992, 1995).[10] A few studies of state supreme courts suggest the importance to judges of

---

9. Because federal and state court systems are separate, it is impossible to order courts precisely from lowest to highest. If the higher prestige of federal courts is taken into account, it is clear that state trial courts are the lowest level and the Supreme Court the highest level. The relative positions of courts in between—state supreme courts and federal courts of appeals, for instance—are less clear.

10. However, some scholars suggest that on most issues, electoral pressures are weak (Jaros and Canon 1971; Glick 1992, 159).

political elite groups that influence their electoral prospects (Schubert 1959, 129–42; Adamany 1969). Some research on federal district judges indicates that judges may be responsive to their districts because of a desire for public support and approval (Cook 1977). This is particularly true of studies of racial issues in the South during the 1950s and 1960s (Peltason 1961; Vines 1964; Giles and Walker 1975).

Still other studies point explicitly or implicitly to goals connected with the quality of life within courts. One such goal is limiting work loads (Sickels 1965; Atkins 1974). Concern with work loads comes through most clearly in accounts of structural and procedural changes in intermediate courts of appeals, which demonstrate that judges are willing to change the decisional process substantially—transferring considerable power to central court staffs—to reduce their own burdens (Baker 1994). Another quality-of-life issue is the maintenance of intracourt harmony, which is sometimes treated as a high priority for judges (Beiser 1973; Howard 1981; Brace and Hall 1993, 1995).

Thus the empirical research on mid-level courts does not fit into a single mold. When the various depictions of these courts are averaged out, however, this scholarship as a whole suggests that judges on these courts stand between the two extremes of the highest and lowest courts: their operative goals are broader than those of Supreme Court justices but narrower than those of state trial judges. Scholarship on these courts also points to variation among judges in goal orientations, though seemingly within a narrower range than in state trial courts (Glick and Vines 1969; Howard 1981; D. Klein 1996a). To that degree, then, the picture of mid-level courts that emerges from the research on them is consistent with the pyramid metaphor.

Of course, that metaphor greatly oversimplifies the research on judicial behavior, which is far from homogeneous in its depiction of courts at any level.[11] Still, the metaphor highlights an important pattern in scholarship on judges. Scholars think quite differently about courts at different levels, and they tend to ascribe

---

11. It is also true that the difference in the typical depictions of courts at the highest and lowest levels of the system reflects differences in research focus and methods to some degree. At both levels, analyses of decisional outputs tend to emphasize attitudes toward legal policy, while analyses of decision processes tend to produce more complex pictures of the considerations that influence decisions. Most Supreme Court scholarship is devoted to analysis of outputs, while a great deal of trial court scholarship involves analysis of processes.

increasingly narrow and homogeneous sets of operative goals to judges at higher levels.

This metaphor leads to two issues, the subjects of the sections that follow. The more general issue is why courts might differ substantially in the operative goal orientations of their judges. What mechanisms could account for intercourt differences in judges' goals, whether or not they follow the lines of the pyramid metaphor?

The second issue concerns the Supreme Court specifically. We have a large and impressive body of empirical evidence on Supreme Court behavior. The standard depiction of Supreme Court justices holds that their behavior reflects only their concern with the content of legal policy; how well does the empirical evidence support that depiction?

Sources of Intercourt Differences in Goal Orientations

In the model presented in figure 1.1, the mix of operative goal orientations on a particular court is a product of the recruitment processes that staff the court and the situations in which its judges work. Each, of course, can create differences in orientations from one court to another.

Recruitment

The potential impact of recruitment is straightforward. People differ a great deal in what they seek to accomplish, in their inherent motives or goals (Winter 1973; Boyatzis 1973; Payne et al. 1984). Recruitment processes might bring to different courts people with different inherent goal orientations.

Arguably, such differences are limited by a degree of homogeneity among judges as a whole. With the exception of some state trial judges, they have all sought out membership in the legal profession and have experienced training as lawyers. Further, those lawyers who seek or accept judgeships may tend to share certain priorities such as an interest in respect from the general public (see Greenberg and Haley 1986). Yet these similarities are not so great that they preclude substantial variation in goal orientations. In turn, that variation allows for the possibility of systematic variation among courts.

Such variation could arise on the "supply side," in that different courts are attractive to different kinds of people. Of course, there is a general preference for courts that stand higher in the hierarchy. Large numbers of federal district judges accept appointments to the courts of appeals, but it appears that no judge has moved in the opposite direction (Goldman 1995b). Still, lawyers undoubtedly vary in their preferences among different kinds of courts (see Wyzanski 1979; Wald 1992, 174–75). Those preferences inevitably affect the composition of different courts. Watson and Downing (1969, 72–73) found little overlap between the set of applicants for trial judgeships and the set for appellate judgeships in Missouri, so that lawyers in effect sorted themselves out among courts. Such sorting out, like similar processes in other spheres of life, has a purposive element: people seek out situations that are consistent with their goals (see Buss 1987; Waller, Benet, and Farney 1994).

The "demand side" involves choices by people who recruit judges. The identities of the recruiters themselves vary. The sharpest difference is between states in which voters often make the final choices of judges and systems (federal and some states) in which public officials fully control the selection process. Further, any particular set of selectors may apply different criteria to different courts. Justice Department officials look for somewhat different qualities in district judges and Supreme Court justices.

There is a substantial body of research on judicial recruitment (Sheldon and Lovrich 1991; Goldman 1991). Most studies examine recruitment processes and outcomes in single courts or court levels, but their findings provide raw materials for intercourt comparisons. Some studies make direct comparisons, either among formal selection systems (Canon 1972; Dubois 1980, 1983; Slotnick 1984; Glick and Emmert 1987) or between levels of courts within the same formal system (Slotnick 1983; Goldman 1995a).

But the research on judicial recruitment is not aimed at identifying variation in goal orientations. Indeed, this research generally incorporates the same kind of assumption that underlies studies of judges' background characteristics: recruitment processes are important because they influence the mix of policy preferences on particular courts and sets of courts. This assumption is exemplified by Levin's (1977) insightful comparison of trial courts in Pittsburgh and Minneapolis, which showed how recruitment processes

in the two cities brought to the bench people with different attitudes toward criminal sentencing.

Still, the research on judicial recruitment provides a basis for
speculation about its effects on goal orientations in different
courts. To take one important example, there are reasons to posit
that the lawyers who populate the highest courts care more about
the content of legal policy than do those who sit on the lowest
courts. That hypothesis merits discussion because of its importance, and it also illustrates the ways that recruitment might bring
about differences among courts.

One basis for this hypothesis is intercourt differences in
lawyers' status: both supply and demand favor the recruitment to
higher courts of lawyers who have enjoyed more success in law and
public life. On the demand side, the degree of success typically
required of candidates for judgeships is greater for higher courts.
On the supply side, judgeships become increasingly attractive to
successful lawyers at higher court levels. Few leading partners in
prosperous firms would be willing to consider a judgeship below
the top level of a state court system, but many such lawyers would
happily join a federal appellate court. The same is true of people in
government. Senator George Mitchell turned down President Clinton's offer of a Supreme Court appointment, but he seemed to
reach that decision with some difficulty. Presumably, he would
have had no difficulty in turning down an offer to join the Superior
Court of Maine. In conventional terms, then, the résumés of judges
on the federal courts of appeals are considerably more impressive
than those of judges on state intermediate courts.

This difference might have no impact on judges' goal orientations. But it may be that the people who reach high levels in law
and politics differ from their less successful colleagues in relevant
ways. One possibility is that both lawyers who practice at high levels of the profession and people who work at high levels of government tend to develop strong views about public policy issues. As a
result, they might give a higher priority to policy goals on average
than do other lawyers.

Probably more important than lawyers' status as a basis for
intercourt differences are the images of higher and lower courts. As
most people see it, the opportunity to shape law and public policy
grows at increasingly higher levels of courts. On the supply side,
perceptions of this difference might affect the kinds of people
attracted to various courts. The highest courts may draw people

for whom legal policy is very important (Watson and Downing 1969, 73). In contrast, lawyers may seek to join lower courts for a variety of reasons, with the opportunity to shape policy ranking relatively low.

On the demand side, the people who select judges typically are quite interested in the policy views of candidates for the highest courts. As a result, they might tend to favor candidates who have expressed their policy positions often and clearly, people who are likely to care a great deal about the content of public policy (see Schmidhauser 1979, 98).[12] On the whole, policy views are less important to those who choose judges for lower courts, where partisan and personal ties between selectors and recruits often are of much greater relevance (Goulden 1974, 21–74; New York State Commission on Government Integrity 1988). That reality is captured in a judge's widely cited observation that a "judge is a member of the Bar who once knew a Governor" (Bok 1941, 3).

The hypothesis on which I have focused is of special interest because it is consistent with the pyramid metaphor: if judges on higher courts focus more on the content of legal policy than do their counterparts on lower courts, recruitment could help to explain that difference. Students of judicial behavior might posit other types of differences between higher and lower courts as well as variation along other lines, such as differences between trial and appellate judges or between courts with broad and narrow jurisdiction. But all this is highly speculative, since there has been very little research on the relationship between recruitment and judges' goal orientations.

Court Situations

Some psychologists have argued that the situations in which individuals act have a more critical impact on behavior, and intrinsic traits of individuals less, than most people realize (Patry 1989; L. Ross and Nisbett 1991). Indeed, the tendency to give undue weight to intrinsic traits has been labeled the "fundamental attribution

---

12. One prominent exception to this generalization was David Souter's appointment to the Supreme Court. President George Bush nominated Souter in part because he lacked an extensive record of positions on legal policy issues, thus providing fewer points of attack for potential opponents. But Souter's surprising degree of liberalism on the Court underlines the costs of this strategy.

error" (L. Ross 1977, 184–85).[13] On the whole, this argument seems convincing. More specifically, recruitment is probably less powerful as a source of intercourt differences in judicial behavior than are judges' situations.

There is no doubt that judges' situations differ enormously among courts. For instance, there are very substantial differences between trial and appellate courts in the form and setting of decisions. Courts vary in such other respects as the composition and volume of their caseloads, the resources available to judges, the proportions of their decisions that undergo appellate review, and the kinds of interactions that occur between judges and other court participants. Because of such differences, it can be argued that the Supreme Court resembles Congress and a municipal court resembles other "street-level bureaucracies" (Lipsky 1980) far more than the two courts resemble each other.

Because court situations determine how inherent goal orientations translate into operative goal orientations, differences in these situations can create intercourt variation in the mixes of goals that judges actually pursue in their judicial work. The most obvious effect of this sort, and perhaps the most important, concerns judges' career goals. Most students of Congress give a prominent place to re-election as a goal driving legislative behavior (e.g., Mayhew 1974; Fiorina 1989). That treatment of re-election is quite reasonable: members of Congress hold an attractive office (though perhaps less attractive than it once was) and face its potential loss at frequent intervals.

Of course, courts vary in both respects. I have already noted differences in the attractiveness of courts, differences that affect judges' interest in retaining their positions. Differences in job security are even greater. Most federal judges and those in a few states hold office for life or until retirement age. Other judges hold office for fixed terms, but there is considerable variation in the difficulty of winning new terms. A member of the Texas Supreme Court can anticipate a heated and expensive battle for re-election (see Donald W. Jackson and Riddlesperger 1991). A Minnesota trial judge is unlikely even to face an opponent (Benson 1993, 765 n. 2).

The importance of prospects for promotion also varies. Some promotions are more attractive than others; in a state without intermediate appellate courts, promotion from a trial court to the

---

13. If people tend to put themselves in situations congruent with their own goals and needs, however, the distinction between personal and situational characteristics is not as sharp as it initially appears.

supreme court is a very big jump in prestige. Further, the chances for promotion differ with the numbers of judgeships at different levels and the extent to which particular courts are staffed through judicial promotion. To take one example, federal district judges have a better chance of promotion to the next level than do members of the courts of appeals (see Posner 1985, 17).

While variation in career goals is especially easy to discern, the importance of other types of goals is also likely to differ among courts. Various characteristics of court situations help to determine what goals are relevant to judges in their judicial work and how much weight is given to particular goals.

If the operative goal orientations of state trial judges and Supreme Court justices differ fundamentally, characteristics of their situations probably are the primary reason. The judge who serves in an urban trial court typically must think about a good many things. In some courts re-election is problematic. An appellate judgeship or a well-paying nonjudicial position is worth striving for. The work load is probably heavy, resources to cope with it limited. Trial lawyers have considerable control over cases and court proceedings, especially on the criminal side. A chief judge may hold power over a judge's working conditions, even over where the judge works. Decisions can be overturned on appeal. Because of these conditions, a great many of the goals that judges bring with them to the bench remain relevant to the choices they make as judges (see A. Smith and Blumberg 1967, 99).

Typically the situation of Supreme Court justices is viewed as very different. Most students of the Court take the implicit position that the justices' situation makes most of their inherent goals largely or entirely irrelevant, leaving only their interest in the content of legal policy—whether they are interested in it as law or as policy. Rohde and Spaeth (1976, 72–74) and Segal and Spaeth (1993, 69–72) made this conception of the Court explicit. Both books cited a lack of electoral accountability and a lack of ambition for higher office as conditions that free justices to focus on the content of legal policy. In effect, they argued that these characteristics render justices' self-interest irrelevant to their judging. Since all justices work under these conditions, it follows that they share the same narrow set of operative goals. The two books also cited characteristics of the justices' situation that arguably reduce the relevance of legal considerations and the need for strategic behavior, issues to be considered in chapters 3 and 4. Table 2.1 summarizes and extends the arguments made in Rohde and Spaeth 1976 and Segal and Spaeth 1993, describing them in terms of the justices' goals.

For now, the only issue is the relevance of goals other than the content of legal policy. As some of the entries in table 2.1 indicate, there is a very plausible rationale for placing the Court at the top in the pyramid metaphor: Supreme Court justices have a considerable degree of insulation from career concerns that are quite relevant to most people, including most judges. In itself, then, the possession of a highly prestigious position for life makes an enormous difference.

Yet it is not self-evident that justices act only on their interest in legal policy. For one thing, justices might not be entirely free from concern about their careers. Despite the Court's prestige, for instance, it might be common for justices to aspire to other positions. More important, the Court's institutional characteristics do not render irrelevant such goals as personal popularity or limited work loads. Such goals might be inherently important to justices, and they might affect the behavior of justices on the Court.

Thus the abundance of empirical evidence on the Supreme Court is welcome. For no other court do we know so much about patterns of judicial behavior. That evidence can be combed for what it tells us about the operative goal orientations of the justices, specifically about the relative importance of goals connected with

TABLE 2.1.   Characteristics of the Supreme Court's Situation That May
Reduce the Operational Relevance of Certain Goals

Situational Characteristic	Goals That Are or May Be Rendered Less Relevant
Lifetime term and very limited prospect of impeachment	Continued tenure in position
High prestige	Securing nonjudicial positions
Discretionary jurisdiction	Legal accuracy
Absence of higher courts	Judicial promotion
	Legal accuracy (due to lack of review of decisions)
Infrequent review and limited control by other branches[a]	Court resources
	Strategic behavior in relation to the other branches[b]

Source: Based in part on Rohde and Spaeth (1976, 72–74) and on Segal and Spaeth (1993, 69–72).

[a]Rohde and Spaeth and Segal and Spaeth posit this condition, which is disputed by other scholars.

[b]This is, of course, not a goal but the way in which justices act on their interest in the content of legal policy (especially the goal of achieving good policy). Like its antecedent condition (see previous note), this result is disputed.

the content of legal policy and of other types of goals. That is the subject of the next section.

The Goals of Supreme Court Justices: Empirical Evidence

The Content of Legal Policy

Scholars who believe that legal policy is the dominant concern of Supreme Court justices find empirical support primarily in two related bodies of research: dimensional analyses of individual votes on the outcomes of cases that are decided on the merits and causal analyses of relationships between those votes and justices' policy preferences. The evidence from these bodies of research merits close examination.[14]

The classic mode of analysis in political science research on the Supreme Court is dimensional. Pritchett (1941, 1948, 1954) was the major pioneer with his analyses of interagreement patterns among justices and scales of their policy positions in votes on the merits. Using techniques such as bloc analysis and Guttman scaling, students of the Court have continued to probe voting behavior in dimensional terms. In the years after Pritchett's work, there was a movement toward increasingly complex modes of dimensional analysis (Thurstone and Degan 1951; Schubert 1962a, 1965, 1974; Rohde and Spaeth 1976).

Schubert provided an explicit theoretical framework for the findings from dimensional analysis, most extensively in *The Judicial Mind* (1965). Drawing from attitude theory in psychology and from Coombs's (1964) theory of data, Schubert (1962a, 90–91; 1965, 26–28) portrayed each case as a stimulus or *j*-point in a space that is based on the issue dimensions in the case. Each justice has an ideal or *i*-point in the same space. If we simplify to a single dimension and treat that dimension as ideological, the justice can be expected to cast a liberal vote if the justice's *i*-point is to the left of the *j*-point for the case. In a modified version of this formulation, depicted in figure 2.1, each of two alternative outcomes in a case has its own *j*-point, and the relationship between the justice's *i*-point and the midpoint between these *j*-points determines the

---

14. The same evidence is widely interpreted to demonstrate the dominance of policy goals over legal goals, and it also relates to the extent of strategic behavior among justices. Its implications for these two issues are discussed in chapters 3 and 4.

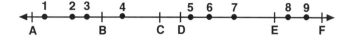

Fig. 2.1. Representation of ideal or *i*-points for justices and midpoints between *j*-points for cases on a single policy dimension. (Numbers represent *i*-points on the dimension for each justice, letters represent the midpoints between the *j*-points (not shown) for the two alternative outcomes in each case. If this is a liberal-conservative policy dimension, each justice casts a liberal vote in each case in which the midpoint between *j*-points is to the right of the justice's *i*-point. From Baum 1988, 906. Reprinted by permission.)

justice's vote (see Coombs 1964, 376–77). This spatial representation of responses to cases has powerfully influenced scholars' thinking about judicial decision making since that time.

Findings of dimensional analyses differ somewhat from study to study, but scholars consistently find that votes take a relatively simple structure (see Spaeth 1979, 109–39).[15] The justices' votes in specific categories of cases, such as double jeopardy and business mergers, generally have structures that seem to approximate a unidimensional form. Most of these categories can be combined into two or three larger dimensions, based on intercorrelations among the voting patterns for different categories. These dimensions are readily interpreted in terms of their subject matter. One contains primarily cases with economic issues. The other one or two contain primarily civil liberties issues. If there are two civil liberties dimensions, issues of equality generally fall into one set and those involving various individual freedoms into the other.

Findings from dimensional analysis in themselves are only descriptive: they depict patterns in votes rather than causal relations between votes and their determinants (see Schubert 1974, xi–xii). But descriptive patterns may lend themselves to interpretation as explanations. The standard interpretation of the dimensional findings on the Supreme Court is that the patterns of votes reflect patterns of policy preferences (or, as they are usually called, attitudes or values).[16] To the extent that cases fall within the major policy dimensions, votes in those cases are thought to be explained

---

15. In recent years the structure of votes in economic cases appears to be relatively complex; that development is discussed later in this section.

16. Gibson 1983, Goldman and Jahnige 1985, and Segal and Spaeth 1993 referred to attitudes, Rohde and Spaeth 1976 to relatively specific attitudes and more general values as well as policy preferences.

by the dimensions. For instance, Rohde and Spaeth (1976, 137–38) concluded that cluster analysis, metric multidimensional scaling, and factor analysis "revealed that three major values explain more than 85 percent of the Court's decisions during both the Warren and Burger Court periods" (see also Pritchett 1941, 895).[17]

This interpretation of the findings from dimensional analyses has been challenged on the ground that the scaling techniques employed and the criteria used to identify acceptable scales over-simplify the dimensionality of justices' votes (Tanenhaus 1966; see Spaeth and Peterson 1971; Stouffer et al. 1950, 77–87; Schooler 1968). There certainly is some validity to this challenge, but there can be no definitive judgment on this matter. The debate over the dimensionality of congressional votes (Poole and Daniels 1985; Koford 1989; J. Snyder 1992a) is a reminder that the findings of dimensional analysis are subject to multiple interpretations even at the descriptive level. The congressional research also points to the possibility that agenda-setting processes create "artificially unidimensional" patterns of votes (J. Snyder 1992a, 1992b; but see H. Rosenthal 1992). For several reasons, such as simplification of decision making (Poole and Rosenthal 1987, 35), justices might be inclined to reject cases and issues that do not fall into familiar attitudinal dimensions.

The simplicity or complexity of dimensions in Supreme Court votes is significant, but it is not as critical a question as it might seem. A complex pattern of votes does not mean that justices vote on some basis other than their policy preferences; the structure of preferences itself might be complex. For example, some studies indicate that voting in economic cases has moved away from a basically unidimensional pattern (Ducat and Dudley 1987; Hagle and Spaeth 1992a, 1993). Almost surely, the primary reason for this change is that political leaders—including Supreme Court justices—have become less inclined to view the range of economic issues in terms of a single attitudinal dimension. Justices' votes in economic cases may express their preferences as directly as they ever did, even though the resulting patterns are not as neat as they once were.

In any event, it is noteworthy that disagreements in voting largely follow lines that can be interpreted in terms of policy

---

17. Schubert (1962a, 104) took a somewhat different approach, concluding from the correlation between justices' positions on content-based and non–content-based dimensions that attitudes toward policy are the bases for voting choices.

dimensions. As Goldman and Jahnige (1985, 137; emphasis in original) argue,

> we cannot say that attitudes *cause* votes when we have defined those attitudes in terms of the same votes. Nevertheless, it is clear that if the attitudinal hypothesis were invalid, neither repeated findings of bloc voting, scale patterns, nor consistent issue-oriented voting would be found. It is therefore reasonable to suggest that judges tend to behave *as if* their attitudes and values governed their voting choices.

Put another way, the patterns of votes disclosed by dimensional studies seem more consistent with attitudes about public policy than with other possible explanations. In this important respect, these studies support the conclusion that policy goals are important bases for Supreme Court behavior. However, several caveats are needed.

First, if justices' policy preferences are the primary source of these patterns of votes, they might be augmented by other sources. For instance, some justices may give a high priority to pleasing audiences that have strong collective preferences themselves, and they could best do so by taking ideologically consistent positions on the Court. To take an unlikely possibility, if Antonin Scalia's only goal were to win the favor of conservative legal scholars, his voting probably would fit into dimensional scales as well as it actually does. To take a more likely possibility, Scalia's own conservative views may be reinforced by the importance to him of audiences whose views also are conservative. As in Congress, it is difficult to separate out the effects of personal attitudes and constituencies as sources of ideologically consistent voting (see Peltzman 1984).

Second, the dimensionality of votes tells us about forces that operate differently on different judges, but it tells us nothing about forces that affect all the justices similarly. To the extent that certain goals have uniform effects on the justices, those effects cannot be discerned from patterns of disagreement. For instance, trends in societal or congressional opinion could move justices in the same direction and to about the same degree, thus creating no serious disturbance in dimensional patterns.

Third, although scaling techniques tend to minimize the numbers of apparent deviations from consistent voting, deviations from unidimensionality do appear. Those deviations could reflect idiosyncratic policy preferences, but they might result instead from the systematic effects of other influences and goals. Thus these "residuals" from dimensional analysis are theoretically significant and merit closer attention (see Schubert 1963a).

Finally, votes on the outcomes of cases represent only one part of Supreme Court decision making. A focus on votes excludes the content of legal rules that justices support, the more consequential component of the Court's decisions on the merits. It also excludes decisions to accept or reject petitions for certiorari, whose significance for the Court's role as a policymaker is self-evident. It is not at all certain that the relative weights of different goals are uniform across all the aspects and stages of decision (Baum 1993).

Despite the inherent limitations of dimensional analysis in explanation, dimensional analyses of votes do provide strong evidence that justices' policy preferences influence their behavior substantially. But the findings from these analyses do not establish that the content of legal policy is the only consideration that motivates Supreme Court justices to a significant degree. The evidence is too ambiguous and too limited to support that conclusion.

If scholars often infer more from dimensional studies than is strictly justified, one unstated reason is that they read the dimensions of voting in terms of an implicit causal analysis. Justices' behavior away from the Court and prior to joining the Court provides more direct evidence of their policy preferences, and in turn those apparent preferences typically are consistent with the positions that justices take as members of the Court (Kritzer 1996, 17). We see William Rehnquist as acting on conservative values, for instance, because those values were evident during his pre-Court career. There was no doubt about the personal liberalism of William O. Douglas when he expressed that liberalism consistently in his extrajudicial writing. While dimensional analysis often is used for exploratory purposes, in effect students of the Supreme Court have used it to confirm their own impressions from observation of the justices.

Systematic causal[18] research on the relationship between justices' policy preferences and behavior has been limited by the difficulty of measuring preferences directly. A few scholars, however, have undertaken such research. An important early study was David Danelski's (1966) analysis of Pierce Butler and Louis Brandeis, which identified for each justice a similarity of themes

---

18. I should note that by "causal" I mean only that possible associations between independent and dependent variables are analyzed, not that such associations necessarily establish causal relationships.

between the speeches they gave as lawyers and their work as justices.

Jeffrey Segal and Albert Cover (1989) took a more comprehensive approach, analyzing the relationship between policy preferences and voting behavior for justices who joined the Court between 1953 and 1988. Their measure of preferences was based on content analysis of newspaper editorials after a justice was nominated. Segal and Cover found a strong statistical relationship between preferences and voting behavior. A follow-up study (Segal, Epstein, Cameron, and Spaeth 1995) extended analysis to earlier and later appointees. It also identified some complexities in the relationship between measures of preferences and voting behavior while confirming the basic thrust of the original study (see L. Epstein and Mershon 1996).[19]

These studies are important because they provide hard evidence of the connection between justices' views about policy and their behavior that scholars have long inferred from their own observations. If confirmation was needed, they confirm that preferences have a great deal of impact on behavior. But each caveat discussed in connection with the findings of dimensional research applies to the causal studies as well. Thus these studies support the conclusion that justices are strongly motivated by their policy goals, but they leave open the question of whether other goals have a significant impact on the justices' behavior.

Career and Standard of Living

Without question, Supreme Court justices care about a good many things other than legal policy. As scholars have argued, however, their situations as justices render some of those goals largely irrelevant to their behavior on the Court. This seems to be true of goals connected with careers and standard of living.

As discussed earlier, career goals generally are viewed as inoperative for contemporary justices, because justices hold their positions for life and because the Court's prestige and power leave them uninterested in other positions. Lifetime tenure could be overcome by impeachment and conviction in Congress, but it is

---

19. Another type of causal analysis focuses on consistency over time in the justices' relative positions on an issue or set of issues (Hagle and Spaeth 1992b; see Segal and Spaeth 1993, 255–60). Such analyses demonstrate high consistency, from which one can infer that the sources of voting differences among the justices are basically stable. But this finding does not provide direct evidence about the identity of those sources. On the role of past behavior in explanation of current behavior, see Ajzen 1991, 202–4.

doubtful that the desire to avoid removal through impeachment affects justices' positions in cases except in rare instances. Congressional interest in impeachment of William O. Douglas over the years and the potential impeachment of Abe Fortas in 1969 stemmed in part from their liberal positions on the Court. Yet removal through impeachment is not only quite unlikely but easily averted through careful behavior outside the context of decision making (see Eisler 1993, 212).

Ambition for other positions might be more consequential, because some justices undoubtedly have that ambition. For one thing, an associate justice can be promoted to chief justice, and at any given time there probably are a few justices who keep that goal in mind. Robert Jackson's desire for promotion and his unhappiness at failing to win it in 1946 became a matter of public interest after he disclosed his feud with Hugo Black (Gerhart 1958, 235–88; John Frank 1949, 123–31). Further, at least a few justices have contemplated candidacies for president or vice president. Douglas seemed to have considerable interest in both offices (J. Simon 1990, 257–75), and Black had wanted the vice presidential nomination that went to Harry Truman (H. Black and E. Black 1986, 216). More recently, some observers perceived that Sandra Day O'Connor was interested in the vice presidency (R. Davis 1994, 128).

Occasionally, justices do leave the Court for other positions. Charles Evans Hughes resigned in 1916 to run for president. And once in a while, a justice finds the Court an unfulfilling setting and takes a federal administrative position, as James Byrnes did in 1942 (Robertson 1994, 311–19). A more ambiguous case is that of Arthur Goldberg, who left the Court in 1964 to become U.S. Ambassador to the United Nations; Goldberg may have been unaware of his unhappiness on the Court until President Lyndon Johnson informed him of it (B. Murphy 1988, 163–71).[20]

To the extent that justices care about other positions, that concern might affect their behavior on the Court. Since presidents appoint chief justices and high executive-branch officials, justices may cast votes and write opinions that are intended to please current or prospective presidents. Federal judges who seek judicial promotions are sometimes suspected of that behavior (Safire 1985; Kaplan 1990). Justices who seek promotion to chief justice might

---

20. There is some reason to posit that the Court has become more attractive and thus that justices have become less inclined to leave for other positions. But there has not been a clear decline over time in the rate of departures for other positions—though Goldberg's departure was the last case of a voluntary departure to take on other full-time responsibilities (L. Epstein, Segal, Spaeth, and Walker 1994, 338–42).

also try to avoid displeasing senators; the Senate failed to confirm Fortas's promotion in 1968 and allowed William Rehnquist's promotion in 1986 only after a heated battle. Similarly, justices who have ambitions for high elective office may take positions designed to appeal to public opinion, just as elected judges may do in order to secure re-election (Reidinger 1987; Hall 1992).

Thus there is a possibility that career goals significantly affect the choices made by some justices. But that effect probably is limited even for those justices with an interest in other positions (see Rohde and Spaeth 1976, 96 n. 8). And it appears that most justices care too little about other offices for career goals to have any meaningful effect on their behavior.

A second goal with little apparent impact is maximizing income and its equivalents. Supreme Court justices would be unusual people indeed if they did not care about material matters—and clearly they do. In an earlier era, many justices resisted retirement in order to maintain their income; the provision of attractive pension benefits has increased the retirement rate substantially (D. Atkinson 1976; see Squire 1988). Busy as justices are, most of them find time to participate in remunerative activities such as law school lectures. Abe Fortas, eager for additional income, engaged in activities that raised ethical questions and that ultimately brought about his resignation from the Court (B. Murphy 1988, 545–77; Kalman 1990, 359–78). William O. Douglas also made himself vulnerable to calls for impeachment with his moneymaking activities (J. Simon 1980, 391–411).

Perhaps concern with income occasionally affects justices' choices. In 1995 questions were raised about denials of certiorari favoring the West Publishing Company. The company had provided travel and other benefits to several justices who helped to select recipients for a West-sponsored annual award to a federal judge (*Washington Post* 1995). And it might be that the desire to retain opportunities for lucrative law school visits or speeches to bar associations affects responses to cases involving law schools or lawyers' groups (see Mauro 1992a). But such possibilities involve too narrow a range of cases to be significant in Supreme Court behavior as a whole.

Limiting Work Load

Some other goals are not so easily dismissed. Of all the considerations other than legal policy that might influence the justices, three seem most plausible: the justices' work loads, their relations with fellow justices, and their standing with audiences outside the Court. Relations with colleagues and standing with Congress, one important audience, both are considered in connection with strategic behavior in chapter 4. In this section I discuss relations with other external audiences and work load.

Judicial concern with work load is a strong theme in trial court research (e.g., Feeley 1979, 196; Lynch 1994, 120). While Supreme Court justices might care less about their work load, in part because it exerts less pressure on them, it seems reasonable to assume that nearly every justice prefers less judicial work to more (see Posner 1995, 123–26). Indeed, there is considerable evidence for this assumption. Justices sometimes complain about the burdens created by their work loads (Powell 1982; Stevens 1982; Burger 1985). An interest in minimizing work loads is reflected in the limited hours that some justices devote to their Court work, in delegation of significant responsibilities to law clerks, and in the development and exercise of discretionary jurisdiction. The question in each of these instances is the extent to which the goal of limiting work loads has an independent effect on the justices' behavior as decision makers—particularly an effect that conflicts with their pursuit of legal and policy goals.

While some members of the Court are willing to work very long hours, others are not. In the latter group, the most visible are those who spent much of their time on other activities—for instance, Douglas on his writing and travel (J. Simon 1980), Fortas on his consultations with President Johnson (Kalman 1990, 293–318). Those justices who devote less than full time to the Court are making something of a trade-off. If they devoted more time to study of cases, they might better identify the positions that are most consistent with their legal or policy goals. If they gave more time to persuasion of their colleagues, they might enhance collective support for their positions. It may be that the trade-off is slight, that the effective justice would gain little by working additional hours, but this is not necessarily true.

Concern with work loads has led to increased delegation of major responsibilities to law clerks—a development decried by some legal commentators (e.g., Kester 1983; Starr 1993). A good case can be made that justices lose little control over the Court's work through this delegation (Tushnet 1992). But they lose *some* control, particularly in the case selection process. This is probably a very sensible trade-off, yet its existence calls into question the justices' complete devotion to law and policy.

The century-long evolution from a jurisdiction that was primarily mandatory to one that is almost entirely discretionary resulted largely from lobbying by the justices themselves (O'Brien 1993, 135). The successive reductions of mandatory jurisdiction appear to be quite consistent with justices' concern for the content of legal policy, because discretionary jurisdiction enables them to concentrate their time on cases that have the greatest potential impact on law and policy (Gressman 1964).

More ambiguous in its impact is the recent decline in the number of cases that the Court accepts for full decisions on the merits (Biskupic 1994a). The mean number of cases accepted per term was 180 in the 1984–87 terms and 99 in 1992–95. That reduction occurred even as the number of petitions for hearings grew, so that the proportion of petitions accepted by the Court declined from 4.2 percent in 1984–87 to 1.5 percent in 1992–95. The great majority of cases accepted by the Court derive from paid petitions, and the number of those petitions has remained stable since the mid-1980s. Even so, the proportion of paid petitions accepted by the Court fell from 7.8 percent in 1984–87 to 4.1 percent in 1992–95.[21]

Such a massive change must reflect a conscious decision by several justices. Perhaps they are motivated by a concern with legal policy. For instance, justices who prefer the legal status quo to most of the doctrinal changes that result when the current Court decides cases might be the strongest proponents of a smaller docket on the merits; in other words, "defensive denials" of certiorari (see Perry 1991, 198–207) may be standard practice for some members of the Court. Some justices may have concluded that the best way to advance a systematic policy agenda is to limit their work loads so they can analyze each case carefully for its implications. Or they might want to focus their efforts on a limited number of policy issues that they care the most about.

But these explanations seem less plausible than the straightforward goal of reducing work loads. And the decline in the Court's collective willingness to hear cases seems to indicate that at least some justices sacrifice opportunities to advance their legal or policy goals in order to reduce their work loads. After all, the volume of petitions aside, the number of cases that raise important issues can hardly be declining and almost surely has increased considerably. Moreover, the Court's capacity to oversee lower courts

21. These figures are calculated from data collected by the Court and published annually by *United States Law Week*. They exclude original jurisdiction cases and those summarily decided by the Court. The numbers of summary decisions are fairly unstable from term to term but show no clear trend over this period.

is increasingly limited as it reviews a smaller proportion of their decisions (see Strauss 1987). The possible effects of work load concerns that have been discussed thus far might be considered peripheral, in that they would not systematically affect justices' positions on the merits of cases. But there are a few ways in which work load concerns could have such an impact. One is that justices might be more willing to join the opinions of colleagues in order to save the time involved in writing separate opinions (Posner 1995, 123–26). It is likely, however, that the availability of law clerks reduces any effect of this sort. Indeed, work load concerns might actually encourage the writing of separate opinions and move the Court further from unanimity, because it is time-consuming to seek consensus (see Bator 1990, 687).

Another possibility is that the justices sometimes choose doctrinal positions with the aim of limiting the need to decide future cases and thus reducing their work loads. At least a few opinions have described this aim explicitly. In *Paris Adult Theatre v. Slaton* (1973, 93), for instance, Justice William Brennan cited "the burden of deciding scores of obscenity cases" as a reason for his own change of position in the field. Even if these opinions depict the justices' motive accurately, however, it is unclear how often they act on this motive.[22] Like other possible effects of the justices' interest in their work loads, this practice merits more study.

The Court's Audiences

There is no doubt that Supreme Court justices care about their standing with audiences outside the Court. They frequently speak to legal groups and sometimes speak to other interest groups. They often work to obtain positive reactions from such groups; Benjamin Cardozo, for instance, "cultivated the good opinion of academics" (Posner 1990, 132). Many justices pay attention to their depiction in the mass media (R. Davis 1994, 38–40), some grant interviews to journalists (R. Davis 1994, 105–107, 119–22; Glendon 1994, 113–14), and some respond to criticism in the press (Jeffries 1994, 278–80; R. Davis 1994, 112–13). Harry Blackmun read his mail from the public (Koh 1994, 20), and William Brennan cared about his portrayal in biographies (Mauro 1995). Several

---

22. It should be noted that a justice who pursues legal clarity as a goal also would favor doctrinal positions that minimize the need to decide future cases.

justices have maintained personal relationships with presidents, even at the risk of creating conflicts of interest (John Frank 1970). This interest in the approbation of certain audiences gives those audiences potential influence over the justices' decisional behavior. Indeed, scholars who study interactions between the Supreme Court and external groups have posited various ways that these groups influence the Court's decisions. The extent and forms of that influence can tell us something about the justices' motivations.

At the outset, a distinction should be made between congruence or covariation on the one hand and influence on the other. Congruence refers to similarity between what an external group wants and what the Court does, covariation to similar trends in the position of an external group and in Court decisions. Neither, of course, necessarily connotes influence. It is influence that helps to illuminate the justices' goals, because the influence of an external group must have a motivational basis.

If justices are influenced by their audiences, that influence could have any of several bases. One possibility is that justices take positions preferred by their audiences as a means to advance their interest in the content of legal policy. Thus they might favor the executive branch in litigation in order to maintain support from policymakers who implement many Court decisions. Similarly, their opinions might follow trends in public opinion as a means to build public approval of the Court as an institution and thus to deter attacks on its decisions by elected officials.

Alternatively, justices could seek the approval of particular audiences as a way to advance goals other than shaping legal policy. For instance, they might try to build support for the Court in Congress in order to maximize the Court's budget, because a higher budget makes their life more comfortable. And justices may respond to audiences because they like approval from those audiences for its own sake. A justice may enjoy the privilege of interacting with the president or accolades from legal academics or positive coverage in the mass media.

It seems highly unlikely that justices care about approval from their audiences only as a means to other ends. Harsanyi (1969, 524) argued plausibly that "[p]eople's behavior can be largely explained in terms of two dominant interests: economic gain and social acceptance." As discussed earlier, economic gain may have little relevance to Supreme Court justices. Social acceptance *is* relevant, and justices would be a singular group of people if none of them were concerned with respect and popularity outside the Court.

Still, the mix of motivations responsible for any influence of external groups on the Court is an open question to be determined empirically. Leaving Congress aside until chapter 4, there are substantial bodies of empirical findings on three other sets of external groups: the general public, interest groups, and the federal government as participant in litigation. That research can be analyzed for what it tells about the extent of influence and about its motivational sources.

The great difficulty of ascertaining influence and its sources should be emphasized. It is not necessarily easy even to ascertain congruence or covariation between a justice's positions and those of an external group. Further, it can be quite difficult to determine whether congruence or covariation actually reflects group influence. Finally, the task of identifying the sources of any influence is even more perplexing: patterns of influence that result from justices' interest in legal policy often would look quite similar to patterns resulting from their interest in personal respect and popularity. If influence reflects a combination of motives, as it probably does in most instances, determination of their relative strength may be particularly difficult. Thus it should not be surprising if our understanding of external influence on the Court is quite incomplete.

On the *general public* as one audience, there are now several studies of the relationship between public opinion and Supreme Court decisions. Some studies examine congruence between the Court's positions on specific issues and public opinion on these issues (Barnum 1985; Marshall and Ignagni 1995; Weissberg 1976, 110–26, 135–36), and a book-length study analyzed congruence in considerable depth (Marshall 1989). The results are mixed, but overall these studies show more agreement than disagreement between the Court and the mass public. Other studies have analyzed covariation over time between broad patterns of public opinion and of Court policy (Mishler and Sheehan 1993; Link 1995; Stimson, MacKuen, and Erikson 1995; Flemming and Wood 1997), each concluding that there is substantial covariation between opinion and policy.

To the extent that policy and opinion are related, some of the possible sources of that relationship involve no direct influence for public opinion (Dahl 1957; Marshall 1989). For example, justices may respond to the same societal events and trends that affect public opinion. Alternatively, they may respond to other policymakers who themselves are influenced by the general public. Presidential elections are an expression of public opinion, so the effects of new appointments on the Court may track changes in opinion (Norpoth and Segal 1994).

The various possible linkages between opinion and decisions are difficult to disentangle. The studies of congruence and covariation provide evidence suggesting that public opinion has an impact on the Court, but it remains uncertain whether opinion has a substantial effect that is independent of other forces on the Court (see Caldeira 1991, 313–16; Norpoth and Segal 1994). In any case, to the extent that the general public does influence the Court, we know little about the motivational sources of that influence (Flemming and Wood 1997, 471).

Scholars have given considerable attention to *interest group* activity in the Supreme Court (see L. Epstein 1993).[23] Much of this research focuses on particular sets of groups or policy areas (e.g., Sorauf 1976; O'Connor 1980; Olson 1984; Wasby 1995). Other research considers group activities and interactions with the Court more broadly (e.g., Barker 1967; Vose 1972; L. Epstein 1993). On the success of groups in the Court, a form of congruence, many studies suggest a positive picture—at least for certain groups— based on major victories such as *Brown v. Board of Education* (1954) for the NAACP Legal Defense Fund (Kluger 1976) or on high winning percentages over time (Lawrence 1990, 98–122). That success underlines the possibility that individual groups, or interest groups as a whole, actually influence the Court's behavior.[24]

Some scholars who analyze interactions between interest groups and the Court in particular fields have concluded that groups do exert substantial influence. In their study of abortion and capital punishment, Epstein and Kobylka (1992) argued that group arguments help to frame issues for the Court. And several

---

23. Interest groups can be defined in a variety of ways. For this discussion I include all organized entities that participate in litigation before the Court. Among the categories of entities submitting amicus curiae briefs that Caldeira and Wright (1990b, 791) described, I exclude only individuals and corporations—though the United States and the Solicitor General as its representative will be discussed separately.

24. One way that interest groups affect the Court is outside the scope of this inquiry: groups can bring to the Court cases and issues that otherwise would not have reached it. Without question, group sponsorship provides an important base for the Supreme Court's work in fields such as civil liberties by assisting litigants in reaching the Court (Vose 1972, 337; Lawrence 1990, 71).

scholars have deduced that group participation affects outcomes and doctrinal positions (e.g., Kobylka 1995). In his study of church–state litigation, Sorauf (1976, 352) concluded that group activity has a powerful effect on courts.

> Courts cannot ignore the demands placed upon them. As sophisticated groups and individuals bring litigation whose primary purpose is to overturn some public policy, they create enormous pressures on the courts to take precisely that activist step.

Such judgments should be given considerable weight because of the rich evidentiary base on which they rest, but there is room for differing judgments about the extent of group influence (see L. Epstein and Rowland 1991).

Some studies have assessed the impact of interest groups by measuring the effect of amicus curiae briefs on case selection or outcomes on the merits when other relevant variables are held constant. McGuire (1990) found that the relative support of amici for the two sides had a statistically significant effect on outcomes in obscenity cases. In a series of studies, Caldeira and Wright (1988, 1990a, 1994) found that amicus support for petitioners substantially increased the likelihood of a certiorari grant during two Court terms (see also McGuire and Caldeira 1993). To some degree, amicus briefs might be indicators of other case characteristics that actually influence justices. Nonetheless, these findings provide strong evidence that interest groups make a difference.

Influence on the Court by interest groups could flow from justices' interest in the content of legal policy. Caldeira and Wright (1988, 1112) viewed justices as acting to achieve policy goals; groups affect their selection of cases by giving them cues about which cases would be most useful to advance their conceptions of good policy. Similarly, the positions that interest groups take on the merits of cases might provide cues to justices about how particular cases relate to their policy preferences. Taking a different perspective, Sorauf (1976, 352) argued that courts that fail to respond to group demands for activism "risk losing support in that part of the public that expects an activist judiciary." In turn, loss of that support might diminish courts' effectiveness in shaping public policy.

Yet just as justices may court popularity in the general public for its own sake, they might seek the approval of interest groups for the same reason. They may be particularly interested in their standing with prestigious legal groups such as the American Bar Association. On the whole, however, it seems more likely that the influence of interest groups rests on justices' interest in the content of legal policy. The motivational sources of group impact have not been probed empirically. It is probably easier to distinguish among sources of influence for interest groups than it is for public opinion, because different sources may lead to different patterns of behavior: the justice who courts a group for personal reasons is likely to give more distinctive support to the group itself than is the justice who acts on the basis of a policy goal. But here too, research has concentrated thus far on the prior question of ascertaining the existence and extent of influence.

Among all the litigating groups that might influence Supreme Court policy, scholars have treated the *federal government* as unique. That treatment is appropriate, because the federal government stands out for its frequent involvement in Supreme Court litigation and for its close relationship with the Court. The government's role as a participant in litigation and the role of the solicitor general as its legal representative in the Court are familiar to students of judicial politics (see Scigliano 1971, 161–96; Salokar 1992). Equally familiar is the federal government's extraordinary success in the Court, both as party and as amicus. That success is reflected in decisions on the merits and, more dramatically, in the Court's selection of cases to hear (Salokar 1992, 106–50).

Scholars have offered several explanations for the solicitor general's success, and they disagree a good deal about the importance of particular explanations (see Tanenhaus, Schick, Muraskin, and Rosen 1963, 122; Segal 1991, 376–82; McGuire 1996). One explanation not involving direct influence is that by screening cases carefully the solicitor general brings an unusually strong set of petitions to the Court (O'Connor 1983, 259–60). Another, involving influence of a sort, is that presidential appointments produce similar perspectives in the solicitor general's office and the Court (Scigliano 1971, 182; but see Segal 1990).

Explanations that point to direct influence include the expertise of the solicitor general's office in litigation (Provine 1980, 86–92); its perceived expertise, which gives greater weight to its positions (Scigliano 1971, 182–91); the justices' gratitude to the government for its self-restraint in petitioning for certiorari (Scigliano 1971, 182–91); and the Court's dependence on the executive branch to help implement and legitimate its decisions (Puro

1981, 228–29; Salokar 1992, 177). The gratitude explanation relates most directly to work load, while the others are more closely linked with justices' interest in the content of legal policy. More broadly, a number of scholars have suggested that justices' deference to the executive branch or a general affinity between the executive and judiciary help to account for the government's success in the Court (Scigliano 1971, 182–91; Segal 1990, 147–49; Salokar 1992, 176–80); these links between Court and executive might have several motivational bases.

The most significant empirical evidence on the solicitor general's influence comes from multivariate studies of case selection (Caldeira and Wright 1988) and of decisions on the merits (Segal 1984; Segal and Reedy 1988; McGuire 1990; George and Epstein 1992). These studies indicate that, when other factors are held constant, the federal government still fares considerably better than other litigants. This finding suggests that the federal government's success reflects real influence and not just the cases it brings or the positions it takes.

But what are the sources of this influence? Little has been done to distinguish empirically among the many possible sources of the solicitor general's advantage. The most systematic research was undertaken by McGuire (1996), who analyzed decisions on the merits in the 1977–82 terms. McGuire concluded that the expertise of lawyers in the solicitor general's office based on their experience before the Court accounted for at least the preponderance of their high rate of success. This finding is important, because it suggests that the executive branch exerts no pull on the Court beyond that available to other litigants. It may be that this is true for decisions on the merits but that there are multiple sources for the much greater advantage of the federal government in getting its cases accepted by the Court.

This discussion of the Court's audiences has underlined the difficulty of ascertaining external influence on the Court and, even more, of identifying the motivations that allow any influence to occur. Two factors further complicate these tasks. First, justices may well vary in both the identities of the audiences that influence them and the extent of this influence, in part because they have different mixes of goals. Thus it is important to probe the impact of external forces on individual justices, as several studies have done (e.g., Segal 1988; Marshall 1989; Lawrence 1990; Caldeira and Wright 1994; Mishler and Sheehan 1996). These studies show differences among justices in the congruence and covariation between their positions and such external forces as majority opinion in the general public, though this variation may not result from differences in influence. In any event, analysis routinely should extend to the individual level. More fundamental is a second complication: if justices *are* influenced by audiences outside the Court, those groups do not necessarily fit the categories on which scholars have focused. For instance, legal academics may be quite important to some justices (W. Murphy 1964, 63; Posner 1990, 132; see Fuld 1953, 915–16). It appears that some justices care about their place in history, so that they pay attention to an amorphous and somewhat inchoate audience (see Mauro 1995; B. Schwartz 1996b, vii–xii). Even justices who care about public opinion may aim at particular segments of the public rather than the general population. For this reason, the analyses of external influence that have been done so far may miss much of the influence that actually occurs.

Two current justices illustrate these complications. In their orientations toward the world outside the Court, President Bush's appointees seem to differ a good deal. David Souter surely cares about audiences outside the Court; after all, he helped to write an opinion that is striking in its concern with public perceptions of the Court (*Planned Parenthood v. Casey* 1992). But his outside activities appear to be quite limited (Biskupic 1994b), and he may orient himself heavily toward the Court itself. If so, external audiences might be only moderately salient to him. It also seems likely that their influence is relatively complex and nuanced.

In contrast with Souter, Clarence Thomas clearly is very interested in audiences outside the Court (M. Fisher 1995; A. Williams 1995). He has given several speeches to conservative organizations and received an award from one (Biskupic 1993). He had a meeting with African Americans, including journalists, at which he defended his positions on the Court (Biskupic 1994c). He reportedly described himself as "a very good friend" of conservative commentator Rush Limbaugh, and he officiated at Limbaugh's wedding (Mauro 1994, 51).[25] It is quite uncertain how much these audiences influence Thomas's behavior as a justice, but the potential for influence seems greater than it does for Souter. More important, the audiences about which Thomas seems to care most

---

25. It may also be relevant that Virginia Lamp Thomas, Clarence Thomas's wife, wrote an article for *People* magazine about the battle over his confirmation shortly afterward, one that understandably portrayed the justice in a very positive light (V. Thomas 1991; see R. Cohen 1991).

do not fit the categories on which research has focused, and their influence would be quite difficult to measure.

Summing up

I have emphasized how little we know about the motivational sources of any influence on the Supreme Court from the Court's audiences. The same can be said about other issues discussed in this section, including the broadest issue: the relative importance to the justices of goals connected with the content of legal policy and other types of goals. Students of the Court generally assume that justices act to advance their conceptions of good law or good policy, and supporting that assumption are strong theoretical arguments and considerable empirical evidence. But those arguments and evidence are not conclusive.

One reason is that justices clearly care about things other than the content of legal policy. Despite a substantial degree of insulation from their environment, many justices show serious interest in the ways that various audiences perceive them as individuals and the Court as an institution. They also show serious interest in their work loads. It would be surprising if they did *not* care about the length of their days at work or their standing with external groups.

This does not necessarily mean that personal standing or limited work loads are important operative goals for the justices, independent of their interest in the content of legal policy. It is quite possible that the goals of pleasing audiences and limiting work loads for their own sake have only a peripheral effect on justices' behavior in deciding cases, sufficiently limited that their impact can safely be ignored. But that is not self-evident from what we know about the Court. Both theoretically and empirically, the breadth of the justices' operative goals remains an open question.

Conclusions

Judges differ in their inherent goals, and court situations differ in the ways they translate inherent goals into operative goals. For both reasons, diffcrent courts may feature quite different mixes of operative goals.

The scholarship on judicial behavior suggests the metaphor of a pyramid to describe differences in judges' goals across court levels. In particular, there is a striking difference between the breadth and heterogeneity of goals depicted collectively by students of state trial courts and the narrowness and homogeneity depicted by students of the Supreme Court.

The depiction of state trial courts suggested by the relevant scholarship should be regarded as tentative, because research on those courts has given limited attention to judicial behavior as such; we need to learn more. Still, this depiction is consistent with the situations of judges in those courts. Working in a complicated situation, state trial judges could be expected to act on a wide range of goals. Further, they would seem likely to differ considerably in their priorities among these goals.

Although scholarship on midlevel courts is far from any consensus about the forces that influence judges, taken as a whole that research is also consistent with the pyramid metaphor. However, there remains a great need for more research with a broad focus, aimed at sorting out the relative importance of different considerations in the decisions of courts such as state supreme courts and federal district courts. Because these courts differ in important respects, such as their positions within judicial systems, the picture that emerges from additional research may be of considerable intercourt variation in operative goal orientations.

Having just said a great deal about the Supreme Court, I want to make only one additional point. The strong basis for accepting the dominance of legal and policy goals in the Court has deterred scholars from considering directly the impact of other motivations on the justices. Despite all the research that has been done on Supreme Court behavior, this is one set of issues that is understudied and that merits more concerted research.

The issues on which Supreme Court scholars *have* focused follow the assumption of primacy for the content of legal policy. One central question for students of the Supreme Court, a question applied to other courts as well, is the relative importance of legal and policy considerations in shaping judges' choices. That issue is the concern of chapter 3.

CHAPTER 3

Law and Policy

Judicial power, as contradistinguished from the power of the
laws, has no existence. Courts are the mere instruments of the
law, and can will nothing. (Chief Justice John Marshall for the
Supreme Court in *Osborn v. U.S. Bank* 1824, 866)

Were my purely personal attitude relevant I should wholeheart-
edly associate myself with the general libertarian views in the
Court's opinion, representing as they do the thought and action
of a lifetime. . . . It can never be emphasized too much that one's
own opinion about the wisdom or evil of a law should be
excluded altogether when one is doing one's duty on the bench.
(Supreme Court Justice Felix Frankfurter, dissenting in *Board
of Education v. Barnette* 1943, 646–47)

My fundamental commitment, if I am confirmed, will be to
totally disregard my own personal belief. (Supreme Court nom-
inee William Rehnquist, testifying before the Senate Judiciary
Committee in 1971 [Mason 1979, 293])

The study of judicial behavior in political science is rooted in skepticism about the theory of judging reflected in those three statements. For several decades, political scientists have agreed on the
proposition that judges do more than apply the law, that their conceptions of good policy influence their choices. But scholars have
disagreed vehemently about the relative importance of judges'
interests in good law and good policy.

This debate has focused most heavily on the Supreme Court.
One reason is that most scholars treat the content of legal policy as
the only important consideration in the justices' choices, so the distinction between law and policy is especially sharp in the Court.
But the debate extends to other courts as well, and appropriately
so: even if lower-court judges act on a wide array of goals, the balance between law and policy is still important to their behavior.
This chapter addresses that debate by considering the impact of
legal and policy goals on judicial behavior.

Conceptual Issues

The meaning of legal and policy goals requires some discussion. On its face, each may seem quite simple. Policy-minded judges take positions that reflect their conceptions of desirable public policy, while law-minded judges take positions that reflect their conceptions of the law's dictates. Because of this apparent simplicity, scholars generally do not define what they mean by law-oriented and policy-oriented behavior (but see Segal and Spaeth 1993, 32, 65). But neither concept is that simple.

Complications on the policy side arise from the different objects on which a policy-oriented judge could focus. Such a judge might care primarily about the outcome of specific cases, wins and losses for litigants. A judge may like to see personal injury plaintiffs win, for instance. Alternatively, a judge might concentrate on the Court's promulgation of legal doctrine because rules that extend beyond a specific case have a broader potential impact on government and society. In turn, judges might care about doctrine for its effects on particular groups such as corporations and racial minority groups or for its impact on general values such as freedom and equality.[1]

Legal goals are even more complicated. Table 1.1 distinguishes between two kinds of legal goals, legal accuracy (accurate interpretation of the law) and legal clarity (clear and consistent interpretation of the law). Accuracy and clarity have much in common. For one thing, in some respects they produce similar behavior. Judges may adhere to precedent in order to maintain clarity and consistency in the law or because they seek to follow applicable legal rules. Moreover, accuracy and clarity both contrast with policy goals: law-oriented judges eschew opportunities to make what they see as good policy in order to make good law. For this reason, it seems likely that judges who give a high priority to one type of legal goal do the same for the other. But the distinction between the two should be kept in mind. A judge who approaches antitrust law with the goal of interpreting the Sherman and Clayton Acts accurately might reach different results from the judge who wants to minimize ambiguity in the law.[2]

---

1. This distinction among three types of objects is somewhat parallel to Casper's (1972) typology of orientations for lawyers in Supreme Court cases.

2. Another difference between the two types of legal goals is that judges who act solely to advance their conceptions of good policy might see legal clarity (e.g., adherence to precedent) as one means to that end, while an effort to maximize legal accuracy conflicts more directly with the goal of achieving good policy.

Judicial restraint, an object of considerable scholarly attention (Halpern and Lamb 1982), should be fitted into the distinction between law and policy. Restraint and its antithesis, judicial activism, have been given a variety of meanings (Canon 1982). Judicial restraint sometimes means that judges assign a high priority to legal accuracy or legal clarity (see Canon 1982, 392–98). In this sense, it simply refers to elevating legal considerations over policy considerations.

In contrast, scholars often speak of judicial restraint as deference to the policy choices of other institutions (see Flango and Ducat 1977). This latter meaning is the primary object of the debate about whether Justice Felix Frankfurter was a supporter of judicial restraint or simply a belated conservative (Grossman 1962; Spaeth 1964). Deference to other institutions "looks" legal, in that the judge who engages in it subordinates policy considerations to a more fundamental principle. For this reason, those who make normative arguments for law-oriented behavior frequently argue for judicial deference as well (McDowell 1985; Wolfe 1991). Similarly, scholars who are skeptical about law as a motivating force for judges tend to question the existence of judicial deference (Rodell 1962; Spaeth and Altfeld 1986).

Conceptually, deference to other institutions should not be treated as a form of law-oriented behavior. Rather, this type of judicial restraint is best understood as a particular kind of policy-oriented behavior, one based on concern for the structure of government power rather than substantive policy goals (see L. Cohen and Spitzer 1994, 71). In this respect it is similar to positions on other structural issues such as federalism and the balance between congressional and presidential power.

Yet it is true that political leaders who care a good deal about policy typically subordinate structural to substantive considerations. For instance, liberals and conservatives both tend to support federalism only when it serves their ideological purposes. For this reason, judges' willingness to deviate from their substantive policy preferences in order to follow structural preferences might serve as one indicator of their willingness to subordinate policy to law. But that indicator should be interpreted with considerable caution.

Legal and policy goals are parallel in their application of different criteria to the content of legal policy. One important difference concerns levels of interpersonal disagreement (see Schofield 1995, 205–6). Different judges who seek legal accuracy or clarity are trying to reach the same end. Thus, disagreements among them are not in their preferences but in their beliefs about what actions are most consistent with their preferences. In contrast, the preferences of policy-oriented judges differ, often a great deal: one gives a high priority to the rights of criminal defendants, another to crime control. Thus, a set of nine Supreme Court justices could share the goal of legal accuracy, but nine policy-oriented justices would have different sets of policy goals.[3]

Judges who care about the content of legal policy could act sincerely, simply taking the positions that accord with their conceptions of good law or good policy. Or they might behave strategically, taking positions that they think will best advance their goals in the collective choices of their court and other institutions. Strategy is usually associated with policy goals, and chapter 4 examines the use of strategy to advance policy goals. But law-minded judges might also act strategically (Ferejohn and Weingast 1992a, 1992b).

As is true of other issues, it is difficult to infer the relative importance of legal and policy goals from patterns of judicial behavior. The multiple forms and manifestations of these goals add to this difficulty. This is also an issue on which judges' own descriptions of their motivations must be interpreted with particular care. As the quotations at the beginning of the chapter illustrate, the norm that judges *should* base their decisions on legal considerations biases the ways that they describe the sources of their behavior. The state of our knowledge about law and policy in judges' decisions reflects these difficulties.

Taking these difficulties into account, this chapter considers the evidence on this issue. Setting aside other goals that shape judicial behavior, the chapter examines the balance between legal and policy goals. The most direct contrast in goals, and the one that scholars have emphasized, is between good policy and accurate interpretation of the law; the chapter focuses chiefly on that contrast. The next section considers theoretical issues concerning the balance between law and policy. The two sections that follow analyze relevant empirical evidence, first on the Supreme Court and then on other courts.

---

3. This distinction should not be overdrawn. Two judges who seek legal accuracy might be so strongly attached to different modes of legal interpretation that, in effect, they hold different goals. For that matter, differing preferences about public policy might be regarded as differences over means to achieve the shared goal of good policy. In practice, however, disagreements about the means to achieve good policy run considerably deeper than disagreements about the means to achieve good law.

Theoretical Issues

The distinction between inherent and operative goal orientations is especially relevant to the balance between legal and policy considerations. In examining that balance theoretically, I begin by considering law and policy as inherent goals and then probe their operative impact on judicial behavior.

Inherent Goals

How much do judges care about advancing legal and policy goals? Of course, most scholars are highly skeptical of judges' claims that they want only to interpret the law accurately (see Haines 1922, 96–98; Segal and Spaeth 1993, 33–53). For the most part, however, students of judicial behavior focus on the operative impact of these goals rather than their inherent importance to judges. Yet that inherent importance merits consideration.

The most striking characteristic of legal and policy goals is their basic similarity. Both involve a desire to shape the content of legal policy. Neither involves self-interest in any direct way. In these senses they rest on the same premises, and they are equally plausible as inherent goals.

If we think of legal accuracy and good policy as proximate goals that are connected to more distal goals, many of the likely connections also look similar. In one of the few efforts to articulate the functions of policy goals for judges, Landes and Posner (1975, 887) suggested the possibility that a judge "derives personal satisfaction from preferring one party to the lawsuit over the other or one policy over another . . ." (see also Higgins and Rubin 1980, 130). Judges also could gain personal satisfaction by taking positions that they regard as good law. As Judge Posner (1995, 131) noted, "The pleasure of judging is bound up with compliance with certain self-limiting rules that define the 'game' of judging," rules that may include adherence to the dictates of law (see Curtis 1959, 156–57). Put in other terms, it pleases judges to carry out what they conceive as the judge's role.

Alternatively, judges might pursue legal or policy goals to obtain the approbation of audiences that are important to them. Groups with particular views about public policy may give support to a judge whose decisions are consistent with those views, support that sometimes is as concrete as official recognitions and awards (see Biskupic 1993). Audiences within the legal community also may be impressed by what they perceive as a judge's ability to interpret the law accurately, and to a degree the law reviews serve as evaluators of judges' skill as interpreters. Even if judges do not act consciously to please such audiences, feelings of accountability to a particular audience can affect their reasoning in cases, causing an increased effort to reach the "right" legal result or to reach an outcome consistent with the policy preferences of that audience (see Tetlock 1983, 1985a, 1985b; Mero and Motowidlo 1995). There is good reason to think that most lawyers care a good deal about both law and policy. All lawyers undergo law-school training that emphasizes the value of legally oriented judging (Stinchcombe 1990; see Howard 1981, 115–24; M. Miller 1995, 17–28). Most engage in the practice of law, which requires them to consider issues in legal terms. As a result, lawyers are likely to develop the feeling that judges should pursue legal accuracy and clarity. At the same time, one attraction of the legal profession for people is their interest in politics and policy, an interest often reinforced by lawyers' practices and avocations.

Undoubtedly, these and other influences operate to create differences among lawyers in the relative importance they ascribe to legal and policy goals. Thus recruitment is important in determining the mix of these goals in the judiciary. As noted in chapter 2, scholars have given little attention to the impact of judicial recruitment on judges' inherent goal orientations; once again, that impact can be discussed in speculative terms.

On the supply side, the question is the kinds of lawyers who are attracted to judgeships. One possibility is that judgeships are most attractive to lawyers who like to analyze issues in legal terms and who are oriented toward legal audiences. In contrast, policy-oriented lawyers might prefer arenas other than the judiciary. That preference may be symbolized by former Senator Howard Baker's expression of his lack of interest in a nomination to the Supreme Court: "I've seen funeral homes that are livelier than that court" (*California Lawyer* 1987, 12). Yet judgeships provide good opportunities to express policy positions and perhaps to shape public policy, and for this reason a lawyer who cares primarily about policy could find a judicial position quite fulfilling.

On the demand side, policy is typically a more important consideration than law for political leaders who help to select judges. Presidents are fond of talking about their Supreme Court nominees' skill in the legal craft, but Democrats seldom choose highly skilled conservatives, and Republicans typically refrain from nominating equally impressive liberals. This emphasis on policy might favor the selection of judges who give a high priority to policy, because their positions on relevant issues are relatively visible and stable. As suggested in chapter 2, such a tendency would operate primarily in higher courts, for which selecting officials pay more attention to potential judges' policy views.

Potential judges' orientations may differ with their career experiences. Lawyers who spend their whole pre-judicial careers in legal practice might tend to think about legal policy from a legal perspective, while those who have devoted themselves to politics and government might be more policy-oriented. Studies of judges' backgrounds show that neither type of background predominates. The most extensive study of state trial judges indicates that most come from private practice but that past involvement in partisan politics is at least as extensive as it is for federal judges (Ryan, Ashman, Sales, and Shane-DuBow 1980, 124–27). In the state supreme courts and lower federal courts, the primary subjects of background research, some judges have records of substantial experience and achievement in the practice of law, others have engaged in a great deal of political and government activity, and many have a mix of the two (Goldman 1995a; Glick and Emmert 1986). The same is true of the Supreme Court, though historically there has been something of a shift away from pre-appointment political careers and toward careers in legal practice and the judiciary (Schmidhauser 1959, 32–34).

This discussion leads to no definitive conclusions, but it suggests the possibility of wide variation among judges in inherent goals. Judges who announce that they (unlike their baser colleagues) are following the dictates of the law usually deserve the scorn they receive, but in fact some judges might be more inclined than others to seek legal accuracy as opposed to good policy. Still, it seems reasonable to assume that most judges—like most lawyers—give a high priority to both law and policy. The question, then, is how characteristics of judges' situations affect the operative importance of legal and policy goals.

Judges' Situations and Operative Goals

One pervasive characteristic of judges' situations is that decisions are framed in legal terms. Lawyers' arguments for their positions typically are arguments about the state of the law. Judges themselves talk and write about their choices primarily in legal terms, not only in opinions but in their communications with each other during the decision process (Murphy 1964, 44 n.*; Brenner and Stier 1995, 4; Knight and Epstein 1996a). This placement of decisions in a legal context can have a powerful effect on judges' choices, giving greater weight to their interest in legal accuracy and clarity (see G. Rosenberg 1994).

For many scholars, however, the effects of the legal context are outweighed by the legal ambiguity of cases: relevant legal rules do not lead clearly to a particular decision. One contribution of the legal realists was to emphasize the existence of legal ambiguity (Rumble 1968, 48–106; see Fisher, Horwitz, and Reed 1993). This emphasis has been renewed by the critical legal studies movement (C. Dalton 1985; Solum 1987). Scholars in that movement have gone so far as to argue that even seemingly clear legal provisions such as the Constitution's minimum age for presidents are in fact indeterminate in meaning (D'Amato 1989).

While most students of judicial politics would stop short of that position, there is widespread agreement among them that legal ambiguity limits the impact of legal goals on judicial decisions. For example, Segal and Spaeth (1993, 70) stressed the effects of the Supreme Court's discretionary jurisdiction. They argued that legal goals have no impact in the Court because the cases that the Court chooses to hear "tender plausible legal arguments on both sides." It follows from this argument that if Supreme Court justices care more about policy than law, it is easy for them to find legal justification for whatever positions they prefer. But even if justices give a higher priority to legal accuracy, they have no choice but to decide between plausible arguments on the basis of their views about policy. In this way policy wins out as an operative goal no matter what weights the justices accord to legal and policy goals.

Yet this is not the only possible effect of legal ambiguity. Even when the state of the law does not dictate a particular result, often (perhaps usually) it provides more support for one litigant than for the other, more support for one legal rule than for an alternative rule. To the extent that judges care about interpreting the law accurately, that they want to reach the "best" result in legal terms, their choices are influenced by their reading of the law.

Thus, even if the law is always indeterminate in the sense that it does not lead inevitably to one result, judges may still act on their own perceptions of the law. Scholars can construct an argument that the Constitution does not forbid a thirty-year-old person from serving as president. But a judge who does not find this argument credible would see a case involving the candidacy of a thirty-year-old as an easy one in legal terms.

One way to understand the interplay of legal and policy considerations in decision making is through the theory of motivated reasoning in psychology (Kunda 1990; see also Showers and Cantor 1985; Pyszczynski and Greenberg 1987; W. Klein and Kunda 1992; Ditto and Lopez 1992; Baumeister and Newman 1994).[4] Judges are likely to hold both the "accuracy" goal of interpreting the law accurately and the "directional" goal of reaching a result consistent with their policy preferences. Even when people are strongly motivated by an accuracy goal, the several stages of their decision processes are biased powerfully—though perhaps unconsciously—by their directional goal.

Yet the accuracy goal constrains this bias, because decision makers want to reach results that they can accept as correct. "People will come to believe what they want to believe only to the extent that reason permits" (Kunda 1990, 483). This idea was expressed in less theoretical terms by a California judge who complained about lawyers' failure to supply her with good legal arguments for their positions: "Many times I'd like to get where they were going but they wouldn't spout law to show me how to get there" (Felitti 1995, 110).

Thus the ambiguity that typically exists in application of legal rules to a case gives judges great freedom to reach the result they prefer on policy grounds, whether or not they recognize that they are doing so. But judges' desire to reach legally accurate results, if it is substantial, makes this freedom less than absolute.[5] Even when it is possible to find some legal justification for either of two alternative results, the result for which there seems to be a better justification has an advantage.

Variation among Cases and Courts

One important aspect of judges' situations is variation in the characteristics of the cases to be decided. All else being equal, the relative importance of legal accuracy and good policy as operative judicial goals is likely to differ considerably among cases (Lindquist and Songer 1994).

---

4. Some political science accounts of judicial decision making track the theory of motivated reasoning in part. See, for instance, R. Smith 1995.

5. As suggested earlier in other terms, judges' perceptions of their audiences probably affect the balance between accuracy and directional goals in their reasoning processes.

For one thing, the importance of policy considerations varies with the relevance of judges' policy preferences. Judges may find it relatively difficult to ascertain how their preferences apply to some cases, particularly when the issues do not relate directly to conventional ideological dimensions. Like scholars, Supreme Court justices undoubtedly have trouble superimposing an ideological framework on boundary disputes between states: the Island Exception to the Rule of the Thalweg, for example, is not easily classified as a liberal or a conservative doctrine (*Louisiana v. Mississippi* 1995). In such cases, judges might be more inclined to decide on the basis of legal considerations (Macey and Miller 1992).

Further, judges' policy preferences on some issues may be considerably more important to them than their preferences on other issues (Schauer 1991; Pickerill 1996; see Petty and Krosnick 1995; Boninger, Krosnick, and Berent 1995). The federal judges who addressed the issue probably did not have strong feelings about whether brokerage subsidiaries of national banks could sell annuities (*Nationsbank of North Carolina v. Variable Annuity Life Insurance Co.* 1995). Nor are state judges likely to be stirred by disputes between businesses over responsibility for sales taxes (*Continental Eagle Corp. v. Tanner & Co. Ginning* 1995) or the apportionment of fault for a collision between two trucks (*Kilpatrick v. Alliance Casualty Reinsurance Company* 1995).

Perhaps the most important source of differences among cases is variation in legal ambiguity. Judges and commentators often distinguish between "easy" and "hard" cases, a distinction based chiefly on the extent of legal ambiguity (Cardozo 1924, 60; Easterbrook 1982, 805–7; Lyons 1984; Coffin 1994, 275; see Dworkin 1975). This distinction oversimplifies a continuum into a dichotomy. But it suggests that judges who care about both law and policy may apply these goals differently in different cases. The easy case gives precedence to legal considerations, because judges are directed to the result that has greater legal support. From the perspective of motivated reasoning, judges are unlikely to reach a decision consistent with their policy preferences when they would have great difficulty justifying it in legal terms. In contrast, the very hard case gives judges free rein to justify whatever decision best accords with their policy views.

Differences among cases translate into differences among courts based on the mixes of cases they hear. The primary source of such differences among appellate courts is discretionary jurisdiction. For one thing, in state courts whose jurisdiction is chiefly mandatory, the narrowness of issues in many cases may reduce the overall relevance of judges' policy views. This seemed to be true of the Rhode Island Supreme Court described by Beiser (1973). In contrast, the Supreme Court's jurisdiction is almost entirely discretionary, and its exercise of that discretion ensures that the average case it decides is considerably more important than the average case heard by most other appellate courts (see Gressman 1964; Caldeira and Wright 1988).

More important, the extent of a court's discretionary jurisdiction affects the mixes of easy and hard cases. The Supreme Court's criteria for case selection, such as the existence of doctrinal conflict between lower courts, favor cases in which strong arguments can be made on both sides (see Caldeira and Wright 1988; Perry 1991). As Segal and Spaeth (1993, 70) suggested, the justices ordinarily see no reason to decide cases in which the weight of the law lies heavily on one side. In contrast, judges on intermediate appellate courts, whose jurisdiction is mostly mandatory, contend that high proportions of their cases are easy—typically, easy victories for appellees (Aldisert 1987, 462, 466; Edwards 1991, 856–58; see Schick 1970, 314; Wold 1978, 61–62).

Intercourt differences in the mix of easy and hard cases should not be exaggerated. A California study indicated that judges on state intermediate appellate courts overstate the obviousness of results in "easy" cases (Davies 1982), and the same may be true of the federal intermediate courts. Moreover, it has been argued that some Supreme Court cases are relatively easy in legal terms (Tate 1981, 356). Still, the mix of cases in the Supreme Court seems less favorable to decision on the basis of legal considerations than the mix in intermediate courts. At least to that degree, scholars who argue that Supreme Court justices enjoy a special freedom from legal constraints are correct.

A complication should be brought in. When commentators speak of easy and hard cases, they are referring primarily to the outcome for the litigants. But for appellate courts in general, and certainly for supreme courts, the promulgation of legal doctrine usually is a more important component of legal policy than is the aggregate of wins and losses for litigants. In patent law, for instance, we (or at least those few people with an interest in patent law) care less about the proportion of cases won by patent owners than about the rules that the courts establish for patent validity and infringement.[6] Undoubtedly, there is a correlation between the extent of legal ambiguity concerning the outcome and the extent concerning doctrine. But the two do not coincide perfectly—as suggested by unanimous Supreme Court decisions in which there is no majority opinion.

This complication is of little relevance to trial courts, in which case outcomes typically are far more important than doctrine. State trial judges seldom pronounce doctrine in published opinions, and publication is relatively uncommon even in federal district courts (Olson 1992). Another difference between trial and appellate courts is that a great deal of what trial judges do involves ascertaining facts.[7] While they must deal with the ambiguity of law, they also deal with the ambiguity of facts, an ambiguity captured (though certainly exaggerated) by Jerome Frank's (1949, 14) famous dictum that "Facts Are Guesses."

The ambiguity of trial-court outcomes in civil cases has been a distinct and major issue in the field of law and economics.[8] Priest and Klein (1984; see Priest 1980) argued that, as a general tendency, litigants bring to trial only those cases that are "close" and thus hard, because they find it much easier to settle cases in which one side clearly has a better chance to win. For this reason, Priest and Klein said, plaintiffs and defendants in a particular field each tend to win about 50 percent of the cases that actually go to verdict. But they pointed to conditions that would cause deviation from a 50–50 split of outcomes, and other scholars have argued with considerable force that even the general tendency does not exist (Wittman 1985; Eisenberg 1990; Gross and Syverud 1991; see Kessler, Meites, and Miller 1996). If this argument is valid, then it might be that trial judges face a significant proportion of easy cases. In part because this picture is uncertain, comparison between trial and appellate courts in the degree of ambiguity in case outcomes is difficult.[9]

The differences among courts that I have discussed so far stem

---

6. Presumably, this is true of judges as well. However, this point should not be overstated. Judges may develop a "rooting interest" in the outcome of the case for the litigants, and competition to win a majority in appellate courts may accentuate their interest in outcomes as distinct from doctrine.

7. On the importance of fact-finding in trial courts and its implications for the decision-making process, see Rowland and Carp 1996, 136–73.

8. Other social scientists have done empirical research on the kinds of cases that go to trial on both the civil (H. Ross 1980) and criminal (Mather 1979) sides of the law.

9. Certainly there is not a 50–50 split of outcomes between appellants and appellees in decisions by appellate courts: appellants win far less than half the time in most intermediate courts (see Chapper and Hanson 1989, 34–35; Administrative Office of the United States Courts 1996, 108; Judicial Council of California 1994, 86). And if

from the cases they hear. Another source of intercourt variation is the frequency with which decisions are reviewed by higher courts. In this respect the Supreme Court is unique, because it faces no appellate review at all. Other courts vary considerably in the numbers and proportions of their decisions that undergo review. For example, federal district judges receive far more appellate scrutiny than do most municipal court judges.

It seems reasonable to posit a correlation between the frequency with which judges undergo appellate review and their compliance with the doctrinal positions of higher courts. Thus appellate review could be said to strengthen judges' interest in legal accuracy, at least insofar as accuracy means adherence to the legal positions of the reviewing court. But the strength of appellate review as a control mechanism is a matter of debate. Further, judges who act to avoid reversal by higher courts may be motivated by goals other than legal accuracy. These issues are considered in chapter 4.

I have referred to two characteristics that may operate to give policy considerations a special importance in the Supreme Court relative to legal considerations, characteristics noted in table 2.1: the lack of higher-court review of the Court's decisions and its possession and use of discretionary jurisdiction. Because of these characteristics, some scholars argue explicitly that the Court is unique in the dominance of policy over law (Segal and Spaeth 1993, xv–xvi, 70–72; see Rowland and Carp 1996, 139).

Indeed, most students of judicial behavior implicitly treat the Supreme Court as different from other courts in this respect. On the whole, lower-court research ascribes some importance to judges' legal goals, and most texts that look at the judicial process across all courts treat both law and policy as important elements in judges' choices.[10] In contrast, Supreme Court scholarship—includ-

the Supreme Court accepted a random sample of petitions rather than looking for hard cases, the success rate for appellants probably would be quite low. This pattern of outcomes is consistent with the widespread perception that a high proportion of appellate cases are easy.

Why do appellants bring and carry forward weak appeals? They often have high stakes in a case that justify appeal even when the chances of success are limited. Delaying the final outcome also may be attractive to the appellant. Other reasons include exaggeration of the chances of success and the expressive value of appeal (see Mann 1983). Priest and Klein (1984, 28–29) themselves argued that systematic deviations from a 50–50 split of outcomes between appellants and appellees are likely because of differences in the stakes that the two sides have in legal precedent.

10. See Ball 1987, 232–36, 249–50, 281–82; Carp and Stidham 1991, 160–64; Louthan 1991, 153; and Tarr 1994, 291, 294. Some texts, however, emphasize policy considerations (C. Smith 1993, 129–30, 133, 141–43; Glick 1993, 305, 346).

ing the most influential books—generally emphasizes justices' policy goals (e.g., W. Murphy 1964; Schubert 1965; Rohde and Spaeth 1976; Segal and Spaeth 1993). Indeed, scholars who think that legal considerations influence the justices in significant ways tend to write in the spirit of fighting against a conventional wisdom (e.g., Brigham 1978; Perry 1991; Gillman 1993).

If there are good theoretical reasons for this distinction among courts, the empirical support for it remains to be considered. What evidence is there for the dominance of policy goals in the Supreme Court, and what do we know about the importance of legal and policy goals in lower courts? Those questions are considered in the next two sections.

Empirical Evidence: The Supreme Court

General Analyses of Voting

On any issue that concerns the determinants of Supreme Court behavior, the first sources of evidence to be considered are the dimensional analyses of justices' votes on case outcomes and causal analyses of relationships between votes and policy preferences. As noted in chapter 2, the findings of these analyses suggest the centrality of justices' policy preferences in determining their votes on case outcomes. The question in that chapter was how much room these findings leave for goals unrelated to the content of legal policy; my conclusion was that they left enough room for these other goals to play a significant part in decision making. If this conclusion is justified, it follows that these findings allow for legal goals to exert considerable impact as well. But the caveats raised in chapter 2 about interpretation of these findings should be applied specifically to legal goals.

One caveat concerns the potential impact of forces that affect all the justices in similar ways. It is true that justices do not undertake the task of legal interpretation in uniform fashion. The current debate in the Supreme Court over the use of legislative history in statutory interpretation is an example of divergence in their approaches (see *Conroy v. Aniskoff* 1993; *Bank One Chicago v. Midwest Bank & Trust Co.* 1996). But for the most part, justices were trained in similar ways to read the law. Thus, to the extent that their judgments in a particular case incorporate assessments of the state of the law, those assessments are likely to have similar effects on different justices—to move them in the same direction, at the least. If so, legal goals could have substantial effects on the justices' votes, but effects that cannot be detected from voting differences among justices.

In contrast, it is unlikely that the differences among justices found by dimensional studies are reinforced by legal considerations. Even if justices do differ consistently in their modes of legal interpretation, the differences in voting that result should cut across ideological lines rather than reinforcing them. A refusal to consider the legislative history of statutes, for instance, would favor conservative results in some cases and liberal results in others.[11] In turn, this means that goals of legal accuracy and clarity might help to explain deviations from ideologically consistent voting (see Schubert 1963a).

A final caveat concerns aspects and stages of decision making other than votes on the outcomes of cases, votes that are the focus of the dimensional and causal studies. Certainly legal considerations could affect the content of opinions to a greater, and more measurable, degree than they affect votes. It is also possible that they have a greater impact in case selection than in votes on the merits (Baum 1993). Little systematic evidence exists on the content of opinions, but it appears that justices' positions in opinions follow ideological lines in the same general way that their votes do.[12] Evidence on case selection is considered later in this section.

---

11. Of course, a particular approach to interpretation may tend to favor one side ideologically. For instance, some commentators have ascribed Justice Antonin Scalia's refusal to consider the legislative history of statutes to a perception on his part that this refusal makes it easier to reach conservative results (Liess 1993, 584–85). But truly consistent adherence to a particular approach would produce mixed results ideologically. Indeed, Scalia's refusal to consider legislative history sometimes leads him to adopt liberal positions (Eskridge 1990, 669 n. 193).

12. Indeed, my impression from reading of cases is that positions taken by justices in opinions are more consistent ideologically than are their votes. Seemingly anomalous votes often are accompanied by opinions that follow the justice's general predispositions more closely. An example is Harry Blackmun's vote to allow all the criminal prosecutions involved in *United States v. Dixon* (1993), rejecting a double jeopardy challenge, while five colleagues (including Antonin Scalia and Anthony Kennedy) voted to bar at least some of the prosecutions. Blackmun wrote a separate opinion largely agreeing with the doctrinal position of the justices who would have barred all the prosecutions but arguing that this case was different because it involved criminal contempt.

Wahlbeck (1997) provided evidence that change in the Court's membership strongly affects the doctrinal positions announced in opinions, just as it affects case outcomes.

Substantive and Structural Policy

Beyond the dimensional and causal studies of Supreme Court votes on the merits, some separate bodies of research are designed to provide more direct evidence about the impact of legal goals on justices' choices. One set of studies examines the relative importance of justices' attitudes toward substantive policy and toward structural policy. Harold Spaeth and other scholars have studied this issue by analyzing the behavior of justices who espouse support for such structural principles as federalism and judicial restraint, examining situations in which these principles conflict with a justice's apparent policy preferences on substantive issues such as labor relations (Spaeth 1963, 1964; Spaeth and Teger 1982; Spaeth and Altfeld 1986; S. Davis 1992). These studies consistently find that structural policy is subordinate to substantive policy in justices' votes (see also Cohen and Spitzer 1994, 71).[13]

Because structural policy is different from law, these findings do not tell us anything directly about the weight of legal considerations in the justices' choices. They do, however, provide additional evidence of the heavy weight of substantive policy preferences in those choices. As suggested earlier, if justices subordinate structural policy to substantive policy, there is reason to posit that they subordinate legal accuracy and clarity as well.

Precedent

The Supreme Court has overruled its own precedents with unusual frequency in the past few decades. By one careful count, there were 106 overrulings between 1960 and 1992 (Brenner and Spaeth 1995, 23, 113–21). This record has raised questions about justices' commitment to legal goals (Maltz 1980).

Justices' treatment of precedents is more ambiguous theoretically than it may seem initially. If justices depart from precedent, they might do so based on their interest in legal accuracy rather than their conceptions of good policy (see Segal and Spaeth 1996a, 975). And justices have multiple reasons to follow precedent, including an interest in simplifying the decision task (Brenner and Stier 1995, 5). Still, the treatment of precedents in subsequent cases provides important evidence about the relative importance of legal

---

13. Spaeth 1962 presented evidence suggesting that considerations of judicial power outweighed substantive policy in a small number of cases.

and policy goals, and some recent studies have examined this issue closely.

Segal and Spaeth (1996a) analyzed the subsequent behavior of justices who dissented from landmark Court rulings that had been issued since 1953. Once the ruling is made, it stands as a precedent. When the Court decides another case to which that precedent is relevant, do the dissenting justices change their position to support it or do they follow the preferences reflected in their original dissent? The findings are striking: in cases that were "progeny" of landmark decisions, 91 percent of the time justices adhered to their original positions rather than shifting to support the precedent. In a less extensive analysis of precedents established in nonlandmark cases, Segal and Spaeth (1996a, 986) found even greater adherence to justices' original positions.

Two studies replicated the Segal and Spaeth study with some modifications. Brenner and Stier (1996) focused on moderate justices, whom they saw as most likely to conform to precedent. Their coding rules differed somewhat from those used by Segal and Spaeth; most important was their exclusion of subsequent cases in which precedents were overturned, an exclusion that reduces the numbers of votes against precedents. They also included brief memorandum decisions or summary decisions.[14] Brenner and Stier found that four moderate justices adhered to their original positions 53 percent of the time; the comparable proportion for the same justices in the Segal and Spaeth study was 85 percent.

Songer and Lindquist (1996) began with the same set of cases analyzed by Segal and Spaeth but conducted two new analyses, in each of which they made one methodological change. First, they adopted coding rules under which a wider range of behavior was counted as following precedent. Doing so reduced votes that supported preferences over precedent from 91 percent to 72 percent. Second, they added to the analysis the summary decisions that were progeny of the landmark decisions while maintaining the original coding rules. This step reduced the proportion of support for preferences over precedent from 91 percent to 69 percent when the large number of summary decisions that followed one death penalty decision were excluded.

These differences in findings are striking, and these scholars sharply debated the divergent methodological choices that led to

---

14. The inclusion of summary decisions in analyses of legal and policy considerations is discussed later in this section.

the differences (Brenner and Stier 1996; Songer and Lindquist 1996; Segal and Spaeth 1996b). Yet, with one partial exception (Songer and Lindquist 1996, 1060), the three studies agreed that the pull of precedent on justices is quite imperfect, a result that is important in itself. Of course, as noted earlier, findings of these studies are subject to multiple interpretations in terms of justices' goals.

Brenner and Spaeth (1995) examined Supreme Court decisions from 1946 to 1992 that overruled past precedents. Two of their inquiries are particularly relevant to the roles of law and policy in justices' behavior. In one, they found that in nonunanimous decisions to alter precedents, there is a strong tendency for justices to take the same general ideological positions that they do in their votes across all cases. In the other inquiry, they showed that in these overruling cases justices more often follow "personal stare decisis" (adhering to their position in the case whose precedent was overruled) than ordinary stare decisis (voting to support the precedent that was overruled). Brenner and Spaeth pointed out that their sample of cases is biased because it includes only those in which precedents were overturned. For that reason their findings, though noteworthy, cannot be generalized to the justices' behavior as a whole.

These studies provide some evidence of differences among justices in adherence to precedent. In the Segal and Spaeth (1996a) study, Potter Stewart and Lewis Powell stood out for the frequency with which they changed positions to support a precedent that they had originally opposed (see also Dorsen 1993, 118). This evidence is too limited to support strong conclusions about the extent of individual differences, let alone their sources. Still, it is consistent with the view that justices differ in their mix of goals.

Legal Arguments

A different way to assess the impact of legal accuracy as a goal is to examine the types of legal arguments that justices make. In an innovative study, Phelps and Gates (1991) compared the arguments used by William Rehnquist and William Brennan. Phelps and Gates inferred from writings by the two justices that Rehnquist advocated an emphasis on what they called "textual" and "historical" arguments (those related to the intent of the framers) in constitutional cases, while Brennan favored "extrinsic" arguments based on extralegal sources. Yet a paragraph-level analysis of constitutional opinions showed only minor differences between the justices in their use of different types of arguments. In a related analysis, Gates and Phelps (1996) found that both Rehnquist and Brennan tended to reach results compatible with their ideological positions when they employed historical arguments. The implications of this study are limited by its analysis of only two justices. Neither Brennan nor Rehnquist would be among the justices most likely to subordinate policy goals to legal accuracy. And the findings do not establish that either justice was uninterested in legal accuracy. Still, the evidence analyzed by Phelps and Gates indicates that for at least two justices, commitment to an ideological direction was far stronger than commitment to a mode of constitutional interpretation. Equally important is the study's methodological contribution: Phelps and Gates showed that close textual analysis can be used to probe the impact of legal goals on decisions.

Case Facts

Several scholars have sought to measure the impact of case facts on Supreme Court decisions. Some years after the first body of systematic research on facts and decisions (Kort 1963a, 1963b, 1966, 1973; Lawlor 1963), Segal (1984) initiated a new wave of research on the subject. Seeking to identify the conditions under which the Court found searches and seizures acceptable under the Constitution, Segal looked primarily at an array of variables related to factual characteristics of cases. He treated these variables as legal because the Court's decisions established them as important criteria for decision. The fact variables included the "nature of the intrusion" (such as home, business, or person), the "extent of the intrusion," prior justification (warrant or probable cause), the arrest situation, and the existence of exceptions to the warrant and probable-cause requirements (such as "hot pursuit" of a suspect or a border search). Segal found that most of these variables had statistically significant relationships with the Court's decisions and concluded that "[t]he legal model was quite satisfactory" (1984, 900).

Several other studies have used variables based on the facts of cases to explain Supreme Court decisions. Among them are George and Epstein (1992) on capital punishment, Ignagni (1994) on establishment of religion, Segal and Reedy (1988) and Wolpert (1991) on gender discrimination, and McGuire (1990) on obscenity. The most common interpretation of case facts in these studies is as legal considerations, though the studies are not always explicit about the theoretical meaning of case facts.

When certain case facts reflected in the Court's legal doctrines affect its decisions in a consistent way, it is quite reasonable to interpret that impact as a function of the justices' interest in legal accuracy or clarity—either of which could lead them to adhere to the Court's doctrinal positions. But that is not the only plausible interpretation. Alternatively, justices may follow doctrinal rules based on case facts because those facts are relevant to their policy preferences; the existence of those doctrinal rules may simply reflect the same widely shared preferences (but see Knight 1994). Thus it is impossible, at least at this point, to reach firm conclusions about the meaning of case facts as influences on decisions. Esler (1994) argued convincingly that the findings of the case-fact research are theoretically ambiguous, and Segal and Spaeth (1993, 362 n. 16) were on firm ground in concluding that "fact models are consistent with both legal and attitudinal models."

Variation among Cases

As discussed earlier, the balance between legal and policy considerations may vary among cases, based on the clarity of applicable legal rules and the relevance of justices' policy preferences. A few studies have investigated such variation.

One focus of investigation is unanimity in the Court, which has been interpreted in quite different ways. Some scholars (Pritchett 1941, 890; Tate 1981, 356) have seen unanimous decisions as the product of relatively clear legal rules that override justices' policy preferences. At least implicitly, many scholars treat unanimity instead as a reflection of agreement based on policy preferences—in scaling terms, a j-point for a case, based solely on policy considerations, that is to the left or to the right of all the justices' i-points. In this conception, cases with unanimous decisions are not distinct from other cases. For instance, some unanimous decisions of the mid-1990s might not have been unanimous if Thurgood Marshall or William Brennan were still on the Court (e.g., *Whren v. United States* 1996).[15]

---

15. Pickerill (1996, 11–13) summarized this position and developed an argument that it is not entirely credible. He also pointed to a third possible source of unanimity: the justices have relatively weak policy preferences in some cases, so it is easier for them to reach agreement.

Studies of intermediate appellate courts have probed unanimous decisions by analyzing the relationship between the membership of court panels and the ideological direction of their decisions (Atkins and Green 1976; Songer 1982; Dubois 1988). Their findings make it clear that unanimity is promoted by similarity in judges' policy preferences. Yet these studies may have limited application to the Supreme Court, since it is far more likely that three judges will agree on a decision because of similar preferences than it is that nine will do so.

A few studies have considered unanimity in the Supreme Court itself. Brenner and Arrington (1987) analyzed unanimous decisions in 33 Court terms between 1946 and 1984, focusing on ideological patterns in case outcomes. Their most striking finding was a high proportion of liberal outcomes across the period as a whole. They interpreted this finding as incompatible with the view that unanimous decisions are the result of legal clarity, "unless one assumes that in the period under investigation, the law in the cases heard by the Court was predominately liberal" (Brenner and Arrington 1987, 82). Rather, they concluded from this and other findings, unanimity reflects the application of justices' attitudes to the stimuli of particular cases.

Spaeth (1989) sought to determine whether unanimous decisions during the Warren and Burger Courts were "truly consensual" (Songer 1982, 231, 233), with consensus suggesting that there was legal clarity on the issues involved in these decisions. Spaeth applied several indicators of an absence of consensus, including disagreement between lower-court judges and the existence of concurring opinions in the Court. He ultimately concluded that only 2 percent of the unanimous decisions were truly consensual. Even if one might disagree with some of Spaeth's criteria, he established that the great majority of unanimous decisions involved some kind of disagreement—most often between the Supreme Court and the lower court decision it reviewed. In general, such disagreements seem incompatible with legal clarity.

These studies probably rule out a simple dichotomy of decisions based on unanimity. But they do not rule out all variation in decision processes across cases, including variation that is correlated with the presence or absence of unanimity. Lindquist and Songer (1994) borrowed Perry's (1991) conception of "outcome" and "jurisprudential" modes of decision, modes that approximate the distinction between policy and legal considerations. They posited that "when precedent is clear or when the justices have little ideological concern about the outcome, the justices will operate in the jurisprudential mode" (1994, 7). They tested this hypothesis by analyzing death penalty cases from 1968 to 1988. They found a sharp contrast between dissensus in most of the major decisions and unanimity in the great majority of summary decisions that were decided on the basis of rules established in major decisions. On the basis of this finding, they concluded that justices abandoned their usual preference-based behavior in the summary decisions and acceded to clear precedents even if they disagreed with those precedents.

The validity of this conclusion depends on the motivations that underlie low dissent rates in these summary decisions. The dearth of recorded dissents in the summary cases may reflect a greater willingness to accede to precedents in summary decisions. Alternatively, it may indicate only an accepted Court practice of eschewing recorded dissents in at least some types of summary cases.[16] In any case, the Lindquist–Songer study underlines the value of investigating possible variation in decision processes.

Case Selection and its Implications

Case selection presents justices with a more complex domain in which to advance their goals than does decision on the merits, since the Court's choice of cases only sets the stage for action on the merits. Empirical studies of case selection indicate that the justices employ several criteria, which can be probed for their underlying goals. In this stage of decision, the distinction between legal accuracy and legal clarity is quite relevant.

One criterion is case importance. It is clear from simple observation that the Court tends to hear cases whose potential impact is relatively great. Further, Caldeira and Wright (1988, 1994) found that the likelihood of a certiorari grant increased with the submission of any amicus briefs and with larger numbers of briefs. This finding supports the conclusion that case importance is a powerful criterion for justices. Especially striking is the fact that briefs *against* a certiorari grant improved the chances that a case would be accepted. This criterion is consistent with an interest in good policy, legal accuracy, or legal clarity: justices who give priority to any of those criteria would look for consequential cases. However,

---

16. On the interpretation of summary decisions, see Songer and Lindquist 1996, 1055–61; Segal and Spaeth 1996b, 1077–80; and *Lawrence v. Chater* 1996.

interest groups care about cases chiefly for their impact on policy, so the Caldeira–Wright findings suggest that policy considerations are at least a substantial part of the justices' motivations in selecting cases. A second criterion, consistently found to be quite weighty, is doctrinal conflict between federal circuits (S. Ulmer 1984; Caldeira and Wright 1988, 1990a, 1994; Perry 1991). This criterion is compatible with efforts to achieve good policy and legal accuracy, but it is connected most directly with an interest in maximizing legal clarity. It seems unlikely that justices would give such a high priority to resolving intercircuit conflict if they did not attach considerable weight to legal clarity as a goal.

Two other criteria, error correction and outcome prediction, have been associated with policy goals. Error correction involves voting to hear cases in which the justice disagrees with the lower-court outcome. Outcome prediction involves voting to hear cases when the justice expects to be on the winning side if the case is decided on the merits (see Schubert 1962b).

Without question, error correction is important to the justices. The Court's high reversal rates in themselves establish its importance: in light of the large number of weak cases brought by petitioners, it is striking that annual reversal rates dip below 50 percent only occasionally (see Segal and Spaeth 1990). Studies have taken several analytic approaches to probe more directly whether justices are more inclined to hear cases in which they think that the lower-court decision was in error (S. Ulmer 1972; Songer 1979; Provine 1980, 105–13; J. Palmer 1982; Cameron, Segal, and Songer 1995; Caldeira, Wright, and Zorn 1996). Taken together, these studies provide powerful evidence that justices do engage in error correction. Studies that distinguished among justices also found that they varied in their use of error correction (see S. Ulmer 1972; Provine 1980, 108; J. Palmer 1982).

The evidence on outcome prediction is mixed. Quantitative studies have analyzed the relationship between votes to grant hearings and support from colleagues for the justice's position on the merits (Brenner 1979b; J. Palmer 1982; Brenner and Krol 1989; Krol and Brenner 1990; Boucher and Segal 1995; Segal, Boucher, and Cameron 1995; see also Provine 1980, 158–72). Although studies differ in their findings, they make it clear that justices engage in outcome prediction to some degree. The evidence of outcome prediction obtained by Caldeira, Wright, and Zorn (1996) is noteworthy because they used estimates of the justices' policy positions to analyze cases that the Court rejected as well as those that it accepted.

Some studies indicate that outcome prediction is situational (Brenner 1979b; Boucher and Segal 1995; Segal, Boucher, and Cameron 1995). Justices who favor reversal seem inclined to accept cases without taking into account the Court's potential reaction on the merits, perhaps because reversal is the more likely outcome on the merits. When they agree with the lower court, however, at least some justices consider the likely result if the Court decides the case (Boucher and Segal 1995).

Based on his interviews of justices and clerks, Perry (1991, 272–84) made the distinction between two modes of decision that Lindquist and Songer later applied to decisions on the merits. Perry concluded that once justices dispose of cases they see as frivolous, they analyze most of the remainder in a jurisprudential mode. In this mode, the first question that justices ask is whether there is a doctrinal conflict between federal circuits. But less often, when justices care a great deal about the outcome, they use the outcome mode: here, the first question they ask is whether their position is likely to win a majority on the merits. Perry (1991, 265–68, 270, 279–80) noted that the Court engages in error correction as well, but the correctness of the lower-court decision was not a criterion in either of his decision modes. Its exclusion apparently reflected a judgment that it was not an important consideration.[17]

Although error correction and outcome prediction have been identified with policy goals, they are also compatible with the goal of legal accuracy. Justices who seek to get the law "right" would also want to correct erroneous interpretations in the lower courts and might well consider the interpretation that the Supreme Court itself was likely to adopt. Accounts of the case selection process suggest that policy considerations are the dominant reason for the use of these criteria (e.g., Lewin 1973, 18), and Perry's analysis (1991, 198–207, 257, 265–66) suggests that justices' concern about outcomes stems primarily from an interest in good policy rather

---

17. Making a distinction analogous to Perry's, Pacelle (1991) concluded from his analysis of agenda change that the Court accepts some cases to serve the justices' policy goals, others to resolve lower-court conflict. Provine's (1980) depiction of case selection differed considerably from Perry's, but she also concluded that justices balance competing considerations—in her view, their policy preferences and their "conceptions of the judicial role and the Supreme Court's role" (1980, 8). Provine also found evidence of substantial differences among justices in criteria for case selection, differences that may be related to their goal orientations.

than legal accuracy. But the relative weight of these two criteria in correction and prediction has not been firmly established. The success of the federal government as a petitioner was noted in chapter 2. The extent of that success is worth reiterating: in the 1995 term, to take one example, the government won hearings with 78 percent of its petitions, compared with 1 percent for other petitioners.[18] As suggested in chapter 2, at least part of this advantage may result from direct influence on the Court, an influence that might not rest entirely on the justices' legal or policy goals. To the extent that legal or policy considerations do account for the government's advantage, their relative importance is very difficult to sort out.

The empirical research on case selection is ambiguous in its implications for judges' goal orientations. But this research provides evidence that justices' policy goals and their interest in legal clarity are both significant motivations in this process. Thus there is some disparity between the empirical evidence on justices' goals in decisions on the merits and the evidence on their goals in case selection. At the merits stage the existing evidence suggests the dominance of policy goals. In contrast, the evidence on case selection suggests something of a balance between legal and policy goals as influences on justices' choices.

It is true that the legal goal more relevant to decisions on the merits is accuracy, not clarity. But even the goal of legal clarity could have some impact at the merits stage, particularly by increasing regard for precedent. More important, justices who give weight to one legal goal are likely to give weight to the other. Thus the disparity in the evidence on the two stages of decision seems real.

There are several possible explanations for this disparity (see Baum 1993). The most relevant possibilities begin with the same premise: the case selection process tends to eliminate easy cases, those in which the applicable legal rules weigh very heavily on one side. The explanations diverge in their implications for the justices' goals in deciding cases on the merits.

In one explanation, the predominance of hard cases gradually reduces the justices' interest in legal accuracy. As they learn that few cases heard by the Court can be resolved easily on the basis of applicable legal rules, they increasingly approach cases in terms of their policy preferences. In a sense, even their inherent interest in

18. These figures are based on a table compiled and provided by the Office of the Solicitor General.

legal accuracy is worn away by the difficulty of resolving cases on the basis of legal rules.[19] Thus, if some jurisdictional change caused the Court to begin hearing many easy cases, at least for some period of time the justices would continue to emphasize policy over law.

A second explanation makes a sharper distinction between inherent and operative goals. This explanation best captures the arguments about the Court's situation made by Rohde and Spaeth (1976, 72–74) and Segal and Spaeth (1993, 69–72). Justices care about legal accuracy, but the legal ambiguity of the cases before them makes that goal irrelevant. Faced with nothing but hard cases, they have no choice but to take positions on the basis of their policy goals. In terms of the theory of motivated reasoning, the selection of cases with high levels of ambiguity elevates policy as a directional goal over the goal of legal accuracy.

But if the Court began to hear a random sample of the cases brought before it, most of them easy, the justices' interest in legal accuracy would come out immediately. The results might be striking: a high proportion of unanimous decisions, relatively few concurring opinions, and only moderate differences between the voting records of the Court's liberals and conservatives. Of course, that is a description of the Court's decisions when its jurisdiction was primarily mandatory.[20]

A final explanation is the most complex: legal accuracy is an important operative goal to the justices, but its impact is obscured. The Court's selection of close cases makes it harder to discern the impact of legal considerations in the cases that it decides, because the weight of the law seldom lies overwhelmingly on one side. In other words, since there is only moderate variance in how much existing legal rules favor one party or the other, it is particularly difficult to measure this variable and analyze its impact.[21] But the

---

19. Handberg (1991) posited a different but analogous effect of case selection, one in which the composition of the Court's cases fosters activism.

20. The dramatic increase in dissensus did not begin until more than a decade after the final major addition to the Court's discretionary jurisdiction (Walker, Epstein, and Dixon 1988; see Haynie 1992). This lag strongly suggests that change in the Court's jurisdiction was not a sufficient condition for such an immense increase in dissensus. In all likelihood, however, it was a necessary condition.

21. Further, even if we could measure the weight of the law in the cases heard by the Court, analysis of its impact on decisions might lead to misleading results. The statistical literature on selection effects demonstrates that the nonrandom elimination of some cases from analysis threatens internal validity by distorting relationships between variables even within the set of cases that can be analyzed (Heckman 1979; Berk 1983). Of course, the Court's selection of cases to hear on the merits eliminates cases in a highly nonrandom fashion; especially important is the Court's strong tendency to reject seemingly easy cases.

weight of the law may still exert a real impact on justices' choices, one that could be identified more easily even in close cases if the Court heard many easy cases. If so, our current picture of the balance between law and policy in Supreme Court behavior is misleading.

Empirical Evidence: Lower Courts

Arguably, scholars have exaggerated the difference in goal orientations between Supreme Court justices and judges on other courts. Still, there are good reasons to posit that legal goals exert a greater impact in lower courts. In any case, several types of studies have probed for their impact on lower-court decisions.

Research on lower courts can make use of the opportunity to compare courts that are subject to different legal rules. The ideal unit of analysis is the state. States differ in their constitutional and statutory provisions on the same issues: to what extent are these differences reflected in the doctrinal positions and decisional records of state supreme courts?

Some studies have addressed this question. In research on judicial expansion of the "public trust" doctrine in environmental law, Lawler and Parle (1989) included in their statistical model a variable measuring whether the state's constitution or statutes recognized the public trust concept. Swinford's (1991) analysis of judicial doctrine on inequalities in school funding included as variables the content of state constitutional provisions that could be used to challenge inequalities. In their analysis of individual votes on death sentences, Brace and Hall (1995) included the presence or absence of certain aggravating circumstances in capital punishment statutes as well as interactions between statutory provisions and related case facts. Each study found that the state of the law had some independent impact on doctrine or votes, a finding that suggests the importance of legal accuracy as a goal.

Other multivariate analyses of lower-court decision making have included variables that are designed to capture legal considerations. Two studies (Songer and Haire 1992; K. King and Davis 1995) took the parties' legal claims into account; King and Davis also considered the quality of their evidence. In his study of responses to judicial doctrines by federal courts of appeals, David Klein (1996b) used measures of the prestige and expertise of the judges who had already responded to the doctrine and the degree of consensus among the responding courts to probe for the impact of judges' interest in legal accuracy and coherence. The findings of these studies were mixed; one of their contributions is to suggest ways of measuring legal considerations.

Role Conceptions

Larger bodies of work that analyze the impact of legal accuracy as a goal for lower-court judges include the extensive research on judges' role conceptions and on sentencing behavior.[22] While some scholars have studied role conceptions of Supreme Court justices (Grossman 1962, 1968; James 1968), most research on judicial roles concerns other courts (see Flango, Wenner, and Wenner 1975; Gibson 1981b). Studies using questionnaires or interviews typically find considerable variation among judges in their self-described roles, variation that has been characterized in terms of several typologies (Glick 1971; Ungs and Baas 1972). Most often, the central dimension is interpreted as the relative weight that judges believe they should give to the state of the law as opposed to their own conception of justice (Wold 1974; Gibson 1979). In a typical typology based on this dimension, Glick and Vines (1969; see also Glick 1971; Vines 1969) labeled state supreme court justices as "law-interpreters," "law-makers," and—in a middle category—"pragmatists."

Some studies are designed only to describe patterns of judicial roles, but most examine the relationship between role conceptions and decisional behavior. Theodore Becker (1966) sought to determine whether judges who espoused stronger adherence to precedent would give greater weight to precedent in a hypothetical case designed to pit an established rule of law against a just result. Similarly, Gibson (1979) asked whether trial judges with stronger orientations to follow precedent were less likely to take extralegal variables into account in their sentencing decisions. Both studies found that judges' attitudes toward precedent had a significant impact.

Taking a different approach, Gibson's (1978b) study of Iowa trial judges found that role conceptions mediated between policy preferences and behavior: judges who accepted the legitimacy of acting on their preferences were more likely to do so. Two studies of state appellate judges (Scheb, Ungs, and Hayes 1989; Scheb, Bowen, and Anderson 1991) obtained similar results with measures of role conceptions that captured decisional criteria and

---

22. Also relevant is the research on judges' responses to the rulings of higher courts, research discussed in chapter 4.

related attitudes. Another kind of impact for role conceptions, one more difficult to interpret theoretically, is a direct relationship with the ideological direction of decisions. Howard (1977) found such a relationship, but some other studies (Glick and Vines 1969; Gibson 1978b) have not.

The findings of these studies need to be interpreted with some caution, because judges' self-described role conceptions may not be fully independent of other attitudes that influence their behavior.[23] But these findings are noteworthy, because they provide some evidence that role conceptions make a difference for judging. The studies of concern for precedent suggest directly that some judges give significant weight to legal considerations, enough weight to weaken the link between their preferences and their decisions. The studies of role conceptions as mediating factors between policy preferences and decisions do not have such clear implications, because judges might limit the weight of their policy preferences for a variety of reasons, but it is likely that legal considerations play a part. More broadly, the consistent finding of wide variation in role conceptions suggests that judges also differ substantially in their goal orientations.

Sentencing

Outside the Supreme Court, the form of judicial behavior that receives the most scholarly attention is sentencing (see Blumstein, Cohen, Martin, and Tonry 1983; Dixon 1995). Scholars in disciplines other than political science have done most of the research on sentencing. Like scholarship on plea bargaining, studies of sentencing behavior provide evidence that trial judges act on a variety of goals. Variation in sentencing among judges and courts, for instance, suggests the importance of policy preferences in shaping sentences (Diamond and Zeisel 1975; Levin 1977; Ryan 1980–81; but see L. Myers and Reid 1995). In contrast, the existence of standard sentences for particular offenses and judges' deference to recommendations by prosecutors suggest that judges give weight to other goals; for instance, they may want to limit their work loads by reducing the time and difficulty required to reach decisions (Sudnow 1965; Heumann 1978). Here my concern is with the relative importance of legal and policy goals in sentencing decisions.

---

23. Another reason for caution is that the role conceptions described by judges may relate more closely to their inherent goal orientations than to the operative goal orientations that actually shape their behavior as judges.

One central issue in sentencing research is the relative importance of "legitimate" and "illegitimate" criteria in judges' decisions. The seriousness of the offense and of the offender's prior record typically are considered legitimate criteria, while defendants' attributes such as race are illegitimate. Despite all the research on the use of these criteria in sentencing, there remains some uncertainty about their relative importance. In part, this is because of the serious methodological problems that confront analyses of this issue (Hagan and Bumiller 1983; Klepper, Nagin, and Tierney 1983). One consistent finding, however, is that where judges are given broad discretion in sentencing, the largest portion of explained variance in sentences results from offense seriousness and prior record.

This is an important finding in itself. It may also say something about the importance of legal considerations in judges' decisions, because sentencing statutes typically emphasize offense seriousness and prior record as bases for sentences. But those statutory emphases reflect widely shared values, so judges might make similar distinctions among offenses and offenders even in the absence of statutory encouragement. For that reason, the theoretical meaning of this finding is uncertain.

Also uncertain is how to interpret the evidence of discrimination in sentencing, particularly along racial lines (Myers and Talarico 1986; S. Klein, Petersilia, and Turner 1990; Baldus, Woodworth, and Pulaski 1990). Discrimination might be regarded as a product of judges' policy preferences, but it may constitute unconscious and unintended behavior that reflects no judicial goals (see Pruitt and Wilson 1983). The anecdotal evidence that individual judges are inconsistent in their sentencing choices (Dash 1975; Kunen 1983, 37, 106) is even more difficult to relate to their goals.

In recent years Congress and many state legislatures have reduced judges' discretion through mandatory minimum sentences for specific offenses (United States Sentencing Commission 1991; Tonry 1996) or through general schemes that confine sentences to a narrow range for specified combinations of circumstances (Von Hirsch, Knapp, and Tonry 1987; Griset 1991; United States General Accounting Office 1992; Frase 1995; Tonry 1996). It is noteworthy that judges often protest against such statutes (see Cauchon 1991; *United States v. Concepcion* 1992). It appears that most judges want freedom over sentencing choices in order to advance their policy goals and perhaps to maintain their self-esteem as autonomous decision makers, even though this freedom increases the costs of decision making.[24]

Judges' sentencing behavior under these statutes also yields information about their motivations, because the statutes increase the potential for conflict between legal rules and policy preferences. The evidence is mixed. Studies indicate that judges engage in variable but significant levels of noncompliance with minimum sentencing requirements (Heinzelmann 1985; Ross and Foley 1987; Ross 1992, 57–58; Tonry 1996, 146–61; see Ross 1976). There appears to be a higher level of compliance with general sentencing guidelines that are "presumptive" rather than voluntary (United States Sentencing Commission 1992, 133; Moore and Miethe 1986). One source of this difference is the greater likelihood of review and reversal when judges depart from sentencing guidelines. This suggests that, at least in this situation, adherence to legal rules as a goal in itself may be less powerful than are the motives that make reversal undesirable.

The research on legal and policy goals in lower courts is not extensive. Only a limited volume of research has been done on the wide array of decision-making activity in lower courts, and only a portion of this research is directly relevant to identification of judges' goals. Further, much of what scholars have learned about patterns of lower-court behavior is compatible with multiple interpretations. When judges follow legal rules, for instance, their behavior could reflect the priority they give to legal accuracy, other benefits they gain from adherence to law (including the avoidance of negative consequences associated with reversal), or compatibility between those rules and their conceptions of good policy. The existing evidence is inconsistent with interpretations of judges' goals that treat either law or policy as unimportant, but it provides little basis for determination of their relative weights.

Conclusions

In this chapter, as in chapter 2, one central issue has been differences between Supreme Court justices and judges on other courts.

---

24. At least in part, this desire for discretion seems to conflict with judges' frequent willingness to defer to prosecutors in sentencing. But even where judges defer to prosecutors, they can shape prosecutors' recommendations by making their expectations clear. Further, the power to make independent judgments may be prized even when it is seldom used.

Here too, there is a conventional wisdom that emphasizes differences: the belief that legal goals have far greater operative effect in lower courts than in the Supreme Court. And once again, clear empirical evidence of this difference has not been found. This does not mean that the conventional wisdom is wrong. Although the logic supporting that viewpoint is subject to dispute, there is good reason to think that the unusual content of the Supreme Court's agenda reduces the relevance of legal accuracy to the justices' choices on the merits of cases. Moreover, recent studies of the Court have produced significant empirical evidence that supports this conclusion. Substantial research has been done on issues related to the impact of legal goals in lower courts, some of it suggesting the importance of those goals. But both bodies of work are far from conclusive, largely because of the very difficult conceptual and methodological problems involved. Thus it is appropriate to remain cautious in assessing the relative importance of legal and policy considerations in lower courts and the Supreme Court.

Another open issue concerns differences in the balance between law and policy among judges who serve on the same court. We do not know enough to ascertain the extent of these differences, let alone their causes. At the least, however, assumptions of homogeneity among judges on particular courts seem open to question. Indeed, it would be surprising if differences in personality and experience did not cause judges to weigh legal and policy goals in different ways.

Chapters 2 and 3 have focused on the identity of judges' operative goals. Chapter 4 turns to the ways that judges act on their goals. More specifically, to the extent that judges are motivated by policy goals, how much do they engage in strategic behavior to advance those goals?

CHAPTER 4

Strategic Behavior

Without question, most judges have an interest in making good policy. Indeed, that interest may well be the dominant motivation for many. But what does it mean to make good policy? Policy-minded judges might simply take the positions that accord most closely with their conceptions of good policy. Or they might act strategically, seeking to move their own court and other institutions closer to what they regard as good policy.

The possibility of strategy in the service of policy goals is a long-standing interest for students of judicial politics, and strategic behavior is now becoming a key issue in the field. The attention given to strategy is merited, not only because of its importance in itself but because of its theoretical implications as well. The extent to which judges act strategically tells a good deal about more distal goals, more fundamental motivations. Further, strategy is part of a broader issue concerning the ways that judges act to carry out their goals.

The first section of the chapter discusses the meaning of strategy and its place in the research on judicial behavior. I then consider theoretical issues, focusing on judges' motivations to act strategically. The remaining three sections survey the empirical evidence on judicial strategy in three arenas: within appellate courts, in relation to higher courts, and in relation to the other branches of government.

Strategy and Judicial Behavior

Scholars who employ rational choice models use several terms to characterize the ways that policymakers act on their goals. The usage of these terms varies, creating a certain degree of confusion. Thus it is important to make my own usage clear. I also need to make several distinctions among types of strategy, distinctions that are summarized in table 4.1.

TABLE 4.1.   Dimensions of Judicial Strategy

I.   Form
A. Strategic voting (contrasted with sincere voting)
B. Other forms of strategic behavior (contrasted with nonstrategic behavior)
II. Time horizon
A. Short-term
B. Long-term
III. Target
A. Judge's own court
B. Other institutions (e.g., higher courts, other branches of government)

In the scholarship on judicial behavior, strategy has both narrower and broader meanings—though the distinction between the two often is blurred. The narrower meaning can be labeled *strategic voting,* which contrasts with sincere voting. Judges vote sincerely when they support the case outcomes and doctrines that they most prefer,[1] without considering the impact of their votes on the collective result in their court (if it is an appellate court) or in other institutions. In other words, "their votes are directly in accordance with their preference scales" (Farquharson 1969, 17) because they seek that accord. In dimensional terms, sincere judges automatically support the alternative that is closest to their ideal points.

In contrast, judges who vote strategically take into account the effects of their choices on collective results when they vote on outcomes and write or support opinions. They do so in order to achieve the most desirable results in their own court and in government as a whole. Because of this motivation, the positions they take may differ from the positions that they most prefer.[2]

These definitions follow standard practice in framing the distinction between sincere and strategic voting as a dichotomy: a

---

1. It should be underlined that voting as defined here encompasses not only votes on the outcomes of cases for the litigants but also positions on doctrinal issues, which are not ordinarily thought of as votes. This broad definition of voting is necessary because judges care about doctrine as well as outcomes. Appropriately, much of the research on judicial strategy focuses on doctrine.

2. This definition of the term *strategic* follows one common usage (e.g., Eskridge and Frickey 1994, 36; Rodriguez 1994, 58; Calvert and Fenno 1994, 349). But some scholars use the term *sophisticated* for what I call *strategic* (e.g., Panning 1985, 678; Spiller and Spitzer 1995, 34), while others equate the two terms (e.g., Austen-Smith 1987, 1323). Sophisticated voting is sometimes treated as the behavioral manifestation of strategic planning (e.g., Farquharson 1969, 40; Denzau, Riker, and Shepsle 1985, 1118). Often, strategic or sophisticated voting is defined not in terms of motivation or intention but in terms of result: a vote that differs from the one a person would

judge is either sincere or strategic. But a judge might vote strategically in one setting and not in another. And in any particular setting, a judge might take a mixed approach that is partly sincere and partly strategic.

Strategic voting in courts typically takes a different form from its counterpart in legislatures. The most common locus for strategic voting by legislators is amendment voting. Since the adoption or rejection of amendments affects the prospects for final passage of a bill, legislators may have an incentive to depart from their preferred positions in voting on amendments (Enelow and Koehler 1980). Courts have no full equivalent of amendment voting; the specification of alternatives is more fluid in the judiciary. Further, legislators usually face dichotomous choices, so departures from preferred positions must be sharp and distinct. In contrast, judges often choose from many alternative case outcomes (as in criminal sentencing), and they can usually choose any of several doctrinal positions. Thus, to the extent that judges vote strategically, departures from their preferred positions can be (and probably tend to be) more limited and less stark than in the legislature.

I should emphasize that I define strategic voting in terms of motivation rather than result. In a particular situation the strategic judge might end up behaving the same as a sincere judge with the same preferences: the best strategy may be simply to vote for the outcome and doctrinal position that the judge most prefers.

It should be emphasized as well that the concern in this chapter is only with strategic voting in the service of policy goals. Judges who depart from their preferences are not voting strategically in this sense if their motive is not to influence policy. If state judges who oppose capital punishment vote to uphold death sentences in order to enhance their re-election prospects, or if appellate judges support opinions with which they disagree because they believe that dissents detract from the clarity of legal rules, their actions are not strategic for purposes of this inquiry.[3]

Given that definition of strategic voting, the dichotomy of sincere and strategic voting is comprehensive only if judges have no

---

cast sincerely (e.g., Kornhauser and Sager 1993, 52; Gardner 1995, 48; Morrow 1994, 133–34). It should be noted also that *naive* and *myopic* are sometimes used to refer to what I call sincere voting or to related concepts (e.g., Denzau, Riker, and Shepsle 1985, 1132; Austen-Smith 1987, 1323; Spiller and Spitzer 1995, 35). In this situation, confusion about terminology is inevitable.

3. Of course, re-election makes it possible for a judge to continue shaping judicial policy, and actions to achieve clear rules may advance a judge's policy goals. If a judge cared about re-election or legal clarity only as means to achieve good policy, actions to advance these subsidiary goals would constitute strategic policy-oriented behavior.

motivations other than policy goals. In situations in which policy considerations account for judicial behavior only to a limited degree, as may be the case in state trial courts, it is not very useful to focus on sincere and strategic voting in the service of policy goals. Thus the examination of strategic behavior in this chapter is most relevant to higher courts, where policy goals seem to play more central roles.

Strategic voting is one form of judicial strategy in a broader sense, which can be labeled *strategic behavior*. Judges engage in strategic behavior whenever they take actions intended to advance their policy goals in collective decisions of their own court or in the decisions of other institutions. The strategies and tactics described by Walter Murphy in *Elements of Judicial Strategy* (1964) illustrate the wide range of actions that can fall under this rubric, from arguments in an opinion aimed at winning a colleague's support to efforts at influence over appointments to other courts.

Unlike strategic voting, most other forms of strategic behavior cannot be contrasted with sincere behavior. Although there is room for disagreement on this point, I think that the concept of sincere behavior has no relevance in case selection or opinion assignment. And if it is strategic to work at winning the support of colleagues for one's policy positions, we would not say that it is sincere to eschew such efforts. Rather, in these settings there is a continuum from a judge who engages in no strategic behavior to a judge who is fully devoted to it. Particularly in contexts such as opinion assignment, this continuum can involve trade-offs between policy goals and other goals.

Strategic behavior can be dichotomized as short-term or long-term. Short-term strategy is aimed at the results of a specific case. In the terms of game theory, a judge who engages solely in short-term strategy treats each case as a one-shot game.

Long-term strategy is aimed at future cases. The judge who engages in long-term strategy in the context of deciding cases is playing a repeated game, with each case as one stage of the game.[4]

---

4. Whether or not they engage in strategic behavior, judges can have short-term or long-term orientations in a different sense. In appellate courts, the outcome of a case for the litigants is a short-term concern, while the impact of legal doctrines is felt in the long term. Presumably, judges' preferences among alternative legal doctrines are based primarily on their predictions of the impact of those doctrines in future cases. The relative importance that judges ascribe to votes and outcomes can be conceived as a balance between short-term and long-term considerations.

It sounds strategic for judges to think about the future consequences of their votes. But if they simply support their most preferred doctrinal positions, that is not strategic voting by the definition used here.

A Supreme Court justice might seek to maximize consensus in the Court's decisions in order to strengthen its influence over policy choices by other institutions. If so, a strategic choice to join the majority in a particular case would be aimed at influencing the results of the policy process in future cases (see D. Atkinson and Neuman 1969, 273 n. 8). Of course, strategic behavior outside the context of decisions also can be aimed at the long term. Efforts to influence judicial appointments are a good example.

While the distinction between sincere and strategic voting raises the sharpest theoretical issues, strategic behavior as a whole merits consideration. The extent of strategic behavior tells a good deal both about judges' commitment to policy goals and about the ways that they put these goals into effect. Thus I give attention both to strategic voting and to other forms of strategic behavior.

Strategy holds an ambiguous position in research on judicial behavior. Strategic behavior has been studied extensively in the Supreme Court (Brenner 1979a), particularly in case selection (Schubert 1962b; Brenner 1979b; Brenner and Krol 1989), opinion assignment (McLauchlan 1972; Rohde 1972c; Brenner 1982b; S. Davis 1990), and the formation of coalitions in support of opinions (Schubert 1959, 188–210; S. Ulmer 1965; Rohde 1972a, 1972b; Brams and Muzzio 1977; Giles 1977; Brenner, Hagle, and Spaeth 1990). Biographical and historical studies document the frequency with which justices behave strategically (W. Murphy 1964). Yet analyses of votes on case outcomes in the Supreme Court typically have rested on the assumption that the justices' policy preferences are expressed directly in their votes, without deviations based on strategic considerations (Schubert 1965; Rohde and Spaeth 1976; Segal and Spaeth 1993).

On its face, this difference in the place given to strategy at different stages of decision seems puzzling (see L. Epstein and Knight 1995, 1–11). Segal (1996; see Segal and Spaeth 1994, 11), however, has argued that justices who act strategically in other contexts would express their preferences directly in final votes on the outcomes of cases, since this is the last stage of action and deviations from those preferences no longer have any strategic value: justices are no longer constrained in their choices.[5] In other words, as the

---

5. This argument could be contested on the ground that the vote on the merits is *not* the last stage of action: justices take into account future cases and possible reactions of other institutions to their court's decisions. On the reactions of other institutions,

terms have been defined in this chapter, a justice who votes sincerely and one who votes strategically would cast the same votes on case outcomes. From this perspective the attitudinal model of decision making is consistent with both sincere and strategic voting on the merits.

If the place of strategy in the attitudinal model is complex, its place in rational choice models is clear: in general, people are assumed to behave strategically. As scholars with a rational choice orientation have come to the study of courts in recent years, their work has inspired specialists in judicial politics to look more closely and more systematically at judicial strategy (see L. Epstein and Knight 1998).[6]

Theoretical Issues

To what extent would we expect judges to engage in strategic behavior? This question is most easily addressed in terms of the dichotomy between sincere and strategic voting. The balance between sincere and strategic voting in courts or other settings can be considered a product of both motivational and cognitive factors—judges' interest in acting strategically and their capacity to do so. Students of human decision making have given primary attention to the cognitive side (e.g., H. Simon 1955; Abelson 1976; Dawes 1988), but for purposes of this inquiry it is more useful to consider cognitive issues in the context of motivation.

Assume that a judge's only proximate goal concerns good policy: would such a judge find it more attractive to vote sincerely or strategically? There is a strong logical basis for an assumption of strategic voting. If judges care about legal policy, then it seems self-evident that they want to see good policy adopted by their court and by other institutions. How could a policy-minded judge *not* behave strategically (see L. Epstein and Walker 1995, 322; L. Epstein and Knight 1995, 12–13)? Indeed, judges' policy goals

---

Segal and Spaeth 1993 (238–41) and Segal 1997 suggest that the Court seldom takes such reactions into account because the justices have little need to be concerned about those reactions and (Segal 1997, 31) because congressional reactions are difficult to predict. This view is reflected in table 2.1.

6. Rational choice scholars typically assume that judges behave strategically in order to further their policy goals. But Ferejohn and Weingast (1992a, 1992b) raised the possibility of strategic behavior in the service of legal accuracy, specifically in order to further the intent of the enacting legislature.

often are defined in terms of seeking favorable results (e.g., Rohde and Spaeth 1976, 72).[7] But the validity of this analysis is not self-evident. In chapter 3, I suggested that the distal goals of personal satisfaction and the approbation of important audiences might be served by acting on either legal or policy considerations. The same distal goals might support either sincere or strategic action on behalf of policy goals.

Judges potentially could appeal to audiences that share their policy preferences by taking positions consistent with these shared preferences, or they could appeal to those audiences by acting effectively on behalf of mutually held policy goals. Similarly, judges might gain personal satisfaction by taking what they see as correct positions in cases or by working for broader acceptance of those positions. The relative importance of sincere and strategic behavior, then, is not obvious.

The Attractiveness of Strategic Voting

Since either sincere or strategic voting could serve judges' distal goals, the balance between the two depends in part on characteristics of judges' situations—particularly those that affect the attractiveness of strategic voting. To begin with, the context of judicial decision making encourages efforts to influence collective results. Appellate judges work in a situation that produces competition to achieve majorities for positions within their court.[8] Beyond the judge's own court, reversal by an appellate court carries the mark of a defeat and perhaps even of incompetence. There is an element of defeat in legislative reversal as well. It seems reasonable to assume that most people prefer winning to losing (see Riker 1962, 22). Thus judges have very good reason to engage in strategic voting as a means to gain an image of success with others and to protect and enhance their self-esteem.

---

7. This line of analysis suggests that the difference between sincere and strategic behavior in the service of policy goals might better be conceptualized as a difference between two types of policy goals: expressing one's preferences in decisions and acting instrumentally to advance one's favored policies. For one thing, this alternative conceptualization clarifies why policy-minded judges do not necessarily behave strategically. Because the standard conceptualization is one of differing ways to carry out the same goal, I take that approach.

8. It may be, however, that continued interaction among judges over time lessens the drive to achieve victories in specific cases. Strategic voting aimed at the short term may interfere with effective strategy in the long term as well as with the quality of personal relations among judges.

In some other respects, however, strategic voting may be less attractive. First, judges who act strategically may experience considerable frustration, because their ability to influence collective results is inherently constrained. A single judge has only limited influence over a court's decisions and even less over the actions of other institutions: even the most effective strategies can accomplish only so much. If a conservative Supreme Court justice is surrounded by like-minded colleagues and by a Republican Congress and president, the justice will enjoy more victories than defeats, but the justice can take little credit for those victories. If a justice is in a minority position in the Court and elsewhere, frequent defeats are inevitable. Despite his legendary skills of persuasion, Justice William Brennan was not highly successful when he battled against superior numbers in the early Rehnquist Court. A federal district judge can reach a decision unilaterally, but that judge has limited capacity to influence actions by colleagues at the same level or by policymakers in other institutions. Thus even a judge who obtains satisfaction from exercising influence may gain little by voting strategically, and the absence of more substantial gains may arouse feelings of ineffectiveness.

Second, the compromises needed to secure victories and avoid defeats can be galling to a judge. At least on occasion, appellate judges may need to give up strongly held doctrinal positions in order to secure majorities for their opinions. Judges who seek to minimize the chances of reversal may be required to take positions that are close to those of the reviewing court or of the legislature that oversees the court, positions that sometimes differ substantially from their preferences. For judges whose self-image is one of power and independence, the need to compromise in itself can carry a cost.

Finally, effective strategy requires good prediction of other people's behavior, and difficulty in prediction may discourage judges from voting strategically. The extent of this difficulty differs with the type of strategic voting involved. Easiest to accomplish is short-term strategy aimed at a judge's own colleagues. The Supreme Court justice who constantly interacts with the same set of colleagues can gain a relatively good sense of the consequences of alternative actions (B. Palmer 1995, 9). Further, there are opportunities to obtain feedback on the effectiveness of strategies over the course of the decision process in a single case. In this respect, then, intracourt strategy is relatively attractive.[9]

---

9. The relative ease of predicting colleagues' positions also simplifies the task of strategic voting aimed at other institutions. Analyses of Supreme Court strategy aimed

Strategy aimed at higher courts can be more difficult. Judges who seek to adhere as closely as possible to their preferred policies while avoiding reversal can garner information from past experience with appellate review and from the reviewing court's record of doctrinal positions. Still, a good deal of uncertainty may remain. Moreover, such a judge must predict the likelihood that a decision will be appealed and, if the reviewing court has discretionary jurisdiction, that the case will be accepted. A trial judge often faces an appellate court that sits in panels, and the chances of reversal may vary a good deal with the membership of the reviewing panel.

Prediction of responses by the other branches is the most problematical. The determinants of congressional action on an issue are highly complex (see Kingdon 1995), and this complexity leads to the notorious difficulty of predicting that action—a difficulty that certainly applies to overrides of Supreme Court decisions (see Henschen and Sidlow 1989; Melnick 1994, 263–64).[10] A justice could try to simplify the task of prediction by thinking about Congress solely in ideological terms. As suggested by some scholars (Gely and Spiller 1990; Eskridge 1991a; see Marks 1989), the justice might calculate the ideological positions of Congress and its relevant subunits (and of the president) in relation to the positions represented by doctrines that the Court might adopt. But such calculations are not easy. And the justice would need to predict the outcomes of presidential and congressional elections in the near future in order to make the appropriate calculations for the next few bienniums.

Strategic voting aimed at the long term carries special difficulties even if it is restricted to a judge's own court. Judges must predict the kinds of cases that will arise in the future and how colleagues will react to those cases, including colleagues who have not yet joined the court. For that matter, judges must predict their own preferences as issues evolve (see March 1978).

---

at Congress often treat the Court as a unitary actor (e.g., Gely and Spiller 1990, 1992; Schwartz, Spiller, and Urbiztondo 1994). In reality, of course, individual justices have to take other justices into account when they develop strategies aimed at Congress. But if justices can do so with little difficulty, this complication is less serious than it might be.

10. Some congressional overrides of Supreme Court decisions are so idiosyncratic that they would defy any effort at prediction. One example is the "dark of the night legislation" (Franklin and Weldy 1993; see also Sturley 1993) that reversed *Carnival Cruise Lines v. Shute* (1991) by adding the word "any" to a 1936 statute. This is not to say that congressional reactions to decisions are completely unpredictable; several studies have identified variables that are related to the likelihood of statutory overrides and other kinds of reactions (Eskridge 1991b; Solimine and Walker 1992; Bawn and Shipan 1993; Ignagni and Meernik 1994; Zorn and Caldeira 1995; Meernik and Ignagni 1997).

Judges need not refrain from voting strategically just because it is difficult to choose and implement the optimal strategy. But they may not want to devote all the necessary effort to a course of action that is complicated to chart and that is likely to achieve only limited gains. This is particularly likely when the price is deviation from strongly held positions.

This discussion suggests that judges have good reasons to engage in strategic voting, particularly within their own court. Yet some characteristics of judges' situations could make strategic voting unattractive to them. If so, sincere voting stands as another way to act on their policy goals.

The Possibility of Sincere Voting

Is it reasonable to think that judges might vote sincerely? Can judges find it satisfying simply to take positions consistent with their preferences, whatever may be the results in their court and elsewhere? There is good reason to think so. For one thing, judges can gain the intrinsic pleasure of doing what they think is right in itself (see Riker 1995, 25; Kuran 1995, 30–35). As with voters (Sen 1977, 332–33; Glazer 1993), it may be quite sensible for judges thus to take positions for expressive purposes, rather than acting instrumentally by calculating the impact of their positions on collective results (H. Simon 1985, 298; see Kahneman and Varey 1991; Abelson 1995; M. Taylor 1995, 231).

Judges themselves have indicated the satisfaction that can be derived from expressing preferences directly. Richard Posner (1995, 123), a federal judge and legal scholar, used economic terms to describe this satisfaction: "for judges as for ordinary citizens voting has a consumption value that is independent of its instrumental, power-exercising value . . ."[11] Justice Antonin Scalia (1994, 42; emphasis in original) waxed lyrical in describing why he likes the freedom to write concurring and dissenting opinions:

---

11. To adapt terms that Kahneman and Thaler (1991, 341) used in a somewhat different way, people ultimately seek not "decision utility," the most favorable decisional outcome as assessed by economic analysis, but "experienced utility." It is quite possible that experienced utility is based primarily on decision utility for at least some people, but it is far from certain that this is true of most people. McClintock and Liebrand (1988) took another perspective on this issue, showing that people transform the "objective decision environment" into an "effective decision matrix" in particular ways based on their values; for some people, the effective decision matrix might be based on their deriving utility from self-expression.

To be able to write an opinion solely for oneself, without the need to accommodate, to any degree whatever, the more-or-less differing views of one's colleagues; to address precisely the points of law that one considers important and *no others;* to express precisely the degree of quibble, or foreboding, or disbelief, or indignation that one believes the majority's disposition should engender—that is indeed an unparalleled pleasure.

Further, judges who vote sincerely may well obtain reinforcement from external audiences that share their views of good policy, such as segments of the legal profession or interest groups. Such audiences surely are pleased by a judge who exercises influence over legal policy, particularly if they also think about judicial policy in strategic terms. But these audiences are also likely to applaud judges simply for taking the positions they both favor. Indeed, particular audiences might prefer the purist who refuses to compromise positions in the interest of exerting influence. It may be that one function of impassioned dissents is to allow judges to show their audiences that they will defend the "correct" position despite superior numbers on the other side. Mayhew (1974, 118, 146 n. 133) argued with some force that legislators' constituents reinforce sincere rather than strategic behavior (see also Denzau, Riker, and Shepsle 1985; Wilkerson 1990; Austen-Smith 1992; but see Fiorina 1995a, 309). Judges' audiences may have a similar effect.[12]

---

12. This discussion may seem to rest on a fanciful image of judges and their audiences. But there is considerable evidence that judges gain reinforcement for their policy positions from like-minded audiences. For instance, the conservative individuals and groups with whom Justice Clarence Thomas interacts (discussed in chapter 2) seem to provide welcome support for positions that sometimes command little support on the Court.

Justice Harry Blackmun offers a particularly good example. Once his policy positions shifted in a liberal direction, Blackmun seemed to take considerable strength from approval of his liberalism outside the Court. Consider, for instance, Blackmun's 1992 appearance at the Legal Aid Society in San Francisco (Holding 1992):

"I am a little bit disappointed now about the way the court is going. . . . If I had more sense, I suppose I would turn in my suit," the 83-year-old justice told the assembled judges and lawyers, who responded with a chorus of "No!" Blackmun assured them that he will "stay there for the moment."

The language of some of Blackmun's dissenting opinions on abortion (*Webster v. Reproductive Health Services* 1989) and the death penalty (*Callins v. Collins* 1994) suggests that one of his purposes was to demonstrate to his audience that he was stoutly defending a purist position consistent with their own views.

Thus, to use Robert Frank's (1985) metaphor, judges can choose "the right pond" in which to compete. They may find it fulfilling to focus their energy on efforts to influence the course of legal policy. Alternatively, they may gain fulfillment from taking what they regard as the right positions. Or, to take the most likely possibility, they may favor some mix of the two paths. In any case, it is not self-evident that policy-oriented judges will be fully committed to strategic voting, and it may be perfectly reasonable for a judge to vote sincerely.

The Mix of Sincere and Strategic Voting

As this discussion suggests, judges almost surely vary in their inclinations toward sincere and strategic voting. That variation probably reflects differences in personality to a great extent. Indeed, this may be one of the ways in which judges' personality characteristics make the greatest difference.[13] And judges, like other public officials (see Sinclair 1993, 224–27), undoubtedly differ in their strategic skills.

Even with such variation, it is possible that the recruitment process favors the selection of judges whose motivations lead them to strategic voting and who have high cognitive capabilities for good strategy (see Elster 1989, 71–81; Morrow 1994, 48). To take one possibility, perhaps those who achieve a level of success that makes them candidates for the Supreme Court tend to care more about exercising power than do most other people. But if such tendencies exist, it is far from obvious that all Supreme Court justices—let alone all judges—are strongly drawn to act strategically.

Further, some tendencies may run in the opposite direction. Successful people who seek judgeships might be *less* inclined toward strategy than are their counterparts who choose to remain in more competitive environments. And a lack of interest or skill in strategy has less damaging consequences for judges than it does for legislators. Elections may serve to reduce the proportion of non-

---

13. Strategic voting might be connected with motivation to exercise power, motivation that varies considerably among public officials as it does in the general population (Barber 1965; Donley and Winter 1970; Winter 1973; Winter and Carlson 1988; Winter, Hermann, Weintraub, and Walker 1991). In terms of the framework used here, judges whose policy goals are connected with goals involving power within and outside their court seem more likely to vote strategically.

strategic legislators, but no such mechanism exists for federal judges (see Segal 1995, 5 n. 7).[14]

A judge's mix of sincere and strategic voting might change over time in response to experiences in the job, though the same experiences can have different effects on different people. Confronted with a series of defeats in such forms as appellate reversal, one judge might become more strategic to minimize the incidence of defeats in the future. In contrast, another judge might give up strategy as useless. According to one of his former law clerks, this was Justice Thurgood Marshall's reaction to the increasing conservatism of the Burger and Rehnquist Courts.

> Unable to exert much influence beyond casting his vote, Marshall reacted as many proud people would: instead of futilely trying to influence his colleagues inside the Court, he concentrated on making sure that his views reached the public through the pages of the *United States Reports.* (Tushnet 1992, 2109–10)

If this account is accurate, Justice Marshall engaged in a variant of what Elster (1983b, 25, 109–10) called "adaptive preference change" or, more simply, "sour grapes."

Individual differences aside, different types of strategic voting are likely to vary in their use. Short-term strategy is far easier to undertake than long-term strategy. Further, the tendency to discount the future (see Loewenstein and Elster 1992) reduces the incentive to vote strategically with an eye to cases that come along later. And differences in the difficulty of calculation and immediacy of results suggest that strategic voting oriented toward a judge's colleagues is more common than such voting aimed at the legislature.

Thus far, I have focused on strategic voting. Most of the considerations that I have discussed apply to strategic behavior as a whole. For instance, personality characteristics help to determine the attractiveness of strategic behavior in its various forms, and the

---

14. In this context *strategy* has a broad meaning, encompassing any calculations (including interest in maintaining one's position or moving up) that might move officials away from voting sincerely on the basis of their policy preferences.

If nonstrategic behavior does not have strong negative consequences for judges, this also means that judges have more limited incentives to behave strategically than do legislators.

difficulties involved in strategic voting are relevant to strategies of any type. But there are two important differences. First, opportunities for strategic behavior in contexts other than voting, such as case selection and opinion assignment, ordinarily come at preliminary stages of decision. As suggested earlier, there might be more to be gained from strategic action at those stages than there is when taking final positions in cases. Second, in situations where there is no alternative of sincerity but simply a choice of how much strategy to employ, the policy-minded judge has more reason to act strategically. Thus, to take one example, a judge who cares only about good policy might have no alternative but to behave strategically in the selection of cases to hear on the merits. For these reasons, strategic behavior may be considerably more common in some other contexts than it is in voting on case outcomes and doctrinal positions.

Investigating Strategic Behavior

In the sections that follow, I examine the empirical evidence on judicial strategy in three arenas. At the outset, it is worth underlining the difficulty of identifying policy-oriented strategy. The most fundamental problem is the theoretical ambiguity of behavior: patterns of judicial behavior that are consistent with the assumption of policy-oriented strategy typically are consistent with other explanations as well. If one posits that judges are devoted to strategic behavior on behalf of their policy goals, virtually any action that they take can be interpreted as strategic: a court hears fewer cases so that it can make policy more effectively in the remaining cases; a judge courts legal audiences to strengthen support for the judge's policy positions in other institutions; and so on (see W. Murphy 1964). By the same token, those who are skeptical about the possibility of strategic behavior can easily find alternative explanations for seemingly strategic actions.

One can simplify the problem of interpreting judges' behavior by assuming the primacy of policy goals and focusing on differences between the patterns of behavior that would result from sincere and strategic voting. But these differences may be fairly small. For instance, Supreme Court justices who seek to avoid legislative reversal of the Court's statutory decisions might find it necessary to abandon their most preferred positions in only a small minority of cases (see Segal 1997). If so, the pattern of behavior manifested by strategic judges has the same appearance of general ideological consistency that we would expect of a sincere justice. It is possible to identify strategic legislative voting that diverges sharply from sincerity on particular issues (McCrone 1977), but the more subtle form of strategic voting in courts and the small size of courts may hinder such analysis. Even if judges diverge substantially from their preferences for strategic purposes, it may not be easy to distinguish this divergence from sincere expression of preferences if a single judge regularly engages in it over time or a whole court engages in it in a particular case.

The possibility of imperfections in judges' strategic choices also complicates analysis. Judges frequently are reversed by higher courts, and Congress overrides substantial numbers of the Supreme Court's statutory decisions (Eskridge 1991b). These outcomes might be taken as strong evidence that judges do not vote strategically with an eye to reactions by other institutions. However, such failures may result primarily from imperfections in judges' ability to predict the behavior of other institutions. For that matter, judges may make mistakes in forecasting the effects of their positions on their colleagues.[15]

Thus there is a need for care in interpreting analyses that compare actual patterns of votes with models of effective strategy. In the terms used by Downs (1957, 8–11), what looks like irrational behavior may simply be rational errors. To take one likely possibility, judges may have chosen a course of strategic action that was appropriate in light of their beliefs about the world, but those beliefs turned out to be inaccurate (see Bicchieri 1993, 11–14). Like the other difficulties I have described, this consideration makes it desirable to gather direct evidence on what judges are trying to do along with evidence on their patterns of behavior.

Strategic Behavior Within Courts

Strategic behavior can take a variety of forms, and the empirical evidence on that behavior is diverse. Table 4.2 summarizes the

15. This consideration applies to all forms of strategic behavior. One might conclude from his limited influence on the Court that Justice Felix Frankfurter did not care about influencing his colleagues (see Danelski 1986, 31–32). But in fact he was strongly committed to strategic behavior within the Court; it appears that he simply was a very bad strategist (Hirsch 1981). Alternatively, Frankfurter as a scholar may have sought to determine the limits of negative influence within a nine-member body. Or, having discovered early in his tenure that it was easier to alienate than to attract colleagues, perhaps he took on the guise of a judicial conservative and did all that he could to push other justices in a liberal direction. If this last scenario is accurate, Frankfurter set a standard for strategic success that put to shame his more straightforward colleague William Brennan.

TABLE 4.2. Discussions of Evidence on Strategic Behavior in Last Three Sections of Chapter 4

Target	Strategic Voting[a]	Other Forms of Strategic Behavior[a]
Judge's own court	General voting patterns	Persuasion on the merits
	Size of majority opinion	Opinion assignment
	coalitions	Case selection
	Decisional fluidity	Long-term strategy
Higher courts	(General)	—
Other branches	(General)	—

[a]Strategy aimed at short term unless otherwise indicated.

aspects of strategic behavior to be considered in this section and the two to follow. The primary subject of empirical research on judicial strategy is relations among judges on a single appellate court. As in other arenas, scholars have concentrated on short-term strategy. The great preponderance of research on strategy within courts deals with the Supreme Court, so this section focuses on the Court.

Strategic Voting

Consistent with the definition offered earlier, voting on case outcomes for litigants or on doctrinal positions can be regarded as strategic if it takes into account the effects of those votes on collective results—here, decisions of the Court. As in the rest of the chapter, the concern is strategy on behalf of policy goals.

Once again, it is appropriate to begin by considering *general patterns of votes on case outcomes*. Dimensional analyses of votes are based on a theoretical model in which justices' votes reflect their policy preferences directly, a model that is most compatible with sincere voting. But their findings are consistent with strategic voting as well. The deviations from sincere voting that result from strategic considerations probably would be sufficiently slight or regular in appearance that they barely disturbed the appearance of unidimensional voting.[16] Similarly, causal studies that show a strong correlation between justices' policy preferences and their general voting behavior leave considerable room for strategy to

16. As discussed earlier in the chapter, it has been argued that strategic justices can always take positions consistent with their preferences, because votes on the merits are effectively the final stage of decision. In other words, according to this argument, if sincere voting by a set of justices would result in a particular unidimensional pattern, strategic voting by the same justices would produce exactly the same pattern.

affect votes; overall, a strategic liberal would cast far more liberal votes than would a strategic conservative. For these reasons, more direct evidence on strategic voting is needed.

One small set of studies considers strategic voting in terms of the *size of the coalitions that support a majority opinion.* Using the concept of a minimum winning coalition (Riker 1962), Rohde (1972a, 1972b) posited that strategic voting would result in a disproportionate number of opinions supported by five justices: the opinion writer would compromise on language to the extent necessary to win a majority, but no more.[17]

Rohde tested this hypothesis with civil liberties cases. He separated out classes of cases that involved "threats" to the Court, so that justices had strategic reasons to seek unanimity in order to deter attacks from external sources. His findings for the remaining cases were mixed. In one study (Rohde 1972a), he found more minimum winning coalitions than would be expected by chance; in the other (Rohde 1972b), there were fewer such coalitions than expected (see Brenner 1979c, 385). Analyzing the same cases as in Rohde 1972b, Giles 1977 concluded that coalition size was better explained by an equivalence between the number of justices supporting the outcome for the litigants and the majority opinion.

On the whole, these studies indicate that the Court does not tend toward minimum winning coalitions. To a degree, then, they suggest limits to strategic voting by the justices. On the other hand, it is not clear that strategy-minded judges would seek minimum winning coalitions. For instance, judges concerned with the reactions of other institutions or with long-term developments in their own court might prefer large majorities for majority opinions.

A substantial body of research analyzes change in votes on case outcomes after the Court's original conference vote and change in opinions after circulation of the draft majority opinion, change that is often labeled *fluidity.* Many studies provide illustrative evidence of fluidity (e.g., Howard 1968; B. Schwartz 1985,

---

17. In his second study Rohde (1972b, 216 n. 21) found Axelrod's (1970) analysis of conflict of interest more relevant than Riker's theory of coalitions.

The concept of a minimum winning coalition is related to the Shapley–Shubik (1954) index of power within groups. Several scholars have considered the implications of that index for coalition formation and other forms of behavior in the Supreme Court (Schubert 1964b; Krislov 1963; Brenner 1975). Empirical research includes Schubert's (1959, 188–210) broad analysis of two historical episodes, Ulmer's (1965) study of blocs in the Vinson and Warren Court, and Johnson's (1977) study of opinion assignment in the same period. The findings are too limited to allow clear conclusions about how well the index applies to appellate decision making.

1988, 1996a). More systematic analyses demonstrate that changes in votes on case outcomes, in collective decisions on outcomes, and in opinion language are common (Brenner 1980, 1982a; J. Palmer 1990, 97–123; L. Epstein and Knight 1995; Maltzman and Wahlbeck 1996b; Wood 1996). But these analyses also show that most votes and outcomes do not change, and it appears that most opinions for the Court do not change fundamentally.

Fluidity can result from strategic voting. But strategic voting may be reflected in the original conference vote. Further, changes in position can occur for reasons other than strategy. Justices may reevaluate the merits of cases on their own (see J. Palmer 1990, 110–12). Even when justices change positions in response to interactions with colleagues, the impact of these interactions might be to provide information that clarifies the relationship between justices' preferences and the alternatives in a case.[18] Thus the frequency of changes in votes and opinion content in itself provides only limited evidence about strategic voting.

On the other hand, evidence gathered from justices' papers and other primary sources makes it clear that justices often change their positions for strategic reasons. In particular, it is standard practice to modify the language of opinions in an effort to win colleagues' support. Some studies provide systematic evidence that suggests the importance of such strategic voting in the Court's decision-making process. Epstein and Knight (1995) found that "bargaining statements" in memoranda, in which justices indicated that they would join the majority opinion if the opinion's language were changed, occurred in at least 43 percent of the 1983 term decisions and 65 percent of a set of important Burger Court decisions. Wood (1996) determined that there were requests for changes in majority opinion language in at least 33 percent of the cases decided during the Burger Court as a whole.[19] Of these requests, 85 percent indicated that the requester's joining of the opinion was contingent on the change. Both studies also found that opinion language frequently changed during the decision process; approximately two-thirds of the requests for changes in

---

18. The structure of communication among justices after the conference vote on a case seems well suited to satisfy some of their information needs. In this respect it may be similar to important aspects of congressional organization (see Krehbiel 1991).

19. As the authors of both studies noted, their figures are underestimates because they gathered data from the papers of one to three justices (depending on the study and time period), while some memoranda undoubtedly were sent privately between other justices. They also noted that not all relevant communications among justices are put in writing.

language that Wood analyzed were accepted by the majority opinion author.

Two studies offer other kinds of evidence for a connection between strategic voting and decisional fluidity. Wahlbeck, Spriggs, and Maltzman (1996) found in a study of the Burger Court that opinion authors tended to write more opinion drafts in situations where there was a greater need to accommodate colleagues in order to maintain a majority. For the same period, Wahlbeck, Maltzman, and Spriggs (1996) found patterns in the times at which justices joined majority opinions that were consistent with strategic behavior.

Bargaining over opinions and rewriting them to meet objections may seem unimportant because they are part of the Court's routine, but this behavior is not inevitable. One alternative is the old practice in which all justices wrote opinions expressing their own views directly, a practice revived on rare occasions in recent years (e.g., *New York Times v. United States* 1971; *Furman v. Georgia* 1972). And it appears that until the late nineteenth century, draft opinions for the Court generally were not circulated to colleagues and thus did not become the subject of negotiation or even suggestions (Ginsburg 1995, 2126).

But shifts in justices' positions that appear to stem from policy-oriented strategy might actually have other sources. Judges may vote strategically in that they take their colleagues' positions into account in choosing their own positions, but in the interest of goals other than good policy. They might seek to advance what they regard as legal accuracy rather than good policy. Kornhauser and Sager (1993, 52–53) suggested another possibility: "[t]he simple line between strategic and sincere behavior seems inapt to multi-judge courts, where . . . the decisionmaking process is collegial and it is the norm for judges to sacrifice details of their convictions in the service of producing an outcome and opinion attributable to the court." In other words, appellate judges might depart routinely from their most preferred positions in order to maximize consensus and thus legal clarity—action that can be defined as strategic, but not in the conventional sense. For that matter, justices might modify their positions for quite nonstrategic reasons such as joining the majority in order to avoid the time and effort required to write dissenting opinions.

Just as important, shifts in justices' positions that are intended to influence the Court's collective decision constitute a rather limited form of strategic voting. With occasional exceptions, justices who take a position differing from their preferences for strategic reasons are not voting in a false or deceptive manner in order to gain an advantage at a later stage of decision. Rather, such justices adjust their positions in order to move the Court toward a better collective decision than they could obtain otherwise. Of course, the Court's procedures do not facilitate more dramatic forms of strategic voting. Still, modifying an opinion to gain colleagues' support or supporting an opinion with which one does not fully agree is quite different from voting against a legislative amendment that one actually favors in itself.

This is not to say that the consequences of strategic voting are inconsequential at either the individual or collective levels. Justices sometimes vote for doctrines that differ considerably from their preferred positions, and the Court's position on legal issues sometimes shifts a good deal during the course of the decision process. The gradual shifts in position that produced a unanimous decision in *Brown v. Board of Education* (1954) are well known (Kluger 1976), and the final opinions for the Court in important cases such as *United States v. Nixon* (1974) and *Roe v. Wade* (1973) look quite different from the original drafts (B. Schwartz 1988). To the extent that such results reflect strategic voting to further the justices' policy goals—as they apparently do in large part—they make clear the importance of policy-oriented strategy to the Court's behavior.

The theoretical meaning of decisional fluidity can be probed further by analyzing the patterns it takes. One issue is the ideological form of change. It is unclear whether final votes conform more closely to ideological dimensions than do conference votes, in part because of methodological complications (Brenner 1980, 1982a, 1989; J. Palmer 1990, 120; Dorff and Brenner 1992). However, there is considerable evidence that vote shifts involve ideological "attraction," in that justices are relatively likely to shift when their overall policy position in a field is closer to the positions of the colleagues they are joining than to those of the colleagues they are leaving. The multivariate study of the Burger Court by Maltzman and Wahlbeck (1995) provides the strongest evidence of this relationship (see also Brenner, Hagle, and Spaeth 1989, 1990; Hagle and Spaeth 1991).

This finding is open to multiple interpretations. As suggested earlier, one possibility is that vote changes often reflect further study by justices that clarifies the relationship between their preferences and the facts and issues of a particular case; no strategy exists. But strategic voting by opinion writers—adopting language to attract like-minded justices—might also be involved. Further, justices may be drawn to join colleagues with similar ideological positions as part of a long-term alliance that has strategic elements. A second issue is the direction of change. Justices are far more likely to abandon positions in the original minority than to leave the majority (Dorff and Brenner 1992, 764; Maltzman and Wahlbeck 1996b, 587). Further, justices are more likely to leave a small minority than a larger one (Maltzman and Wahlbeck 1996b; Brenner, Caporale, and Winter 1996). Almost surely, something more than sincere expression of policy preferences is involved.[20]

The most credible explanation is that justices want to be part of the majority (Brenner and Dorff 1992). In turn, that interest could reflect a variety of motivations, from an interest in shaping the majority opinion to an interest in achieving maximum clarity in the law. It is very difficult to distinguish empirically among these motivations, and we have little sense of their relative importance.

Other Forms of Strategic Behavior

Beyond strategic voting, the justices could engage in many other forms of strategic behavior. It is clear that they do so: there is an abundance of short-term strategy in Supreme Court decision making (e.g., W. Murphy 1964; Cooper 1995).

First of all, justices expend substantial effort on *persuasion on the merits,* attempts to win support from colleagues for particular outcomes and doctrines. These efforts are a recurrent subject in biographical and historical studies. Epstein and Knight's (1995) analysis of interactions between justices in the course of deciding cases provides quantitative evidence that attempts at persuasion are a regular feature of collective decision making.

The evidence from primary sources indicates that at least a large portion of the efforts to win colleagues' support for particular positions in cases is motivated by concern about policy. But another motivation for justices may be an interest in achieving what they regard as good law in the Court's decisions. It is worth reiterating that justices make arguments to each other largely in

---

20. It is possible to argue to the contrary: the original majority usually has the better case, and members of the original minority frequently come to recognize this fact after they read the draft majority opinion; in other words, they realize that they had originally misapplied their preferences about law or policy. This process almost surely is involved in some shifts from minority to majority, but it does not seem credible as a full explanation of such shifts.

terms of legal accuracy and clarity rather than good policy (Murphy 1964, 44 n.*; Brenner and Stier 1995, 4; Knight and Epstein 1996a); their doing so suggests that they think their colleagues will be swayed by such arguments. But it is impossible to ascertain the balance between legal and policy considerations in these interactions.

Another possible locus for strategic behavior is the assignment of majority opinions. Research on *opinion assignment* in the Supreme Court ranges widely, reflecting a variety of hypotheses about the goals and strategies of the chief justice and other justices who assign opinions (Danelski 1968; Slotnick 1979; Maltzman and Wahlbeck 1995, 1996a). Among the criteria suggested by scholars are achieving equality of assignments and work load, taking advantage of subject-matter expertise, maintaining and increasing the size of the majority coalition, and securing an opinion that reflects the assigner's own preferences. Each of these criteria could involve strategic considerations by policy-minded assigners, but the most strategic criterion is achievement of an opinion consistent with the assigner's preferences.

Scholars have analyzed assigners' use of this criterion on the basis of justices' voting records. Justices who care about opinion content are expected to assign cases disproportionately to themselves and to the colleagues whose voting records are closest to theirs in a specific subject area or more generally. Like any other strategy tending toward inequality, this assignment pattern would be constrained by the perceived need to assign approximately equal numbers of opinions to the various justices. But inequalities in a chief justice's assignments can be balanced by inequalities in the opposite direction in assignments by senior associate justices (Segal and Spaeth 1993, 265–71).

The research shows that justices do tend to assign opinions to themselves and their ideological allies in more important cases, achieving a degree of equality through their assignments in less important cases. Several studies (Slotnick 1978; S. Davis 1990; Maltzman and Wahlbeck 1995) have found direct evidence of this behavior through measures of case importance.[21] Also consistent

---

21. Maltzman and Wahlbeck (1996a) found that Chief Justice Rehnquist did not favor himself or ideological allies to a significant degree in important cases, but this study covered only three terms. In their study of the 1953–90 terms (Maltzman and Wahlbeck 1995), they found evidence that chief justices favor ideological allies more in ideologically heterogeneous courts, and over the period as a whole chief justices strongly favored allies in policy areas that Maltzman and Wahlbeck identified as politically salient.

with this conclusion is the finding that Earl Warren overassigned to himself and to the justice closest to him in civil liberties cases (Rohde 1972c) but not in economic cases, presumably less important to him (Rathjen 1974a).

Assigners' concern with maintaining a majority has been gauged by the assignment of opinions to justices whose voting records in an issue area are relatively distant from that of the assigner. Rohde (1972c) posited that justices would assign opinions disproportionately to the "pivotal" justice, the one who is fourth closest to the assigner and who thus creates a minimum winning coalition. Other studies (McLauchlan 1972; Brenner and Spaeth 1988a; S. Davis 1990) posited disproportionate assignment to the "marginal" justice in the majority, the one whose position is closest to those of the dissenters (see also Maltzman and Wahlbeck 1995, 1996a). These studies found evidence of overassignment to pivotal or marginal justices, a pattern that can be interpreted as a product of policy-oriented strategy or of other considerations.

One form of strategic voting might occur in connection with opinion assignment: the chief justice could vote "falsely" with the majority in conference in order to assign the Court's opinion. There is sufficient evidence to establish that Chief Justice Burger sometimes used this strategy (Cooper 1995, 43–46). But Burger apparently was the first chief justice to do so frequently, and it appears that William Rehnquist has not followed Burger's example (see Rohde and Spaeth 1989; Eisler 1993, 272). Burger seems to have paid a price for this strategy in the distrust of other justices. His experience illustrates the general point that colleagues' expectations may limit the effectiveness and thus the incidence of some forms of strategic behavior.[22]

Beyond decision making on the merits, scholars have considered strategic behavior in *case selection.* Evidence on the justices' behavior in case selection was discussed in chapter 3; that evidence can be applied to the issue of strategy. Because it involves a preliminary stage of decision, case selection might seem to allow for the kind of strategic voting that scholars have studied in legislative committee decisions (Denzau and Mackay 1983) and amendment voting (Enelow 1981; Krehbiel and Rivers 1990; Calvert and

---

22. A few studies have analyzed the writing of dissenting opinions (Rathjen 1974; Brenner and Spaeth 1988b). In a practice that was institutionalized in the 1970s, the senior dissenting justice on the Supreme Court regularly assigns dissenting opinions (Cook 1995). This assignment practice is a useful subject for analysis of strategic behavior (see Wood and Gansle 1995).

Fenno 1994). Certainly there is a similarity between legislative committee decisions and Supreme Court case selection, in both of which policymakers set an institutional agenda and can do so in ways designed to advance their policy goals. But case selection does not involve sincere and strategic voting as defined in this chapter, because justices who decide whether to hear cases—unlike legislators in committees—do not vote on alternative policies.[23] Certainly, however, justices can engage in strategic *behavior* in their certiorari decisions.

Most of the criteria that scholars have identified in case selection by the Supreme Court might be used by justices who act strategically on behalf of their policy goals. For instance, such justices could be inclined to hear cases containing important issues in order to maximize the Court's impact on policy. They might also engage in error correction, voting to hear cases in which they disagree with the lower-court outcome. But the most strategic practice is outcome prediction: voting to hear cases when the justice expects to be on the winning side on the merits if the case is accepted (see Schubert 1962b). Thus the extent to which justices utilize outcome prediction is a good index of their strategic behavior in case selection.

As noted in chapter 3, the evidence on outcome prediction is mixed. Perry (1991) concluded from his interview data that prediction is the dominant basis for choice in those cases in which justices' policy goals are most relevant. Quantitative studies of case-selection decisions show that outcome prediction occurs (e.g., J. Palmer 1982; Brenner and Krol 1989; Krol and Brenner 1990; Caldeira, Wright, and Zorn 1996), but some studies also indicate that it is an important consideration only when justices are inclined to affirm the lower court (Brenner 1979b; Boucher and Segal 1995; Segal, Boucher, and Cameron 1995). And the justices clearly give considerable weight to other criteria for their choices of cases to hear.

---

23. Some scholars have argued to me that error correction constitutes sincere voting, in contrast with the strategic voting involved in outcome prediction. That I do not treat error correction as sincere is a product of my definition of sincere and strategic voting. In any case, the two forms of behavior in case selection are analogous with sincere and strategic voting. The justice who engages in error correction reacts to a lower-court decision in terms of the relationship between the decision and the justice's preferred policy, without taking into account the Court's prospective decision in the case. In contrast, the justice who engages in outcome prediction does take that prospective decision into account. Certainly, as noted in the text, outcome prediction is considerably more strategic than is error correction.

This body of evidence suggests that justices make some use of their opportunities for strategic action in case selection, but less than they might. However, the evidence is not entirely consistent, and it is not as extensive as it could be. Thus no strong conclusions are appropriate.

In addition to strategic behavior aimed at the current case, justices might engage in strategies oriented toward the future. Of the various forms that *long-term strategy* could take, probably the most likely is to establish good relations with other justices in order to facilitate persuasion of them. It is clear that most justices do care about building and maintaining good relations with colleagues. Some justices seem relatively indifferent to collegial relations (Justice William O. Douglas appears to be a good example), and a few seem intent on fostering bad relations with their colleagues (Justice James McReynolds is the classic example), but such justices are exceptional.[24]

Biographical studies show that strategic considerations sometimes motivate justices to seek good relations with their colleagues (see W. Murphy 1964, 49–54). Justice William Brennan, for instance, used his effective personal skills largely to advance his policy goals (Eisler 1993; H. Clark 1995). Yet justices may also seek good relations as a means to build power within the Court as an end in itself. And efforts to achieve good relations with other judges could also reflect the desire for a pleasant work situation or for personal popularity. Almost surely, those two considerations account for a large portion of what Supreme Court justices do to foster good interpersonal relations (see, e.g., Danelski 1968); it would be quite surprising if most justices did not want a pleasant atmosphere at the Court or the approbation of colleagues for their own sake. The various motivations for good collegial relations are likely to be sufficiently intermixed that scholars—and the justices themselves—would have great difficulty in determining their relative weights.[25]

---

24. Of course, indifference or hostility toward colleagues may itself be a long-term strategy. McReynolds *did* help to drive from the Court a colleague whose policy position differed sharply from his own (see W. Murphy 1964, 56). On the other hand, Justice Douglas (1995, 88) reported that McReynolds "does not know the word 'expediency.'"

25. The motivations for efforts to seek good relations with colleagues relate to the issue examined in chapter 2, the importance of goals other than an interest in the content of legal policy. If justices seek good intracourt relations for reasons such as a pleasant work situation, those efforts could detract at least marginally from their pursuit of good law or good policy. For instance, justices might abandon dissenting positions in cases for reasons other than policy-oriented strategy. Little can be said with confidence

Another possible long-term strategy is to form alliances with like-minded colleagues (see W. Murphy 1964, 78–82). Alliance formation is not easily ascertained from patterns of voting and opinion agreement among justices (see S. Ulmer 1965; Grossman 1968). However, ideological allies sometimes work together to influence decisions on the Court. Like some groups of justices in earlier eras, for instance, Warren and Brennan met to discuss cases prior to the Court's conferences (B. Schwartz 1983, 206; Cooper 1995, 99). Such collaboration is likely to have long-term elements.

Beyond opinion assignment in specific cases, a chief justice can use that and other powers as means to influence colleagues in the long term. There is some anecdotal evidence that associate justices see a connection between their relationship with the chief justice and the assignments they receive. One example is David Souter's joke that he joined William Rehnquist in singing carols at the Court's Christmas party because "I have to. Otherwise I get all the tax cases" (Mauro 1992b). There is also anecdotal evidence that Chief Justice Burger used the power for punitive purposes (Marcus 1986; Rhode 1992). But it is not clear whether Burger or other chiefs sought to influence colleagues' policy positions with their assignments. And we know little about the use of other powers for long-term strategic purposes.

Of course, long-term strategic behavior can take a variety of other forms. Supreme Court justices (and members of other courts) may adhere to minority positions on doctrinal issues in the hope that they will gain majority support in the future (Kozinski 1991).[26] They sometimes offer cues to litigants in order to influence future developments in a legal field. They also engage in advocacy or "entrepreneurship" for policy positions (Cates and McIntosh 1995; McIntosh and Cates forthcoming; see Galanter, Palen, and Thomas 1979). Justice William Brennan's encouragement of the use of state constitutions to expand protections of individual rights is a good example of such entrepreneurship (see Brennan 1977). Judges may also seek to shape judicial organization and procedure in ways that favor their policy goals (Barrow and Walker 1988; E. Schwartz 1993; see Shepsle and Weingast 1995).

---

about the justices' motives in this regard. But it certainly is plausible that an interest in good relations with colleagues has an impact on the behavior of Supreme Court justices and other judges that is independent of, and to some degree in conflict with, their interest in legal policy. Thus, despite the difficulty of distinguishing among different motivations involved in judges' interpersonal relations, efforts to do so would be worthwhile.

26. This may be an example of sincere voting that also constitutes strategic behavior.

Alongside the substantial research on strategy within the Supreme Court is a smaller body of scholarship on strategic behavior within other appellate courts. One important example is research on strategies engendered by the use of three-judge panels on the federal courts of appeals (Atkins 1972; Atkins and Zavoina 1974; Van Winkle 1996). Other lower-court studies deal at least in part with issues related to strategy, such as the impact of decision-making procedures on dissent rates in state supreme courts (Brace and Hall 1990) and the approaches that policy-minded state supreme court justices take in case selection (Baum 1977a).[27] There is insufficient evidence on particular forms of strategic behavior to allow any meaningful conclusions. One result is that we know little about the strategic implications of differences among courts in characteristics such as institutional rules and judges' stakes in case outcomes.

Strategy and Judicial Hierarchy

Scholars have done considerable research on one important context for strategic voting in lower courts: judges' responses to decisions and doctrines of higher courts. This research is based on a variety of theoretical perspectives (Johnson and Canon 1984; Kilwein and Brisbin 1997). Some past studies touched on strategic elements in these responses. Recent research by Cameron, Segal, and Songer (1993, 1995; Cameron 1993; Songer, Segal, and Cameron 1994) and by McNollgast (1995) has focused more directly on strategic voting as an element of judicial hierarchy, conceptualizing the relationship between higher and lower courts as one between principals and agents.

These studies posit that lower-court judges want judicial doctrine to match their policy preferences as closely as possible. But judges cannot simply set doctrine at their ideal points. Rather, because of the threat of reversal by the reviewing court, they must balance their preferences against the preferences of that court: they sometimes take positions that diverge from their own preferences in order to avoid reversals that would move policy even further from those preferences. This, of course, is a form of strategic voting.[28]

Theoretical analyses have reached differing conclusions about

---

27. Other research on lower courts with direct or indirect implications for an understanding of strategic behavior includes Sickels 1965; Schick 1970; Slotnick 1977; Howard 1981; Flango, Ducat, and McKnight 1986; Barrow and Walker 1988; and Dubois 1988.

28. One difficulty for this line of reasoning is that reversal relates to the outcome for the litigants, not to doctrinal disagreement. A strategy-minded judge might reach outcomes consistent with the reviewing court's preferences while deviating on doctrine.

the relative weight of judges' own preferences and those of the reviewing court in determining lower-court decisions. Cameron (1993) presented an analysis in which judges' desire to avoid reversal ultimately leads them to adopt fully the position of their reviewing court, though he did not argue that this result actually occurs (see L. Cohen 1995, 1688). McNollgast (1995) concluded that lower courts have considerable freedom to depart from Supreme Court doctrine, though they are constrained by the prospect of reversal. Songer, Segal, and Cameron (1994) argued that judges' choices substantially reflect both their own preferences and those of the reviewing court.

Empirical studies of this issue have dealt almost solely with lower-court responses to the Supreme Court (see Wasby 1970; Johnson and Canon 1984). They have examined both compliance, adoption of the Supreme Court's doctrines, and "responsiveness" (Songer, Segal, and Cameron 1994, 674–75), shifts in doctrinal positions that track shifts in the Court's positions.[29] Much of the early compliance research was aimed at documenting and analyzing noncompliance, giving primary attention to controversial civil liberties decisions (W. Murphy 1959; Peltason 1961; Canon and Kolson 1971; Canon 1973, 1974). This research demonstrated that the Court's decisions on school desegregation and the rights of criminal defendants, to take two prominent examples, received much less than full acceptance in the lower courts. Some recent studies have concluded that true noncompliance, failure to adopt doctrinal positions already articulated by the Court, is unusual (Tarr 1977; Gruhl 1982; Johnson 1987; Songer and Sheehan 1990; see Songer, Segal, and Cameron 1994; but see Melnick 1994, 253–54). While there is a good deal of research on compliance, it does not yet provide a clear picture of the extent to which judges adopt Supreme Court doctrine.

Studies of lower-court responsiveness gauge doctrinal trends in lower courts by outcomes for litigants. With one partial exception (Songer and Sheehan 1990), these studies consistently have found that lower federal courts shift position in tandem with the Supreme Court across a wide range of policy areas (Stidham and Carp 1982; Songer 1987; see also Songer and Haire 1992; Sanders 1995). And one study found that district courts followed the lead

---

But for a judge who cares only about legal policy, affirmance accompanied by disagreement on doctrine would be a near-equivalent of reversal.

29. Compliance and responsiveness are analogous with congruence and covariation, the terms used in chapter 2 to refer to judicial responses to public opinion.

of their court of appeals (Baum 1980). The findings by Songer, Segal, and Cameron (1994) on search and seizure are especially compelling because their study analyzed the impact of changing Supreme Court policy on court of appeals policy with controls for relevant case facts in decisions at both levels.

If it is assumed that judges act only on the basis of their policy goals, the empirical evidence of compliance with Supreme Court decisions and responsiveness to its doctrinal trends indicates that lower-court judges engage in a good deal of strategic voting. By the same token, the occasional strong resistance of lower courts to Supreme Court decisions suggests that strategic voting may not be universal.

Some forms of resistance can fit within modified strategic models. Many judges in the South balked at school desegregation even though the Fifth Circuit Court of Appeals and the Supreme Court stood ready to reverse them. But undoubtedly some of those judges predicted that they could maintain sufficient control over the ultimate outcomes to delay desegregation despite reversal—a prediction that was largely accurate (Peltason 1961; Paulson and Hawkes 1984). As this situation illustrates, the reviewing court does not necessarily have the last word. Strategic models can take into account both the control of lower-court judges over case dispositions after appellate remands (Beatty 1972; Pacelle and Baum 1992) and, more fundamentally, the limited capacity of appellate courts to review decisions of their subordinates (McNollgast 1995).

More problematic for strategic models are phenomena such as the highly visible resistance of the federal Ninth Circuit Court of Appeals to the Supreme Court in the 1980s and early 1990s (Stewart 1984; Maher 1985; Bishop 1992; *Vasquez v. Harris* 1992; *Gomez v. United States District Court* 1992; Fried 1993; Kozinski 1997), resistance that reached its apogee in a 1992 battle over stays of an execution on the night that it was to take place. The resistance was against conservative Supreme Court doctrine, offered by Ninth Circuit judges with liberal preferences in general or on particular issues. The resisting judges certainly recognized that deviation from the Supreme Court's course was likely to produce bad results for policy from their perspective: review, reversal, and the announcement of nationwide doctrine that ran contrary to their preferences. Yet they persisted to a remarkable degree.

This course of action is difficult to interpret as strategic voting. It is much easier to understand as a product of the satisfaction that judges get from taking positions consistent with their preferences, whatever the ultimate result (see Tarr 1977, 134). And this interpretation is consistent with the statements of some Ninth Circuit judges (Chiang 1992; Noonan 1992; Paddock 1992; Reinhardt 1992; see *Brewer v. Lewis* 1993, 563).

The example of the Ninth Circuit suggests that reversal rates may serve as an indicator of variation in the mix between sincere and strategic voting. All else being equal, judges who take a strategic approach to higher courts will be reversed less often than those who take strictly sincere positions. Analogous comparisons might illuminate variation in strategic voting within courts (as measured by success in achieving majorities) and in strategic voting aimed at the other branches (as measured by success in avoiding legislative overrides). Of course, the task of controlling for other influences on reversal rates and their analogues is not easy.

Lower-court compliance with the rulings of higher courts and responsiveness to doctrinal trends in those courts need not be understood as a product of judges' policy goals; those forms of behavior are consistent with other motives as well (Kilwein and Brisbin 1997). For one thing, while judges generally want to avoid reversal by higher courts (e.g., Schick 1970, 141–53; Satter 1990, 227–35), it is not clear that their policy goals are the primary reason (Caminker 1994, 77–78). Reversal may reduce the self-esteem of judges for whom one measure of successful judging is the ability to follow the law as established by a reviewing court. Further, it may reduce esteem for the judge in relevant audiences that use the same measure. In one extreme case, the Senate refusal to confirm G. Harrold Carswell's nomination to the Supreme Court resulted in part from reports of a high reversal rate for his decisions (Johnson and Canon 1984, 35). Reversal may also increase judges' work loads by requiring them to rehear cases.[30]

Further, a judge who was motivated primarily by legal goals would have powerful reasons to follow the lead of a reviewing court aside from the prospects for reversal. The goal of legal clarity leads judges to accept hierarchical authority as an important value in itself (see Petrick 1968).[31] And if judges seek to interpret

---

30. A work load–related consideration that is unconnected with reversal may also foster compliance: judges might seek to reduce the costs of decision making by using higher-court doctrines as guides (see Macey 1989).

31. Jerome Frank's scholarship helped to raise doubts about the importance of legal considerations in judicial decisions. Thus one commentator said that his appointment to a federal court of appeals "might be likened to the choice of a heretic to be a bishop of the Church of Rome" (Seagle 1943, 664). In light of his writing, Frank might have seemed unlikely to follow the dictates of the law dutifully. But Frank did follow

the law accurately, they are likely to define accuracy largely in terms of following the rulings of higher courts (see Howard 1981, 115–24). From this perspective, then, the obedience of lower-court judges to higher courts could be viewed as powerful evidence for the importance of legal goals to them. Moreover, judges might act strategically to further what they regard as accurate interpretations of the law.

Thus quite different motivations could lead to the same general type of response to higher courts. But these different motivations might produce somewhat different patterns of response. For example, the law-minded judge who strongly accepts hierarchical authority may focus on following the existing rules laid down by a superior court, while the judge who wants to avoid reversal for policy reasons may give greater weight to the predicted decision of the superior court in the case under consideration (see Caminker 1994). To the extent that such differing patterns can be distinguished empirically, doing so may help in identifying the goals that underlie lower-court behavior.

Strategy and the Other Branches

Like lower courts, the president and Congress have substantial powers to shape the ultimate impact of Supreme Court decisions. Students of the Court have long been interested in the use of these powers and in the ways that the Court reacts to their potential and actual use. In recent years, scholars have given considerable attention to strategic behavior by the Court in light of these powers. Most of their research has been concerned with the Court's interpretations of statutes (but see, e.g., Gely and Spiller 1992).

The predominant view in this body of work is that justices regularly take the other branches into account when they set the Court's doctrines on statutory issues, voting strategically to minimize the chances that their decisions will be overridden. If the interpretation of a statute that the justices most prefer is likely to elicit reversal by Congress and the president, they will compromise by adopting the interpretation closest to their preferences that could be predicted to withstand reversal (Gely and Spiller 1990; Eskridge 1991a, 1991b; Spiller and Gely 1992; Eskridge and Frickey 1994; Schwartz, Spiller, and Urbiztondo 1994; see

Supreme Court decisions—even those with which he expressed strong disagreement (see *Hammond-Knowlton v. United States,* 2d Cir. 1941). In the view of one commentator (Glennon 1985, 106–18), this was not because Frank feared reversal but because he thought that adherence to the precedents of a higher court was highly desirable.

McNollgast 1995, 1652–56). The potential for reversal is gauged by the ideological content of actual and potential Court doctrines in relation to the comparable ideological positions of Congress and sometimes of congressional subunits and the president.

This conception is attractive, but it could be contested on two grounds. If justices do not think strategically, of course, they may be quite willing to accept overrides of their decisions (see D. Atkinson 1974, 33). And even strategy-minded justices might give little attention to the possibility of overrides in most cases, for any of several reasons: they view overrides as too uncommon to worry about (but see Eskridge 1991b), they find it difficult to predict the prospects of an override, or they can continue to shape the affected policy in future cases even if an override occurs (Segal 1997, 32). Such justices might be most willing to act on the prospect of reversal when that prospect seems especially likely or when they care a great deal about the policy question in a case.

Research on this issue has been largely theoretical, but there are several empirical studies. Some scholars who argue that the Court systematically takes the other branches into account have supported their general position with close analyses of certain statutory decisions. Gely and Spiller (1990) discussed *Motor Vehicle Manufacturers Assn. v. State Farm Mutual* (1983), involving federal regulation of automobile safety, and *Grove City College v. Bell* (1984), involving the reach of antidiscrimination laws applying to recipients of federal funding. Cohen and Spitzer (L. Cohen and Spitzer 1994) analyzed *Chevron U.S.A. v. Natural Resources Defense Council* (1984), a decision requiring that federal courts give strong deference to administrative interpretations of statutes. Eskridge (1991a) analyzed the Court's interpretations of civil rights statutes between 1962 and 1990. In another article Eskridge (1991b, 379–85) presented briefer discussions of statutory interpretations in six other fields. Eskridge and Frickey (1994) surveyed the Court's statutory interpretations from the 1993 term.[32] All these studies are insightful, but they were intended primarily to demonstrate the plausibility of strategic voting and to explore its workings rather than to test for its existence.

A few studies have undertaken such tests. Spiller and Gely (1992) analyzed the Court's decisions interpreting the National

---

32. In the constitutional arena, political scientists have offered extended case studies of *Marbury v. Madison* (1803) (Clinton 1994; Knight and Epstein 1996b) and of the Court's Reconstruction-era decisions (Epstein and Walker 1995) as games between the Court and other political institutions.

Labor Relations Act between 1949 and 1988. They posited that congressional ideology influences the proportion of pro-union decisions by the Court under conditions in which sincere expression of the Court's collective preferences would result in congressional reversal of the Court. They tested several models based on differing assumptions about the distribution of legislative power, and the hypothesis of congressional influence on the Court—interpreted as strategic voting by the justices—generally was supported. All of the tests were based on the use of closed rules for legislation in Congress. Spiller and Gely could not test for strategic voting under open rules, more commonly used, because sincere expression of the Court's collective preferences would seldom result in congressional reversal under those rules and thus sincere and strategic voting would look about the same (Spiller and Gely 1992, 470 n. 24; see Segal 1997, 34).

Segal (1997) analyzed the Court's statutory decisions in civil liberties for the 1946–92 terms. Using proportions of liberal votes as indicators of the ideological positions of justices and members of Congress, Segal calculated potential constraints on each justice based on the relationship between their own positions and the set of positions that would withstand efforts at congressional overrides. In a series of analyses that varied in several respects, including their assumptions about the distribution of power and their measures of justices' ideological positions, Segal consistently found that potential congressional constraints had little impact on justices' support for civil liberties in statutory cases. Just as important, he found evidence that justices frequently faced no potential constraints; as was true under open rules in Congress for Spiller and Gely, strategy-minded justices could safely cast votes that directly reflected their preferences.

These two studies are important, but empirical research on strategic voting aimed at the other branches is still in its early stages. Further research, with a variety of assumptions and analytic approaches, will tell us more about the Court's attentiveness to the president and Congress in statutory interpretation. One difficulty confronting this research is that justices may respond to the other branches in ways that are not captured by a model based on comparisons of ideological positions across all relevant cases. Ideological analysis is a good shorthand device to calculate the potential for overrides, but justices who are strongly committed to avoiding overrides might include other determinants of congressional action in their calculations. And ideological analysis across the full range of decisions would be problematical if justices are selective in their efforts to avoid reversal, as they may well be. It will not be easy to take these complications into account in analyzing justices' behavior.

A different body of evidence that is relevant to Court strategy in statutory interpretation concerns the frequency with which Congress overturns the Court's decisions and the circumstances under which it does so (Stumpf 1965; Henschen 1983; Eskridge 1991b; Paschal 1991; Solimine and Walker 1992; M. Miller 1992; Hausegger and Baum forthcoming; see Zorn and Caldeira 1995; Ignagni and Meernik 1994). The finding that Congress overrides statutory decisions with moderate frequency (Eskridge 1991b), despite all the impediments to congressional action, presents a challenge and an opportunity. On their face, the occasional overrides suggest that the justices have only limited interest in avoiding reversal or that they do a poor job of forecasting congressional action.[33] But more important, analysis of overrides may provide a way to probe when and how much the Court pays attention to the potential for overrides.

While recent research on the Court and the other branches has focused primarily on routine statutory interpretation, scholars traditionally have given the greatest attention to major interbranch confrontations—most often involving constitutional issues (Pritchett 1961; W. Murphy 1962; see Clinton 1994; Epstein and Walker 1995; Knight and Epstein 1996b). It seems clear that justices sometimes shift their positions in order to defuse conflict with the other branches. During this century, the most prominent episodes in which such shifts seemed to occur involved the constitutionality of New Deal legislation in the late 1930s and an array of

---

33. Alternatively, overrides might be the intended product of complex judicial strategy. Several scholars have suggested that under certain circumstances, at least some of the justices who vote with the majority might want Congress to override the Court's decision (W. Murphy 1964, 129–31; Eskridge 1991a, 388–89; Spiller and Tiller 1996; Spiller and Spitzer 1995). But no strategy based on pure policy considerations seems likely to produce many situations in which members of the Court majority welcome reversal by the other branches.

Indeed, the most straightforward interpretation of the Court's occasional "invitations" to Congress to reverse its decisions is that the justices sometimes follow what they see as the best interpretation of the law even when that interpretation conflicts with their policy preferences (see, e.g., *McCarty v. McCarty* 1981, 235–36; *Department of Defense v. Federal Labor Relations Authority* 1994, 339). The invitations indicate that they care about policy. That they invite Congress to make what they regard as good policy rather than making it themselves suggests that they care about legal accuracy (see Hausegger and Baum 1996).

civil liberties issues in the late 1950s. But the Court has not always retreated in the face of congressional or presidential wrath; its adherence to unpopular doctrines on issues such as school prayer and remedies for school desegregation is noteworthy.

To the extent that the Court does make such retreats, short-term policy considerations are only one possible motivation. Justices may worry about preserving the Court's general institutional powers and prestige more than about reversal of specific doctrinal positions (see Dahl 1957; McCloskey 1960). Institutional standing affects the Court's capacity to shape legal policy, so trimming of policy positions to maintain that standing has elements of strategic voting (W. Murphy 1962, 262–68). But the Court's standing also has consequences for other goals such as individual popularity and limited work loads.[34] In any event, systematic analyses of the justices' responses to confrontations with the other branches complement studies of routine statutory interpretation as means to probe strategic voting oriented toward the other branches.

Conclusions

Models of judges who behave strategically to further their policy goals have become increasingly important. On theoretical grounds there are good reasons to posit that judges regularly engage in strategic voting and other forms of strategic behavior on behalf of their policy goals. But there are also good reasons to posit that judges typically vote sincerely rather than strategically. While strategic voting may seem to be an inevitable consequence of policy goals, judges might find it attractive to express their preferences directly rather than try to shape collective action within their court and in government as a whole.

Empirical analysis of strategic behavior has been sparse in comparison with the ground to be covered. Little has been done on

---

34. Congress can affect the Court's work load through such means as jurisdictional rules and the provision of Court staff.

The sources of justices' interest in good relations with Congress relate to the question in chapter 2 as to how and why the Court responds to important audiences. In all likelihood, any influence on the Court by Congress stems overwhelmingly from its powers over the Court rather than from the justices' interest in friendly interbranch relations for their own sake. It is more difficult to assess the extent to which justices are concerned with those powers because Congress affects legal policy and the extent to which they are concerned because Congress affects the justices' incomes and working conditions. But those differing motives would seem likely to affect Court behavior somewhat differently, so careful analysis of the Court's response to Congress might illuminate the sources of congressional influence.

long-term strategy, and research on strategy aimed at other institutions is still fragmentary. The largest volume of research by far concerns short-term strategic behavior within the Supreme Court. This research indicates that justices routinely engage in a limited but significant type of departure from sincere voting, modifying opinions to garner support from colleagues and joining opinions with which they disagree in part. Research also documents the regularity of other kinds of strategic behavior, such as efforts to win colleagues' support for particular positions in cases. But in all these contexts, it is often difficult to distinguish between attempts to advance policy goals strategically and other motivations.

The ambiguity of the existing evidence helps to sustain fundamentally different judgments about the role of strategy in judicial behavior. Those scholars who assume that judges are devoted to strategic behavior and those who are skeptical about judicial strategy can interpret the same evidence in quite different ways. As scholars amass more evidence about strategic behavior, the room for divergent interpretations is likely to decline only marginally.

The issue of judicial strategy concerns the ways that judges carry out their goals, but that issue has implications for efforts to identify the goals themselves. For the most part, scholars infer the motivations of judges from their patterns of behavior. As chapters 2 and 3 suggest, such inferences are difficult under any circumstances. This chapter points to additional difficulties that result from the complex ways that judges may act on their goals. If judges have multiple ways to advance their goals, if their efforts to do so involve errors, inference of motivations from judges' choices can be quite complicated. These difficulties require flexibility in thinking about, and testing for, the behavioral manifestations of judicial goals.

CHAPTER 5

Looking to the Future

In the last three chapters, I assessed the state of knowledge on three broad issues concerning judicial behavior. This chapter considers the implications of those assessments. The first section discusses how much we know about judicial behavior and why we do not know more. The rest of the chapter examines directions that research might take to enhance our understanding of judges' choices.

The State of Knowledge

There is a large body of solid research on judicial behavior, yet I think that we have made only limited progress in explaining that behavior. To a degree, that judgment reflects rigorous criteria for explanation in two senses. First, I have argued that explanations ideally should reach the fundamental sources of judicial behavior—in terms of the framework used here, the goals that underlie it. From that perspective, successful prediction of judges' behavior and identification of its correlates do not constitute full explanations in themselves. Second, I have assessed empirical findings by a high standard of proof, so that I have emphasized the limits of what can be inferred from those findings. More lenient criteria might have led to more optimistic judgments about the current state of knowledge.

By any criteria, however, the major issues in the explanation of judicial behavior are far from settled. This lack of closure is suggested by the surveys of issues in chapters 2 through 4. In those chapters I considered evidence on the balance between judges' interest in the content of legal policy and other kinds of goals, between legal and policy goals, and between strategic and nonstrategic behavior. Empirical research on each issue provides support for some conclusions, but by no means does it resolve the issue definitively.

To a degree, the absence of greater progress toward explanation can be ascribed to characteristics of scholarship on judicial behavior. Substantively, the emphases on the Supreme Court and on judges' policy preferences have limited scholars' attention to other courts and to other possible influences on decisional behavior. Judicial behavior is a very broad area, and scholars in the field could not cover the whole area well even if their research were spread evenly. Because research focuses so heavily on part of the area, its coverage of others is spotty.

Research in the field also can be criticized on methodological grounds. Among scholars who do quantitative research, movement toward greater analytic rigor has been slower than in some other fields of study. As a result, the evidentiary basis for judgments about judicial behavior is not as strong as it might be.

Finally, scholarship on judicial behavior has given limited emphasis to theory development. Much of the empirical research in the field focuses on particular aspects of judicial behavior without putting them in a broader theoretical context. And students of judicial behavior have made relatively limited use of theoretical developments in other fields and other disciplines. The result is to slow the pace with which scholars build a general understanding of judicial behavior.

But the shortcomings of research on judicial behavior should not be given undue emphasis. For one thing, the methodological quality and theoretical grounding of empirical research have improved markedly in recent years. More fundamentally, weaknesses of research in the field are not the primary source of limitations in our understanding. Some perspective can be gained by looking at other objects of study in political science.

A good comparison with judicial behavior is voting behavior, which would seem far easier to explain (Dennis 1991, 84–85). To begin with, scholars in the voting behavior field study a fairly narrow set of behaviors. If voting is "not so simple" a decision as it might appear (Dalton and Wattenberg 1993), voting is simpler in structure and more discrete than the complex of actions that constitute judicial behavior. Students of voting behavior benefit from a rich body of data, much of it produced to their collective specifications. As a group, those scholars are quite attentive to theoretical issues, and they are among the most skilled political scientists in methods of empirical analysis. As Niemi and Weisberg (1993, 10) said, "One might expect that the combination of sophisticated methodology, high-quality data, and effective theories would yield a commonly accepted understanding of voting and elections."

Yet Niemi and Weisberg concluded that "[t]his has not been the case" (see also Dennis 1991, 85–86). In the mid-1970s they decided to edit a reader on controversies in the voting behavior field; years later they reflected on that decision.

> Perhaps naively, we expected that some of these controversies would soon be resolved. After preparing a second and now a third edition, we recognize that these controversies will remain lively for a long time. Indeed, we expect this edition to be followed in due course by a fourth, a fifth, and even a sixth edition. (1993, ix)

Nor have political scientists achieved definitive explanations of other phenomena they study. Thus the lack of definitive explanations of judicial behavior must reflect something more than special weaknesses of research on that behavior.

In part, this shared gap between aspirations and achievements in explanation reflects shared imperfections in research. But far more important is the fundamental difficulty of explanation, a difficulty that would confront scholars even if there were no imperfections in research. The complexity of human behavior puts heavy burdens on those who seek to understand why people do what they do. This complexity is reflected in the theoretical ambiguity of behavior: the patterns disclosed by research typically are consistent with multiple explanations. Certainly this is true of judicial behavior. As I noted frequently in the last three chapters— undoubtedly, far too often for some readers—empirical findings that scholars use to support a particular interpretation of judges' behavior typically are consistent with other interpretations as well.

One implication of this difficulty is that we should be realistic in our expectations about advances in the understanding of judicial behavior. Research on judicial behavior today is impressive because of the creative and effective ways that scholars are probing major issues in the field. As a result, knowledge about the sources of judicial behavior is growing at a pace that has been unrivaled for many years. But we can expect major issues to remain open for the foreseeable future.

This is hardly a bleak situation. Even as research continues to run up against the barriers to definitive explanations, it can disclose a good deal more about the bases for judges' choices. Besides, the certainty that every significant issue will remain open should gladden scholars' hearts: no research program is likely to end prematurely because the subject of its concern has been settled.

The difficulty of explanation has a second implication: it puts a premium on diversity in research. The relative value of different scholarly approaches to the study of judicial behavior is open to debate, but I think it is clear that no single approach merits universal adoption. Rather, every approach has its own advantages and limitations. It follows that the field will advance most rapidly if issues are probed in multiple ways. C. Herman Pritchett's (1968, 509) famous injunction to "let a hundred flowers bloom" in the study of judicial politics can be read as a plea for tolerance among scholars with different interests and orientations, but I think it is primarily a prescription for scholarly progress.

In the three sections that follow, I consider future directions for the study of judicial behavior. I begin with a brief consideration of methodology, then discuss in greater detail the theoretical orientation and subject matter of research. In each of these sections the central theme is the value of diversity in research.[1]

Future Directions: Methodological

As suggested by the surveys of scholarship in this book, the study of judicial behavior is dominated by quantitative research. Most scholars in the field would readily agree that quantitative research of increasingly high quality has led to enormous advances in our understanding of judicial behavior. Some scholars go further (though seldom in print), arguing that only quantitative research can do much to advance our understanding of judicial behavior.

I disagree strongly with that position. This disagreement rests in part on counterexamples: studies that relied entirely or primar-

---

1. Recommendations for future research such as those offered in the sections that follow have an element of presumption, carrying with them the implication that the author knows more about what other scholars ought to be doing than they do. The act of presenting them also suggests that the author has only a limited grip on reality, because there is little evidence that such recommendations have much effect on the course of research in a field. Scholars do the research that they find interesting and promising, with limited regard to exhortations in the last section of a review article or the last chapter of a book. Thus I should apologize to readers for the presumption and affirm my realism about the likely impact of my suggestions. I offer them nonetheless in the hope that at least some scholars in the field find them useful and as a way of drawing together the implications of the surveys of scholarship in the book.

ily on qualitative methods have made major contributions to our understanding of judicial behavior. In Supreme Court scholarship, important studies of that type include those done by Walter Murphy (1964) on judicial strategy, J. Woodford Howard (1968) on decisional fluidity, H. N. Hirsch (1981) on Justice Felix Frankfurter, and H. W. Perry (1991) on case selection. Moreover, perhaps to a greater extent than most scholars realize, our sense of the Court is informed by historical research (e.g., McCloskey 1960; McCloskey and Levinson 1994; W. Murphy 1962) and biographical studies (see Howard 1971), bodies of work that are mostly qualitative in form.

Research that is chiefly qualitative in form has been at least equally important below the Supreme Court level. Among the most impressive scholarship on mid-level courts is work such as J. W. Peltason's (1961) study of responses to *Brown v. Board of Education* by Southern federal district judges, Marvin Schick's (1970) study of the federal court of appeals for the Second Circuit, Barrow and Walker's (1988) study of the division of the federal Fifth Circuit, and Tarr and Porter's (1988) study of three state supreme courts. Qualitative analysis is most prominent in trial-court research by political scientists and other scholars, and many studies that relied heavily on qualitative data have made major contributions (e.g., Balbus 1973; Heumann 1978; Mather 1979; Eisenstein, Flemming, and Nardulli 1988; McCoy 1993).

Those who favor quantitative approaches might argue that such qualitative studies are merely suggestive, that quantitative analysis provides greater rigor. Even if this were true, suggestions of patterns in judicial behavior are hardly a trivial contribution. Quantitative research has advanced our understanding of decisional fluidity on the Supreme Court since Howard (1968) originally offered arguments about its frequency and the circumstances that favor it (e.g., Brenner 1980; Maltzman and Wahlbeck 1996b). But it was Howard who used qualitative analysis of primary source materials to underline the significance of fluidity in the Court's decision-making process and who thereby encouraged further research.

More important, some scholars' perceptions of differences in the rigor of quantitative and qualitative analysis are at least greatly exaggerated. Kritzer (1994, 1996) has underlined the fundamental similarities between qualitative and quantitative research. The two forms involve research processes that have much in common. Though the need for judgment in interpretation is more obvious in qualitative research, it is just as critical in quantitative analysis. And in broad terms the two confront similar methodological issues and can be assessed by similar standards.[2] Those similarities caution against the assumption that either approach is inherently preferable.

It is true that, because of differences in analytic strategies and in types of data, qualitative and quantitative forms of research often provide different perspectives on an issue (see Rowland and Carp 1996, 149–50). But that difference is a virtue, because it expands scholars' understanding of issues. And to the extent that research with differing methodologies produces similar findings, those findings can be given greater weight. Thus Shively (1995, 1193) concluded that "[i]t is better to have two studies of the same phenomenon, one quantitative and the other qualitative, than to have two quantitative studies or two qualitative studies."[3]

The value of bringing both quantitative and qualitative research to bear on an issue is illustrated by case selection in the Supreme Court. In recent years there have been major quantitative studies of case selection (e.g., Caldeira and Wright 1988, 1994; Krol and Brenner 1990; Boucher and Segal 1995) as well as the study by Perry (1991) that relied on qualitative analysis for its major conclusions. Kritzer (1994, 720) described well the relationship between the two.

> But do we learn more about the agenda-setting process in the Supreme Court from some of the very good quantitative research that has been done, or from Perry's qualitative methodology? My answer is that the two fundamentally complement each other, and if we had one without the other (which we did until Perry's work was published), we would have a picture that omits important dimensions of the certiorari process.

Scholars' choices about styles of research are largely a matter of personal taste. This must be true, because some students of judicial behavior in political science continue to do qualitative research

---

2. This is not to say, however, that qualitative research should look as much as possible like quantitative research (see Bartels 1995; Brady 1995).
3. For the same reasons, I think that the same is true of differing methodologies in general. The distinction between qualitative and quantitative research is only the sharpest and most prominent of many methodological divides in social science, and it is desirable to have work on both sides of other divides.

despite the strong preference for quantitative approaches in the discipline as a whole. Not only is there nothing wrong with their choice, it serves well the task of advancing knowledge (see Perrow 1984, 321–23). I think that Shively (1995, 1193) was clearly right in arguing that "we benefit as a field from having a mixture of quantitative and qualitative work, and we should hope that neither side of the squabble wins."

Future Directions: Theoretical Orientations

Any scholar would agree that the study of judicial behavior should be firmly rooted in theory. But what kind of theory should be used? Within the social sciences, the primary debate is between economic and psychological perspectives, and I focus on those two approaches in this section.[4]

Arguably, this focus is too narrow. As much as psychologists and economists disagree, both typically treat individuals as the primary units of analysis. Alternatively, scholars can take sociological approaches based on larger units of analysis such as organizations. Students of judicial politics have used organizational analysis to understand trial courts (see Mohr 1976), and analysis that focuses on groups rather than individuals has provided important insights on a variety of social behaviors (e.g., Vaughan 1996). But even scholars who treat organizations or other collectivities as their units of analysis must choose an approach to the understanding of individual behavior (see Coleman and Fararo 1992). In that sense, the choice between economic and psychological perspectives is pervasive.

The Economic Perspective

Perhaps the most important development in the study of judicial behavior today is the movement to analyze judges' choices from an economic perspective. Scholars increasingly do research on judicial behavior that employs rational choice models of decision making.[5]

---

4. To make explicit the obvious, it is impossible to consider fully the benefits and limitations of either perspective in a brief section. Segal (1994) presented a short and quite useful survey of applications of economic and psychological theory to the study of appellate courts.

5. As I will discuss, *rational choice* means quite different things to different scholars. The same is true of related terms such as *positive political theory* and *public choice* (see Farber and Frickey 1992).

Many scholars have analyzed the behavior of legal actors other than judges from

Such models are far from new to the field (Schubert 1962b; Murphy 1964). But more economists and legal scholars now study judicial behavior from an economic perspective (Macey 1989; Gely and Spiller 1990; Eskridge 1991a; Kornhauser 1992; L. Cohen and Spitzer 1994), and political scientists who take a rational choice perspective have become more interested in the courts (Ferejohn and Weingast 1992b). Partly as a result, a growing number of scholars within the field of judicial politics have drawn from the rational choice approach in at least a portion of their work (e.g., Hall and Brace 1989; Cameron, Segal, and Songer 1995; L. Epstein and Walker 1995; Caldeira, Wright, and Zorn 1996).[6]

The rational choice approach has both methodological and theoretical components; though the two are not fully separable, the theoretical component is my primary concern. The methodology is that of formal theory or economic analysis, with deductive development of theoretical propositions and the use of analytic tools such as game theory (see Lalman, Oppenheimer, and Swistak 1993, 78). Scholars can adopt this methodology without accepting the theoretical assumptions about behavior that are associated with the rational choice approach (see Bendor 1988).

Those assumptions vary considerably even within the set of scholars who identify their approach as that of rational choice; by no means is there full theoretical agreement among those scholars (see Ferejohn 1991, 282; Noll and Weingast 1991, 238; Abell 1992, 189; Riker 1995, 24–25; J. Friedman 1995, 2; Ferejohn and Satz 1995, 81–82). While some scholars attach a long list of restrictive assumptions to rational choice models (see Monroe 1991b, 4), Fiorina (1995b, 87) suggested that perhaps "the only thing that all [rational choice] people would agree upon is that their explanations presume that individuals behave purposively." For this reason it is difficult to characterize and analyze the rational choice approach.

Still, most research that takes a rational choice perspective shares a set of core assumptions. Individuals hold certain goals that they seek to advance. Those goals are pursued instrumentally: people want to achieve certain outcomes. Typically, it is assumed that goals are limited in number and that people who serve in the

---

an economic perspective. Their work has contributed much to our understanding of actors such as litigants (see, e.g., Posner 1986; Baird, Gertner, and Picker 1994; Songer, Cameron, and Segal 1995).

6. The increasing importance of the rational choice approach in the study of judicial behavior is suggested by the number of scholars at early stages in their careers who have drawn from that approach for their work (e.g., B. Palmer 1995; Comparato 1996; Truelove 1996).

same roles hold the same kinds of goals: they may have different policy preferences, for instance, but they care about policy to the same degree. People act on their goals in light of their beliefs about the options available to them and the outcomes that would result from the options. Usually, though not always, they are assumed to act in ways that maximize the achievement of their goals. Characteristics of the situations in which people act determine how individual actions translate into collective outcomes, and individuals take those characteristics into account in making their choices. Most rational choice analyses also share a particular perspective on explanation and a domain for explanations. Derived from economics is an emphasis on successful prediction as a criterion for explanation and on behavioral outcomes rather than processes as the subject of study. Goals and beliefs typically are analyzed as bases for behavior but not treated as phenomena to be explained.

The value of an economic perspective on behavior and of rational choice models has been discussed at great length (Hogarth and Reder 1987a; Monroe 1991a, 1995; Coleman and Fararo 1992; Ordeshook 1993; Green and Shapiro 1994; J. Friedman 1996). The most visible part of that discussion is a vehement debate between those practitioners of rational choice analysis who essentially claim that their approach is the only way to study politics and those opponents of rational choice who essentially deny its legitimacy. As one scholar said of the disagreement between behavioral and rational economics (Zeckhauser 1987, 251), "[i]n some ways, it is more a debate between religions than between scientific theories." Less visible, but considerably more fruitful, is an exchange among scholars with more nuanced positions, scholars who all recognize that rational choice analysis has strengths and limitations but who differ in their judgments about its value. Drawing from the work of participants in that exchange, let me offer some thoughts about the value of rational choice theory in the study of judicial behavior.

One feature of rational choice analysis is that it offers a broad theoretical framework. As such, it can help to integrate disparate research (see Ferejohn and Fiorina 1975). This feature is especially welcome in the study of judicial behavior, where integration is sorely needed. For instance, a rational choice framework provides a common thread linking the various stages of decision making in an appellate court: voting on case outcomes and opinion assignment can be analyzed in the same terms. To take another example, that framework offers an effective way to analyze linkages between the implementation of Supreme Court rulings by lower courts and the Court's own selection of cases to hear (Cameron, Segal, and Songer 1995).

The strong concern of rational choice analysis with theoretical premises about behavior is equally welcome. Scholarship on judicial behavior often gives little explicit consideration to fundamental premises about the bases for judges' decisions. In contrast, scholars who adopt a rational choice approach typically begin with explicit premises about goals and institutional situations and systematically follow their implications for patterns of behavior. These premises and implications lead to a wealth of ideas that are useful in building theory and guiding empirical analysis, whether or not one accepts rational choice theory as the framework for analysis (Moe 1979; Kavka 1991; see Ferejohn and Satz 1995, 72).

This contribution is exemplified by the explicit consideration of judges' goals. Most rational choice theorists who study the Supreme Court have accepted the majority view that justices act primarily on their policy goals. But with their collective emphasis on goals as bases for behavior, scholars who work from a rational choice perspective have considered and posited a wide range of other motivations for justices and members of other courts. These motivations range from an interest in interpreting the law well to an interest in career advancement (Higgins and Rubin 1980; R. Epstein 1990; Gordon 1991; Eskridge 1991b; Mark Cohen 1991; Macey 1989, 1994; Posner 1995, 109–44). Empirical analyses have probed the impact of judicial goals such as salary and budget maximization (Anderson, Shughart, and Tollison 1989; Toma 1991), retention of judicial positions (Elder 1987), and promotion to higher courts (Mark Cohen 1992). This theoretical and empirical work underlines the need to think systematically and broadly about the goals that underlie judicial behavior.

Similarly, the rational choice assumption that people behave strategically has been a useful stimulus for research. As applied to voting on the merits of cases, that assumption challenged the implicit assumption of sincere voting that characterized much of the research on Supreme Court behavior. As a result, scholars in the field have begun an important debate and body of research on the balance between sincere and strategic voting in the Court.

Any scholarly approach is necessarily limited in its reach. In terms of the framework used in this book, the rational choice approach is especially useful for analysis of the impact of institutional situations on the operative goal orientations of decision makers. Arguably, its greatest contribution is its assistance in relating variation in institutions to variation in behavior. It is much less concerned with the impact of individual characteristics on behavior, and scholars who take a rational choice approach usually rule out some types of individual variation. And as noted earlier, rational choice analysis focuses on behavioral outcomes, giving limited attention to decision processes; it also emphasizes the consequences of goals and beliefs, generally not inquiring into their sources.

While assumptions differ a great deal among rational choice analyses, the realities of human behavior diverge substantially from some widely shared assumptions, particularly the assumption that people behave in a way that maximizes the achievement of their goals. "If the only question posed is, Rational choice, true or false? then the answer is clearly false" (Plott 1987, 117).

The fact that rational choice theory cannot account fully for behavior is treated by some critics as a fatal flaw. But if it is fatal at all, it is only for those who contend that everything can be explained in rational choice terms. Few practitioners of rational choice analysis make that claim. One practitioner (Grofman 1993, 240) asserted that "[o]nly an idiot (or an economist) would claim that rational choice models can explain all of human behavior," and he added that "even most economists are not so foolish."

I think it is clear that, with its limitations, the rational choice approach provides an enormously useful way to analyze the behavior of judges; its value is demonstrated by what we have already learned from its use in the study of judicial behavior. It is equally clear, I think, that the field would not benefit if scholars studied judicial behavior only from a rational choice perspective. Any single approach to explanation has limitations, which can be overcome only if the scholars who study a particular form of behavior adopt different perspectives.

Psychological Perspectives

If it is difficult to characterize economic analysis of behavior, psychological analysis presents even greater difficulties. There is no single framework on which psychologists agree; indeed, there has been something of a gulf between psychologists who emphasize cognition and those who emphasize motivation (Sorrentino and Higgins 1986). For this reason I refer to psychological perspectives in the plural. Taken together, however, these perspectives contrast sharply with that of economics (see Hogarth and Reder 1987b).

One difference between disciplines is in their conceptions of explanation. Psychologists are less likely than practitioners of economic analysis to equate good prediction with explanation. That difference is connected with an emphasis on decision processes as objects of study and sources of explanation (see Fiske and Taylor 1991, 15), an emphasis reflected in the centrality of cognition in psychology today (see Markus and Zajonc 1985, 137–39).

Related to this difference in conceptions of explanation is psychologists' interest in understanding the sources of behavior in themselves. Attitudes and cognitions are studied as independent variables that influence behavior, but they also receive extensive treatment as dependent variables and—more broadly—as objects of intrinsic interest. Among the studies of attitudes, for instance, only a minority concern the relationship between attitudes and behavior (see Eagly and Chaiken 1993).

Psychologists also diverge from economists in their perceptions of human behavior. Psychological research has produced a good deal of evidence that the characteristics of situations exert a considerable impact on behavior, perhaps a greater impact than that of individual traits (Patry 1989; L. Ross and Nisbett 1991). However, psychology leaves considerably more room for individual variation than does economic analysis. That difference is exemplified by the prominence of personality as a subject of research.

Especially relevant to current issues in judicial behavior are depictions of decision making (H. Simon 1985; Hogarth and Reder 1987a; Quattrone and Tversky 1988; Kinder 1993; Monroe 1995). Scholars who take a psychological approach typically see a substantial gap between decisions that would maximize the achievement of goals and the decisions that individuals actually make. Moreover, at least some types of errors in people's efforts to advance their goals are viewed as systematic rather than random.

In themselves, the differences between psychological and economic perspectives suggest the value of using both as means to understand judicial behavior. By depicting decision making in a different way, psychological research provides an alternative to some common assumptions in rational choice analysis. Similarly, its inquiries into issues that are more peripheral to economic analysis help to broaden the scope of explanations.

Students of judicial behavior have drawn from several bodies of psychological theory. Schubert's (1965) use of attitude theory to structure his conception of Supreme Court decision making was quite consequential, because that conception has influenced attitudinal conceptions of decision making since then. To a degree, the widely held assumption that judges vote sincerely reflects Schubert's choice of attitude theory. Scholars have employed psychological theory to analyze other issues, such as the impact of personality on judicial behavior and interpersonal influence in decision making. A sampling of research that makes explicit and integral use of psychological theory is presented in table 5.1. Additional work has drawn on psychological theory in more limited ways or less explicitly.

Still, students of judicial behavior have utilized psychological theory less than might be expected. In the past, one reason was the relative dearth of any type of social science theory in the scholarship on judicial behavior. Research in the field is becoming more explicitly theoretical today, but it is primarily economic theory rather than psychology to which scholars are turning.

Part of the explanation probably lies in the diversity of psychological scholarship. The absence of a general framework for explanation of behavior makes psychology less attractive than rational choice analysis as a means to integrate theory and empiri-

TABLE 5.1. Selected Examples of Uses of Psychological Theory in Research on Judicial Behavior

Approach or Concern	Uses
Psychoanalytic perspective on personality	Lasswell (1948) on three trial judges Hirsch (1981) on Felix Frankfurter
Analysis of motives and incentives for political activity	Caldeira (1977) on New Jersey judges Aliotta (1988) on the Supreme Court
Impact of self-esteem	Atkins, Alpert, and Ziller[a] (1980) on Florida judges Gibson (1981a) on California judges
Attitude theory	Schubert (1965) on the Supreme Court Spaeth and Parker (1969) on the Supreme Court Rohde and Spaeth (1976) on the Supreme Court Mishler and Sheehan (1996) on the Supreme Court
Cognition and decision making	Segal (1986) on the Supreme Court Rowland and Carp (1996) on federal district courts
Integrative complexity in decision making	Tetlock[a], Bernzweig[a], and Gallant[a] (1985) on the Supreme Court Gruenfeld[a] (1995) on the Supreme Court
Interpersonal influence in small groups	Atkins (1973) on federal courts of appeals Main and Walker (1973) and Walker and Main (1973) on federal district courts Walker (1976) on state supreme courts

[a]Psychologists; other scholars listed are political scientists.

cal findings. And the multiplicity of psychological theories makes it more difficult to gain familiarity with potentially relevant work. Also important is the subject matter of scholarship in psychology. Research concentrates most heavily on the situations that "ordinary" people confront in the various aspects of their lives. There has been relatively little attention to the behavior of elite groups such as judges in long-term institutional structures. As a result, the body of psychological theory research is less easily applied to judicial behavior than is rational choice scholarship, which fits well the kinds of choices that judges make.[7]

Yet scholarship in psychology can make a very substantial contribution to the analysis of judicial behavior. Some specific applications of psychological theory were discussed in earlier chapters. Other applications are exemplified by the work cited in table 5.1. A brief survey of selected bodies of theory may suggest additional possibilities.

One relevant body of research is on personality theory. It is reasonable to posit that personality traits studied by psychologists, such as personal needs and cognitive style, can affect the behavior of public policy makers (see, e.g., Barber 1965; Winter 1987; Fiske 1993). The studies by Lasswell (1948) and Hirsch (1981) demonstrate in different ways the impact of judges' personalities on general patterns in their behavior. Two other studies (Atkins, Alpert, and Ziller 1980; Gibson 1981a) show that the specific trait of self-esteem may help to structure judges' orientations to decisions.

Certainly personality is quite relevant to the issues that have been canvased in this book. Judges' goal orientations and the ways they act on their goals undoubtedly reflect their basic needs and motivations. To take one example, suggested in chapter 4, characteristics such as the need to exercise power probably influence the extent to which judges act strategically.

Still, interest in personality lies outside the mainstream of research on judging. One reason may be the apparent difficulty of integrating individual traits into existing theories of judicial behavior. But students of personality have done similar integration of their own, analyzing the interaction between individual traits and

7. Political psychology has become a significant interdisciplinary field, but even within that field most research is on people whose situations are somewhat (or quite) different from those of judges (Hermann 1986; Sears 1987; Kressel 1993). A large proportion of research is devoted to mass behavior in contexts such as elections. Research on decision making by government officials concentrates on single leaders such as presidents and on foreign policy-making.

situations in which people act and working to identify the situations in which those traits have the greatest impact (see M. Snyder and Ickes 1985; Kenrick and Funder 1988). By following their lead, students of judicial behavior can take individual personality into account without ignoring the impact of institutional rules and other elements of judges' situations.

A second body of research is in attitude theory. While this research is reflected in the attitudinal model of judicial behavior, greater use can be made of its insights. Quite relevant to the study of judicial behavior are processes and sources of attitude change, a central concern in attitude theory (Eagly and Chaiken 1993, 219–63; Petty, Priester, and Wegener 1994). Research addresses such issues as the relationship between attitude strength and resistance to change (Eagly and Chaiken 1993, 580–89) and the effects on people's attitudes of their taking positions repeatedly (Downing, Judd, and Brauer 1992). Students of the Supreme Court have been concerned with change in judges' policy preferences (Schubert 1983; Atkins and Sloope 1986; Wasby 1991; Kobylka 1992; L. Epstein, Hoekstra, Segal, and Spaeth 1995); attitude theory provides tools to analyze change processes systematically. Indeed, Mishler and Sheehan (1996) employed theories of attitude change in analyzing the impact of public opinion on justices' attitudes.[8]

Of more central importance to judicial behavior is the approach of attitude theory to the links between attitudes and behavior. Earlier views that attitudes strongly influence behavior or that they have only a weak influence have been supplanted by more complex and nuanced conceptions of their impact (Fazio 1986; Eagly and Chaiken 1993, 155–218), such as the theories of reasoned action and planned behavior (Fishbein 1980; Ajzen and Fishbein 1980; Ajzen 1985, 1991). In these conceptions attitudes may have multiple components, and several other forces may interact with attitudes or intervene between attitudes and behavior.

In a third body of research, cognitive psychology, the relationship between attitudes and behavior typically is even less direct. Attitudes may serve primarily "as information filters or intermediaries that influence the cognitive processes of perception, memory, and influence" (Rowland and Carp 1996, 150) rather than as direct bases for choice (see Markus and Zajonc 1985; Fiske

---

8. Also relevant is the research on learning by government officials, informed by psychology and other disciplines, which examines change in policy positions as a result of experience (Etheredge 1985; Breslauer and Tetlock 1991). For an analysis of preference change from a rational choice perspective, see Gerber and Jackson 1993.

and Taylor 1991). The theory of motivated reasoning (Kunda 1990) exemplifies this conception of attitudes, one that has achieved widespread acceptance in psychology. This conception provides a means to integrate approaches that emphasize the effects of attitudes on judicial decisions into a cognitive perspective on decision making. This is particularly important in light of the current primacy of that perspective in psychology.

Cognitive psychology addresses other issues relevant to an understanding of judicial behavior. One central issue is how people undertake the difficult task of making decisions that involve complex thinking. Even the relatively simple conceptions of decision making that dominate Supreme Court research imply an intricate set of cognitive processes. If justices act sincerely on their policy preferences, they must organize those preferences into a coherent system and analyze the content of cases to see how the available alternatives fit into that system of preferences. If justices act strategically on their preferences, they must also calculate and take into account the possible impact of alternative courses of action on the behavior of other people. If justices seek to make both good law and good policy, their task is even more complicated. Trial judges who must work with the raw evidence in cases to reach a decision have a particularly difficult task. The state trial judge who undertakes that task under heavy time pressures and who seeks to advance a set of disparate goals operates in a world of enormous complexity.

These situations require that decision makers sort out and use large volumes of information, and cognitive psychologists have offered clusters of theory to analyze these processes (see Lodge and McGraw 1995). Schema theory helps in understanding how individuals structure their knowledge and thereby create a context for the analysis of new information (Fiske and Linville 1980; Conover and Feldman 1984; Fiske and Taylor 1991, 96–179).[9] Theories of problem representation analyze the ways that people define or conceive of the decisions they face, including their identification of alternative courses of action (Voss, Wolfe, Lawrence, and Engle 1991; Sylvan and Voss forthcoming). One approach to problem representation is Pennington and Hastie's (1986, 1991, 1992) "story model" for decision making by jurors, a model that might be applied to trial judges as well (Rowland and Carp 1996, 173 n.

---

9. For a skeptical view of schema theory and a set of responses to that view, see Kuklinski, Luskin, and Bolland 1991 and Lodge et al. 1991. A related but alternative conception is the associative network model (McGraw and Lodge 1995).

8). Individual differences in information processing can be taken into account in cognitive approaches, thus linking decision making with personality (Pervin 1985, 93–98).

Related to the process of decision making under complexity are the outcomes of that process. Considerable scholarship has been done from a cognitive perspective on deviations from the behavior that would maximize goal achievement. One body of research deals with heuristics and biases in individual choice that lead to such deviations (Nisbett and Ross 1980; Dawes 1988; Poulton 1994). Prospect theory represents a way to understand the resulting patterns of deviations (Lichtenstein and Slovic 1971; Kahneman and Tversky 1979; Kahneman, Slovic, and Tversky 1982; Quattrone and Tversky 1988). Another perspective is reflected in the work on bounded rationality by Herbert Simon (1955, 1983, 1985, 1987, 1995) and others (e.g., March 1978; see Weiss 1982).

Rowland and Carp (1996, 152–73) used an array of theoretical work in cognitive psychology to analyze the behavior of federal district judges (see Rowland 1991, 78–80). Specific concepts such as heuristics can assist in understanding particular aspects of decision making. Segal (1986) used heuristics as a framework for his analysis of case facts as cues to Supreme Court justices. In light of the difficulty of predicting how other institutions would respond to a court's decisions, strategy-minded judges may employ certain heuristics to make their task manageable. Segal's (1995, 17 n. 37) sketch of one way that justices may respond to the possibility of congressional overrides can be understood as a hypothesis about the heuristics that the justices employ.

Among the applications of psychological theory that I have suggested, undoubtedly some would prove considerably more useful than others. But the applications that have been made thus far demonstrate the value of psychological perspectives on judges' choices. Thus the diverse body of scholarship in psychology constitutes an important resource for further inquiry into judicial behavior.

Economics and/or Psychology?

Psychological and economic perspectives on behavior are not mutually exclusive. Within a general framework such as the one used in this book, both economic and psychological theory can be employed to understand and study the processes and forces that shape judicial behavior.[10] For instance, in analyzing individual choice, one might begin with models based on typical rational choice assumptions and draw on theories of cognition to understand behavioral deviations from those assumptions (see Mueller 1986; J. Friedman 1995, 20–21).

Of course, synthetic work of that type is already being done. In part, psychological research on heuristics and biases and on bounded rationality represents an effort to describe and explain deviations from rational choice assumptions. In turn, some scholars use the tools of economic analysis to understand these deviations (e.g., De Palma, Myers, and Papageorgiou 1994; Bendor 1995).[11] Indeed, there has been a melding of psychological and economic perspectives in an important body of research on economic behavior that goes under the labels of economic psychology and behavioral economics (see van Raaij, van Veldhoven, and Wärneryd 1988; Thaler 1991). This research makes clear the benefits of combining multiple perspectives.

In practice, however, it is unlikely that more than a small minority of individual scholars will synthesize economic and psychological approaches in their own research. The disciplinary training that scholars receive shapes their skills and tastes in research, thereby making one perspective more attractive than the other. And, in part because of this training, scholars develop conceptions of good explanations and perceptions of human behavior that strongly favor a particular perspective (see Lopes 1994; Segal 1994).

The impact of these differing conceptions and perceptions should be underlined. On conceptions of explanation, one important issue is the trade-off between the advantage of the economic perspective in coherence and that of psychological perspectives in comprehensiveness. The simplifying assumptions that one scholar sees as critical limitations in the explanatory reach of rational choice analysis strike another as necessary means to preserve clarity and rigor. The relative lack of tidiness in psychological theory is a very serious disadvantage for some scholars, but for others it is the unavoidable cost of seeking to understand behavior fully.

10. A somewhat different framework that allows for integration of these two bodies of theory is that of situational analysis (Farr 1985) and similar approaches that emphasize the context of decision making (Lane 1990; Huckfeldt and Sprague 1995). On the application of some of these approaches to judicial behavior, see Esler and Stookey 1995 and L. Epstein, Hoekstra, Segal, and Spaeth 1995, 14–16.

11. One early contributor to this research was Daniel Ellsberg (1961), later to gain fame for his part in the Pentagon Papers episode that culminated in *New York Times v. United States* (1971) (see Rudenstine 1996).

A related issue is the importance of successful prediction as a criterion for explanations. For scholars who give heavy weight to prediction, assumptions of rational choice theory that depart from reality are of little concern in themselves if they do not detract from predictive success. Such assumptions are more problematic for those who seek to understand the fundamental sources of behavior. Such scholars are likely to favor psychological theories that probe more deeply into those sources.

The impact of differences in perceptions of human behavior is exemplified by three recent lists of circumstances in which rational choice models are most useful (Green and Shapiro 1995, 267; Kelley 1995, 101; M. Taylor 1995, 225–26). While the lists differed, there were several circumstances that at least two of the three cited: uncomplicated goals, a good understanding of how to achieve those goals, high stakes in their achievement, and the experience of repetitive choices.[12] The first two circumstances involve issues on which scholars differ a good deal: there are strong disagreements about the simplicity or complexity of goals held by people such as judges and about their capability of identifying the best means to advance their goals. The third relates to another issue on which views diverge, the extent to which behavior is aimed at achieving certain decisional outcomes. On these and other issues concerning human behavior, scholars with particular disciplinary backgrounds tend to hold sets of perceptions that are strongly favorable or strongly unfavorable to the utility of rational choice or economic analysis.

Thus it is understandable that individual scholars typically gravitate to either economic or psychological perspectives on explanation. Yet the effort to achieve better explanations will benefit if both approaches are widely used in the study of judicial behavior. It is equally important that the two camps know of each other's contributions and build on them. If the debate between economics and psychology seems to resemble one between religions, there is much to be said for ecumenism (see Bendor 1988, 388–90).

Future Directions: Subject Matter

Throughout the book I have suggested the value of new research about judicial behavior on a wide array of issues and in a variety of settings. Indeed, it is difficult to imagine any topic on which schol-

---

12. For other analyses of the conditions under which rational choice theories are most useful, see Kreps 1990, 139–40; and Satz and Ferejohn 1994, 81.

ars cannot make a contribution with solid and innovative research. Still, some gaps in our knowledge of judicial behavior merit particular attention, because they are especially wide and consequential.

Some Research Areas

One subject on which more concerted research would be particularly beneficial is *recruitment of judges*. Scholars have given extensive attention to some aspects of judicial recruitment—particularly the final stage of the recruitment process, in which judges are chosen from pools of serious candidates. But the full recruitment process and its effects have received little attention.

Students of judicial behavior can learn a good deal by looking more broadly and more deeply at judicial recruitment and its impact. Models of useful approaches and a body of applicable theory can be drawn from the scholarship on political recruitment, careers, and ambition (Schlesinger 1966; Prewitt 1970; G. Black 1972; Rohde 1979; Fowler and McClure 1989; Hibbing 1991; S. Williams and Lascher 1993; Fowler 1993; Kazee 1994).

An important lesson of this scholarship is the value of thinking about recruitment in terms of office-holding careers. What are the patterns of entry points into the judiciary, of promotions from those entry points to higher levels, and of departures from various levels of courts? Description of these patterns in itself may lead to insights about judges' perspectives. It also provides a starting point for inquiry into several issues concerning the orientations of people who serve on particular types of courts.

One such issue is the impact of ambition on the behavior of judges. The holder of any position may seek to remain in that position, to move to a higher position, or to leave government altogether. This issue is especially relevant to state judges, many of whom leave the judiciary voluntarily and who often can take active steps—through electoral candidacies, for instance—to obtain promotions to higher courts. It seems reasonable to posit that judges with differing ambitions tend to undertake their judicial tasks in differing ways (see Barber 1965), and tests of this expectation should help in understanding the mix of goal orientations on particular courts and variation in goals among courts.

Another lesson of the scholarship on recruitment and related issues is that people who seek particular positions in government may differ in important ways from those who seek other positions and, even more, from those who do not seek any positions (see

Jacob 1962). Because of their training and experiences, lawyers as a group may be distinctive (Stover 1989; Kelly 1994). But those sets of lawyers who are interested in serving on higher courts, on lower courts, and on no courts at all may differ significantly among themselves. Some possible differences and their consequences for judicial behavior were discussed in earlier chapters. But with only a little relevant research to draw on (e.g., Watson and Downing 1969), those discussions were quite speculative. On this and other issues, more extensive inquiry into judicial recruitment could produce valuable results.

A second promising area for research concerns the *impact of court situations.* Courts vary enormously in traits such as the extent of appellate review, security of tenure, potential for promotion, subject matter of cases, and control over caseload. One important point of agreement between scholars with economic and psychological perspectives is that those kinds of differences have a fundamental impact on people's choices.

Students of judicial behavior have been quite cognizant of this impact. In particular, the special situation of Supreme Court justices is a recurring subject in scholarship on the Court (e.g., Rohde 1972c, 659–62; Segal and Spaeth 1993, 69–72). Yet there has been little systematic analysis of the relationship between characteristics of court situations and judicial behavior. The paucity of such research reflects scholars' focus on the Supreme Court and the general lack of comparison among courts. Such intercourt comparisons and analyses of particular courts over time could illuminate the effects of differences in the settings for judicial decisions.[13]

One strategy is to compare courts that have similar responsibilities but that differ in institutional characteristics. This strategy has been used to compare state supreme courts that differ in procedural rules on such matters as opinion assignment and voting order (Hall and Brace 1989; Brace and Hall 1993).[14] The scholarship on plea bargaining has given some attention to the impact of variation in work loads (e.g., Feeley 1979). The argument that specialization affects judicial behavior in fundamental ways (Shapiro

---

13. This is not to say that studies of single courts at single points in time cannot be useful in identifying the effects of characteristics such as work loads and procedural rules. But analyses of variation in these characteristics can probe their impact more fully.

14. Comparisons of state supreme courts whose judges are selected in different ways (S. Nagel 1973; Atkins and Glick 1974; Schneider and Maughan 1979; Dubois 1980; Pinello 1995) help to illuminate the effects of both recruitment and judges' situations.

1968, 52–54) has been the subject of limited tests (Baum 1977b, 1994; W. Hansen, Johnson, and Unah 1995). But far more research of this type remains to be done.

The frequent movement of judges from lower to higher courts within particular systems and from state to federal courts creates opportunities to analyze how the same individuals behave within different institutional settings. To take one example, the impact of electoral considerations on state judges can be gauged by studying change in the policy positions of elected judges who move to federal courts. If the Supreme Court's immunity from review by a higher court helps to make it distinctive, the impact of that characteristic should be discernible when judges come to the Court from lower courts. Beyond what they establish about the impact of specific court characteristics, such analyses could shed considerable light on the relative importance of individuals and situations in shaping judicial behavior. The same is true of research on individuals who move from legislatures to courts (Danelski 1970; Gibson 1978a).

Analyses of courts over time can probe the impact of institutional changes. Some types of change seem particularly promising as subjects of analysis. One is growth in courts' discretionary jurisdiction (Halpern and Vines 1977; Walker, Epstein, and Dixon 1988). In appellate courts with little control over their caseloads, one potentially important change is delegation of major decision-making responsibilities to central staffs (see Davies 1981; Stow and Spaeth 1992; Baker 1994). The impact of rules for retention of judgeships can be analyzed over time as well as among courts. What difference does it make, for instance, when states replace partisan elections with retention elections that may be considerably easier for incumbents to win?

Overlapping the two areas for research that I have discussed so far is a third, which concerns the *ways that judges act on their goals*. Thus far, the preponderance of research explicitly addressing this issue has dealt with strategic behavior to advance policy goals. This research has been devoted primarily to the Supreme Court, and even for the Court the results are far from definitive. But there has been considerable progress, and current research will add much to what we know.

This focus on policy-oriented strategy should not obscure the array of other issues concerning linkages between goals and behavior. Even those scholars who believe that Supreme Court justices act only to make good policy recognize the multiplicity of goals that affect the choices of other judges. However, there has been little systematic analysis of the ways that judges act on these other goals. One important example is an interest in securing re-election. Brace and Hall (1995; Hall 1987, 1992, 1995) have examined electoral concerns in the review of death sentences. Several studies have analyzed the impact of public opinion on criminal sentencing in trial courts (Kuklinski and Stanga 1979; Gibson 1980; Pruet and Glick 1986), giving some attention to judges' interest in keeping their positions. But more work on re-election and criminal cases is needed, in light of the growing frequency with which both trial and appellate judges are attacked as allegedly "soft on crime." Personal injury law sometimes becomes a visible campaign issue; more often, it is a basis for substantial campaign contributions. As in the legislature, the impact of past and prospective contributions on judges' positions is a question of both theoretical and practical importance (see, e.g., Wright 1990). It seems unlikely that concern for re-election affects judges' behavior across the full range of issues, since many issues are of little interest to either the public or interest groups that participate in judicial elections. Yet some judges, like many legislators, might adopt a "blame avoidance" strategy (Weaver 1988, 18–37) that leads to caution on even obscure issues in order not to provide potential opponents with ammunition for attacks.

Where judges hold multiple goals, perhaps the central question in explanation of their behavior is how they balance those goals in practice. A good deal of work on judicial behavior touches on this issue. As an explicit issue, it arises most often in scholarship on the nexus between legal and policy considerations in decision making. The balance between goals is at least an implicit issue in research on electoral considerations for judges and in much of the scholarship on state trial judges.

The balancing of goals merits more concerted and more systematic research. If the task of acting on a single goal can be difficult, the task of trying to advance multiple goals that sometimes conflict is far more difficult. How do judges undertake this task? Scholars have offered some ways of thinking about this process (e.g., Denzau, Riker, and Shepsle 1985; Ainslie 1985). Students of Congress in particular have demonstrated that it is both possible and useful to analyze trade-offs between goals (Dodd

1977; Denzau, Riker, and Shepsle 1985; M. Thomas 1985; Poole 1988; see Weaver 1988). Students of judicial behavior can take similar approaches to illuminate this process.

Focusing on Variation

A recurrent theme in this section and in the book as a whole is the value of studying variation among courts. Understanding of judicial behavior is inherently limited by the heavy focus of scholarship on the Supreme Court and the relatively slight attention given to courts below the top few levels of the judiciary. More extensive study of lower courts would provide a more comprehensive picture of the forces that shape judicial behavior. Courts whose institutional characteristics create unusual situations for judges may be instructive.[15] And, as I have argued, explicit comparisons of courts with different characteristics illuminate the impact of court situations. Even if we cared only about the Supreme Court, our ability to explain the Court's behavior would be enhanced by comparing it with other institutions.

I have also given some emphasis to possible variation among individual judges in the same court setting. While individual-level variation has been central to the study of judicial behavior, the great majority of attention has been focused on differences in the specific content of judges' policy preferences. Possible differences in the priorities that judges give to different goals and in their ways of acting on goals generally have been set aside, except in the literature on state trial courts (e.g., Dolbeare 1967, 65–66; Caldeira 1977; Wice 1985, 99–103; Conley and O'Barr 1990, 85–106).

The value of focusing on these kinds of variation can be debated. Arguably, situations have far greater effects on behavior than do the characteristics of individuals. Further, analysis of patterns in behavior becomes more complicated when individual differences are considered.

Yet these considerations should not be overstated. Any scholar who studies an institution closely can attest to the significance of individual differences. Even if all Supreme Court justices share the same goal orientations, a premise whose accuracy is uncertain, there is no doubt that they differ in their ways of acting on those goals. For instance, Danelski (1968) identified major

---

15. One example is specialized courts, mentioned earlier. Another is courts in which judges' income is directly dependent on their caseloads, most judges are non-lawyers, or both (Note 1966; Gorton 1974; Provine 1986).

differences in the leadership styles of chief justices, and what he found about Taft, Hughes, and Stone surely is true of Warren, Burger, and Rehnquist. It is at least desirable, if not necessary, to take such differences into account. Psychological scholarship on issues such as personality demonstrates that the complications involved in incorporating individual differences into analysis can be managed successfully. For their part, legislative scholars have analyzed the impact of differences in goal orientations among members of Congress on their behavior alongside the effects of institutional characteristics (Fenno 1973; Bullock 1976; S. Smith and Deering 1983). The smaller size of courts makes it more difficult to follow that path, but it should still be possible to trace the consequences of differences among judges within the context of court situations. Although the impact of individual traits should not be exaggerated, understanding of individual-level variation is essential to full explanations of judicial behavior.

Conclusions

This book arose from my effort to grapple with the complexity of judicial behavior. The process of assessing our knowledge about judicial behavior has deepened my appreciation of that complexity and of the difficulties it creates for explanation. Despite all the progress that scholars have made, progress that is accelerating today, we are a long way from achieving truly satisfying explanations of judicial behavior.

To borrow a term from Pennington and Hastie (1991), scholars build stories about the phenomena they study. Some stories win support because they provide important insights. But no single story is comprehensive, and alternative stories capture different portions of reality.

Our stories about judicial behavior are getting better—more clearly delineated, more firmly anchored in reality. But they are still incomplete, and the difficulties of explanation ensure that they will remain incomplete. The field will move most effectively toward better explanations if scholars take this reality into account by recognizing both the limitations and contributions of the various conceptions of judicial behavior.

Just as no single explanation can be definitive, neither is any single assessment of the state of knowledge. I have sought in this book to sort out what we know and do not know on the basis of empirical research on judicial behavior. I chose a particular vantage point and framework, and those choices shaped my assessment. Other people with their own perspectives undoubtedly would have reached some different conclusions. Still, my hope is that the book helps to clarify issues and our understanding of them, so that it contributes in a small way to further progress in the field. In any event, it is encouraging to see how much scholars are accomplishing today, and there is good reason to expect those advances to continue. If we cannot expect the puzzle of judicial behavior to be solved, we are gaining a better understanding of the puzzle. That is no small achievement.

References

A list of court cases follows this reference list.

Abell, Peter. 1992. "Is Rational Choice Theory a Rational Choice of Theory?" In *Rational Choice Theory: Advocacy and Critique,* ed. James S. Coleman and Thomas J. Fararo, 183–206. Newbury Park, Calif.: Sage Publications.

Abelson, R. P. 1976. "Social Psychology's Rational Man." In *Rationality and the Social Sciences: Contributions to the Philosophy and Methodology of the Social Sciences,* ed. S. I. Benn and G. W. Mortimore, 58–89. London: Routledge and Kegan Paul.

Abelson, Robert P. 1995. "The Secret Existence of Expressive Behavior." *Critical Review* 9:25–36.

Adamany, David W. 1969. "The Party Variable in Judges' Voting: Conceptual Notes and a Case Study." *American Political Science Review* 63:57–73.

Adamany, David W. 1973. "Legitimacy, Realigning Elections, and the Supreme Court." *Wisconsin Law Review* 1973:790–846.

Administrative Office of the United States Courts. 1996. *Judicial Business of the United States Courts: 1995 Report of the Director.* Washington, D.C.: Administrative Office of the United States Courts.

Ainslie, George. 1985. "Beyond Microeconomics: Conflict Among Interests in a Multiple Self as a Determinant of Value." In *The Multiple Self,* ed. Jon Elster, 133–75. Cambridge: Cambridge University Press.

Ajzen, Icek. 1985. "From Intentions to Action: A Theory of Planned Behavior." In *Action Control: From Cognition to Behavior,* ed. Julius Kuhl and Jurgen Beckmann, 11–39. Berlin: Springer-Verlag.

Ajzen, Icek. 1991. "The Theory of Planned Behavior." *Organizational Behavior and Human Decision Processes* 50:179–211.

Ajzen, Icek, and Martin Fishbein. 1980. *Understanding Attitudes and Predicting Social Behavior.* Englewood Cliffs, N.J.: Prentice-Hall.

Aldisert, Ruggero J. 1987. "Philosophy, Jurisprudence, and Jurisprudential Temperament of Federal Judges." *Indiana Law Review* 20:453–515.

Alexander, Jeffrey C., Bernhard Giesen, Richard Münch, and Neil J. Smelser, eds. 1987. *The Micro-Macro Link.* Berkeley: University of California Press.

Aliotta, Jilda M. 1988. "Social Backgrounds, Social Motives and Participation on the U.S. Supreme Court." *Political Behavior* 10:267–84.

Alpert, Lenore, Burton M. Atkins, and Robert C. Ziller. 1979. "Becoming a Judge: The Transition from Advocate to Arbiter." *Judicature* 62:325–35.

Alschuler, Albert W. 1976. "The Trial Judge's Role in Plea Bargaining, Part I." *Columbia Law Review* 76:1059–1154.

Anderson, Gary M., William F. Shughart II, and Robert D. Tollison. 1989. "On the Incentives of Judges to Enforce Legislative Wealth Transfers." *Journal of Law and Economics* 32:215–28.

Arnold, R. Douglas. 1990. *The Logic of Congressional Action.* New Haven: Yale University Press.

Atkins, Burton M. 1972. "Decision-Making Rules and Judicial Strategy on the U.S. Courts of Appeals." *Western Political Quarterly* 25:626–42.

Atkins, Burton M. 1973. "Judicial Behavior and Tendencies Toward Conformity in a Three Man Small Group: A Case Study of Dissent Behavior on the U.S. Courts of Appeals." *Social Science Quarterly* 54:41–53.

Atkins, Burton M. 1974. "Opinion Assignments on the United States Courts of Appeals: The Question of Issue Specialization." *Western Political Quarterly* 27:409–28.

Atkins, Burton, Lenore Alpert, and Robert Ziller. 1980. "Personality Theory and Judging: A Proposed Theory of Self Esteem and Judicial Policy-Making." *Law and Policy Quarterly* 2:189–220.

Atkins, Burton M., and Henry R. Glick. 1974. "Formal Judicial Recruitment and State Supreme Court Decisions." *American Politics Quarterly* 2:427–49.

Atkins, Burton M., and Justin Green. 1976. "Consensus on the United States Courts of Appeals: Illusion or Reality?" *American Journal of Political Science* 19:735–48.

Atkins, Burton M., and Terry Sloope. 1986. "The 'New' Hugo Black and the Warren Court." *Polity* 18:621–37.

Atkins, Burton M., and William Zavoina. 1974. "Judicial Leadership on the Court of Appeals: A Probability Analysis of Panel Assignment in Race Relations Cases on the Fifth Circuit." *American Journal of Political Science* 18:701–11.

Atkinson, David N. 1974. "Justice Sherman Minton and Behavior Patterns Inside the Supreme Court." *Northwestern University Law Review* 69: 716–38.

Atkinson, David N. 1976. "Retirement and Death on the United States Supreme Court: From Van Devanter to Douglas." *University of Missouri-Kansas City Law Review* 45:1–27.

Atkinson, David N., and Dale A. Neuman. 1969. "Toward a Cost Theory of Judicial Alignments: The Case of the Truman Bloc." *Midwest Journal of Political Science* 13:271–83.

Atkinson, John W., ed. 1958. *Motives in Fantasy, Action, and Society.* Princeton, N.J.: D. Van Nostrand.

Austen-Smith, David. 1987. "Sophisticated Sincerity: Voting over Endogenous Agendas." *American Political Science Review* 81:1323–29.

Austen-Smith, David. 1992. "Explaining the Vote: Constituency Constraints on Sophisticated Voting." *American Journal of Political Science* 36: 68–95.

Axelrod, Robert. 1970. *Conflict of Interest: A Theory of Divergent Goals with Applications to Politics.* Chicago: Markham.

Baird, Douglas G., Robert H. Gertner, and Randal C. Picker. 1994. *Game Theory and the Law.* Cambridge, Mass.: Harvard University Press.

Baker, Thomas E. 1994. *Rationing Justice on Appeal: The Problems of the U.S. Courts of Appeals.* St. Paul, Minn.: West Publishing.

Balbus, Isaac D. 1973. *The Dialectics of Legal Repression: Black Rebels Before the American Criminal Courts.* New York: Russell Sage Foundation.

Baldus, David C., George Woodworth, and Charles A. Pulaski Jr. 1990. *Equal Justice and the Death Penalty: A Legal and Empirical Analysis.* Boston: Northeastern University Press.

Ball, Howard. 1987. *Courts and Politics: The Federal Judicial System,* 2d ed. Englewood Cliffs, N.J.: Prentice-Hall.

Barber, James David. 1965. *The Lawmakers.* New Haven, Conn.: Yale University Press.

Bargh, John A. 1990. "Goal ≠ Intent: Goal-Directed Thought and Behavior Are Often Unintentional." *Psychological Inquiry* 1:248–77.

Barker, Lucius. 1967. "Third Parties in Litigation: A Systemic View of the Judicial Function." *Journal of Politics* 29:41–69.

Barnum, David G. 1985. "The Supreme Court and Public Opinion: Judicial Decision Making in the Post–New Deal Period." *Journal of Politics* 47:652–65.

Barrow, Deborah J., and Thomas G. Walker. 1988. *A Court Divided: The Fifth Circuit Court of Appeals and the Politics of Judicial Reform.* New Haven, Conn.: Yale University Press.

Bartels, Larry M. 1995. "Symposium on *Designing Social Inquiry,* Part 1." *Political Methodologist* 6 (2): 8–11.

Bator, Paul M. 1990. "What is Wrong with the Supreme Court?" *University of Pittsburgh Law Review* 51:673–97.

Baum, Lawrence. 1977a. "Policy Goals in Judicial Gatekeeping: A Proximity Model of Discretionary Jurisdiction." *American Journal of Political Science* 21:13–33.

Baum, Lawrence. 1977b. "Judicial Specialization, Litigant Influence, and Substantive Policy: The Court of Customs and Patent Appeals." *Law and Society Review* 11:823–50.

Baum, Lawrence. 1980. "Responses of Federal District Judges to Court of Appeals Policies: An Exploration." *Western Political Quarterly* 33:217–24.

Baum, Lawrence. 1983. "Judicial Politics: Still a Distinctive Field." In *Political Science: The State of the Discipline,* ed. Ada W. Finifter, 189–215. Washington, D.C.: American Political Science Association.

Baum, Lawrence. 1988. "Measuring Policy Change in the U.S. Supreme Court." *American Political Science Review* 82:905–12.

Baum, Lawrence. 1992. "On the Unpredictability of the Supreme Court." *P.S.: Political Science and Politics* 25:683–88.

Baum, Lawrence. 1993. "Case Selection and Decisionmaking in the U.S. Supreme Court." *Law and Society Review* 27:443–59.

Baum, Lawrence. 1994. "Specialization and Authority Acceptance: The Supreme Court and Lower Federal Courts." *Political Research Quarterly* 47:693–703.

Baumeister, Roy F., and Leonard S. Newman. 1994. "Self-Regulation of Cognitive Inference and Decision Processes." *Personality and Social Psychology Bulletin* 20:3–19.

Bawn, Kathleen, and Charles R. Shipan. 1993. "Congressional Responses to Supreme Court Decisions: An Institutional Perspective." Paper presented at the annual meeting of the American Political Science Association, Washington, D.C., September 2–5.

Beach, Lee Roy. 1985. "Action: Decision-Implementation Strategies and Tactics." In *Goal Directed Behavior: The Concept of Action in Psychology*, ed. Michael Frese and John Sabini, 123–33. Hillsdale, N.J.: Lawrence Erlbaum Associates.

Beatty, Jerry K. 1972. "State Court Evasion of United States Supreme Court Mandates During the Last Decade of the Warren Court." *Valparaiso University Law Review* 6:260–85.

Becker, Gary S. 1976. *The Economic Approach to Human Behavior.* Chicago: University of Chicago Press.

Becker, Gary S. 1993. "Nobel Lecture: The Economic Way of Looking at Behavior." *Journal of Political Economy* 101:385–409.

Becker, Theodore L. 1966. "A Survey Study of Hawaiian Judges: The Effect on Decisions of Judicial Role Variation." *American Political Science Review* 60:677–80.

Beiser, Edward N. 1974. "The Rhode Island Supreme Court: A Well-Integrated Political System." *Law and Society Review* 8:167–86.

Bendor, Jonathan. 1988. "Review Article: Formal Models of Bureaucracy." *British Journal of Political Science* 18:353–95.

Bendor, Jonathan. 1995. "A Model of Muddling Through." *American Political Science Review* 89:819–40.

Benson, Laura. 1993. "The Minnesota Judicial Selection Process: Rejecting Judicial Elections in Favor of a Merit Plan." *William Mitchell Law Review* 19:765–85.

Bergmann, Barbara R. 1987. "'Measurement' or Finding Things Out in Economics." *Journal of Economic Education* 18:191–201.

Berk, Richard A. 1983. "An Introduction to Sample Selection Bias in Sociological Data." *American Sociological Review* 48:386–98.

Berry, Mary Frances. 1978. *Stability, Security, and Continuity: Mr. Justice Burton and Decision-Making on the Supreme Court.* Westport, Conn.: Greenwood Press.

Beveridge, Albert J. 1919. *The Life of John Marshall, Volume IV: The Building of the Nation, 1815–1835.* Boston: Houghton Mifflin.

Bicchieri, Cristina. 1993. *Rationality and Coordination.* Cambridge, England: Cambridge University Press.

Bishop, Katherine. 1992. "After Long Night of Legal Battles, California Carries Out Execution." *New York Times,* April 22, A1, C23.

Biskupic, Joan. 1993. "Thomas's Speech to Georgia Group May Have Violated Judicial Code." *Washington Post,* May 8, A4.

Biskupic, Joan. 1994a. "Justices Take No New Cases as Term Starts." *Washington Post,* October 4, A1, A8.

Biskupic, Joan. 1994b. "Behind the Robes, Songs and Whitewater Rafting." *Washington Post,* October 20, A19.

Biskupic, Joan. 1994c. "'I Am Not an Uncle Tom,' Thomas Says at Meeting." *Washington Post,* October 28, A1, A24.

Biskupic, Joan. 1996. "Justice Makes the Case for Christianity." *Washington Post,* April 10, A1, A7.

Black, Gordon S. 1972. "A Theory of Political Ambition: Career Choices and the Role of Structural Incentives." *American Political Science Review* 66:144–59.

Black, Hugo L., and Elizabeth Black. 1986. *Mr. Justice and Mrs. Black: The Memoirs of Hugo L. Black and Elizabeth Black.* New York: Random House.

Blais, André, and Stéphane Dion, eds. 1991. *The Budget-Maximizing Bureaucrat: Appraisals and Evidence.* Pittsburgh: University of Pittsburgh Press.

Blumberg, Abraham S. 1967. *Criminal Justice.* Chicago: Quadrangle Books.

Blumstein, Alfred, Jacqueline Cohen, Susan E. Martin, and Michael H. Tonry, eds. 1983. *Research on Sentencing: The Search for Reform.* Washington, D.C.: National Academy Press.

Boden, Margaret A. 1972. *Purposive Explanation in Psychology.* Cambridge, Mass.: Harvard University Press.

Bohman, James. 1991. *New Philosophy of Social Science: Problems of Indeterminacy.* Cambridge, Mass.: MIT Press.

Bohman, James. 1992. "The Limits of Rational Choice Explanation." In *Rational Choice Theory: Advocacy and Critique,* ed. James S. Coleman and Thomas J. Fararo, 207–28. Newbury Park, Calif.: Sage Publications.

Bok, Curtis. 1941. *Backbone of the Herring.* New York: Alfred A. Knopf.

Boninger, David S., Jon A. Krosnick, and Matthew H. Berent. 1995. "Origins of Attitude Importance: Self-Interest, Social Identification, and Value Relevance." *Journal of Personality and Social Psychology* 68:61–80.

Boucher, Robert L., Jr., and Jeffrey A. Segal. 1995. "Supreme Court Justices as Strategic Decision Makers: Aggressive Grants and Defensive Denials on the Vinson Court." *Journal of Politics* 57:824–37.

Boyaztis, Richard E. 1973. "Affiliation Motivation." In *Human Motivation: A Book of Readings,* ed. David C. McClelland and Robert S. Steele, 252–76. Morristown, N.J.: General Learning Press.

Brace, Paul, and Melinda Gann Hall. 1990. "Neo-Institutionalism and Dissent in State Supreme Courts." *Journal of Politics* 2:54–70.

Brace, Paul, and Melinda Gann Hall. 1993. "Integrated Models of Judicial Dissent." *Journal of Politics* 55:914–35.

Brace, Paul, and Melinda Gann Hall. 1995. "Studying Courts Comparatively: The View From the American States." *Political Research Quarterly* 48:5–29.

Brady, Henry E. 1995. "Symposium on *Designing Social Inquiry,* Part 2." *The Political Methodologist* 6 (2): 11–19.

Braithwaite, Richard Bevan. 1953. *Scientific Explanation: A Study of the Function of Theory, Probability and Law in Science.* Cambridge, England: Cambridge University Press.

Brams, Steven J., and Douglas Muzzio. 1977. "Unanimity in the Supreme Court: A Game-Theoretic Explanation of the Decision in the White House Tapes Case." *Public Choice* 32:67–83.

Brennan, William J. 1977. "State Constitutions and the Protection of Individual Rights." *Harvard Law Review* 90:489–504.

Brenner, Saul. 1975. "The Shapley-Shubik Power Index and Supreme Court Behavior." *Jurimetrics Journal* 15:194–205.

Brenner, Saul. 1979a. "Game Theory and Supreme Court Decision Making: A Bibliographic Overview." *Law Library Journal* 72:470–75.

Brenner, Saul. 1979b. "The New Certiorari Game." *Journal of Politics* 41: 649–55.

Brenner, Saul. 1979c. "Minimum Winning Coalitions on the U.S. Supreme Court: A Comparison of the Original Vote on the Merits with the Opinion Vote." *American Politics Quarterly* 7:384–92.

Brenner, Saul. 1980. "Fluidity on the United States Supreme Court: A Reexamination." *American Journal of Political Science* 24:526–35.

Brenner, Saul. 1982a. "Fluidity on the Supreme Court: 1956–1967." *American Journal of Political Science* 26:388–90.

Brenner, Saul. 1982b. "Strategic Choice and Opinion Assignment on the U.S. Supreme Court: A Reexamination." *Western Political Quarterly* 35: 204–11.

Brenner, Saul. 1989. "Ideological Voting on the Vinson Court: A Comparison of Original and Final Votes on the Merits." *Polity* 22:157–64.

Brenner, Saul, and Theodore S. Arrington. 1987. "Unanimous Decision Making on the Supreme Court: Case Stimuli and Judicial Attitudes." *Political Behavior* 9:75–86.

Brenner, Saul, Tony Caporale, and Harold Winter. 1996. "Fluidity and Coalition Sizes on the Supreme Court." *Jurimetrics Journal* 36:245–54.

Brenner, Saul, and Robert H. Dorff. 1992. "The Attitudinal Model and Fluidity Voting on the United States Supreme Court: A Theoretical Perspective." *Journal of Theoretical Politics* 4:195–205.

Brenner, Saul, Timothy Hagle, and Harold J. Spaeth. 1989. "The Defection of the Marginal Justice on the Warren Court." *Western Political Quarterly* 42:409–25.

Brenner, Saul, Timothy Hagle, and Harold J. Spaeth. 1990. "Increasing the Size of Minimum Winning Original Coalitions on the Warren Court." *Polity* 23:309–18.

Brenner, Saul, and John F. Krol. 1989. "Strategies in Certiorari Voting in the United States Supreme Court." *Journal of Politics* 51:828–40.

Brenner, Saul, and Harold J. Spaeth. 1988a. "Majority Opinion Assignments and the Maintenance of the Original Coalition on the Warren Court." *American Journal of Political Science* 32:72–81.

Brenner, Saul, and Harold J. Spaeth. 1988b. "Ideological Position as a Variable in the Authoring of Dissenting Opinions on the Warren and Burger Courts." *American Politics Quarterly* 16:317–28.

Brenner, Saul, and Harold J. Spaeth. 1995. *Stare Indecisis: The Alteration of Precedent on the Supreme Court, 1946–1992*. New York: Cambridge University Press.

Brenner, Saul, and Marc Stier. 1995. "Does Stare Decisis Influence the Justices' Voting on the Supreme Court?" Paper presented at the annual meeting of the American Political Science Association, Chicago, August 31–September 3.

Brenner, Saul, and Marc Stier. 1996. "Retesting Segal and Spaeth's *Stare Decisis* Model." *American Journal of Political Science* 40:1036–48.

Breslauer, George W., and Philip E. Tetlock, eds. 1991. *Learning in U.S. and Soviet Foreign Policy.* Boulder, Colo.: Westview Press.

Brigham, John. 1978. *Constitutional Language: An Interpretation of Judicial Decision.* Westport, Conn.: Greenwood Press.

Buckle, Suzann R. Thomas, and Leonard G. Buckle. 1977. *Bargaining for Justice: Case Disposition and Reform in the Criminal Courts.* New York: Praeger Publishers.

Bullock, Charles S., III. 1976. "Motivations for U.S. Congressional Committee Preferences: Freshmen of the 92d Congress." *Legislative Studies Quarterly* 1:201–12.

Burger, Warren E. 1985. "The Time is Now for the Intercircuit Panel." *American Bar Association Journal* 71 (April): 86–91.

Buss, David M. 1987. "Selection, Evocation, and Manipulation." *Journal of Personality and Social Psychology* 53:1214–21.

Caldeira, Greg A. 1977. "Judicial Incentives: Some Evidence From Urban Trial Courts." *Iusticia* 4 (2): 1–28.

Caldeira, Gregory A. 1991. "Courts and Public Opinion." In *The American Courts: A Critical Assessment,* ed. John B. Gates and Charles A. Johnson, 303–34. Washington, D.C.: CQ Press.

Caldeira, Gregory A., and John R. Wright. 1988. "Organized Interests and Agenda Setting in the U. S. Supreme Court." *American Political Science Review* 82:1109–28.

Caldeira, Gregory A., and John R. Wright. 1990a. "The Discuss List: Agenda Building in the Supreme Court." *Law and Society Review* 24:807–36.

Caldeira, Gregory A., and John R. Wright. 1990b. "Amici Curiae Before the Supreme Court: Who Participates, When, and How Much?" *Journal of Politics* 52:782–806.

Caldeira, Gregory A., and John R. Wright. 1994. "Nine Little Law Firms? Justices, Organized Interests, and Agenda-Setting in the Supreme Court." Paper presented at the annual meeting of the Midwest Political Science Association, Chicago, April 14–17.

Caldeira, Gregory A., John R. Wright, and Christopher J. W. Zorn. 1996. "Strategic Voting and Gatekeeping in the Supreme Court." Paper presented at the Conference on the Scientific Study of Judicial Politics, St. Louis, November 15–16.

California Lawyer. 1987. "No Wonder They're So Stiff." December, 12.

Calvert, Randall L., and Richard F. Fenno Jr. 1994. "Strategy and Sophisticated Voting in the Senate." *Journal of Politics* 56:349–76.

Cameron, Charles M. 1993. "New Avenues for Modeling Judicial Politics." Paper presented at the Conference on the Political Economy of Public Law, Rochester, N.Y., October 15–16.

Cameron, Charles M., Jeffrey A. Segal, and Donald R. Songer. 1993. "Law Creation and Signaling in the Judicial Hierarchy." Typescript.

Cameron, Charles M., Jeffrey A. Segal, and Donald R. Songer. 1995. "Signals and Indices in the Supreme Court's Certiorari Decisions." Paper presented at the annual meeting of the Midwest Political Science Association, Chicago, April 6–9.

Caminker, Evan H. 1994. "Precedent and Prediction: The Forward-Looking Aspects of Inferior Court Decisionmaking." *Texas Law Review* 73:1–82.

Canon, Bradley C. 1972. "The Impact of Formal Selection Processes on the Characteristics of Judges—Reconsidered." *Law and Society Review* 6: 579–93.

Canon, Bradley C. 1973. "Reactions of State Supreme Courts to a U.S. Supreme Court Civil Liberties Decision." *Law and Society Review* 8: 109–34.

Canon, Bradley C. 1974. "Organizational Contumacy in the Transmission of Judicial Policies: The *Mapp, Escobedo, Miranda,* and *Gault* Cases." *Villanova Law Review* 20:50–79.

Canon, Bradley C. 1982. "A Framework for the Analysis of Judicial Activism." In *Supreme Court Activism and Restraint,* ed. Stephen C. Halpern and Charles M. Lamb, 385–419. Lexington, Mass.: Lexington Books.

Canon, Bradley C., and Kenneth Kolson. 1971. "Rural Compliance with *Gault:* Kentucky, a Case Study." *Journal of Family Law* 10:300–326.

Cardozo, Benjamin N. 1924. *The Growth of the Law.* New Haven, Conn.: Yale University Press.

Carp, Robert A., and Ronald Stidham. 1991. *The Federal Courts,* 2d ed. Washington, D.C.: CQ Press.

Casper, Jonathan D. 1972. *Lawyers Before the Warren Court: Civil Liberties and Civil Rights, 1957–66.* Urbana: University of Illinois Press.

Cates, Cynthia L., and Wayne V. McIntosh. 1995. "Retail Jurisprudence: The Judge as Entrepreneur in the Marketplace of Ideas." *Journal of Law and Politics* 11:709–50.

Cauchon, Dennis. 1991. "The Scales of Justice May be Tipped Unfairly." *USA Today,* June 24, 8A.

Chaiken, Shelly, Akiva Liberman, and Alice H. Eagly. 1989. "Heuristic and Systematic Information Processing Within and Beyond the Persuasion Context." In *Unintended Thought,* ed. James S. Uleman and John A. Bargh, 212–52. New York: Guilford Press.

Chapper, Joy A., and Roger A. Hanson. 1989. *Understanding Reversible Error in Criminal Appeals.* Williamsburg, Va.: National Center for State Courts.

Chiang, Harriet. 1992. "Judge Explains Stay of Execution." *San Francisco Chronicle,* May 18, A13.

Clark, Hunter R. 1995. *Justice Brennan: The Great Conciliator.* New York: Birch Lane Press.

Clark, John A. 1996. "Congressional Salaries and the Politics of Unpopular Votes." *American Politics Quarterly* 24:150–68.

Clinton, Robert Lowry. 1994. "Game Theory, Legal History, and the Origins of Judicial Review: A Revisionist Analysis of *Marbury v. Madison.*" *American Journal of Political Science* 38:285–302.

Coffin, Frank M. 1994. *On Appeal: Courts, Lawyering, and Judging.* New York: W. W. Norton.

Cohen, Linda R. 1995. "Politics and the Courts: A Comment on McNollgast." *Southern California Law Review* 68:1685–89.

Cohen, Linda R., and Matthew L. Spitzer. 1994. "Solving the Chevron Puzzle." *Law and Contemporary Problems* 57 (Spring): 65–110.

Cohen, Mark A. 1991. "Explaining Judicial Behavior or What's 'Unconstitutional' About the Sentencing Commission?" *Journal of Law, Economics, and Organization* 7:183–99.

Cohen, Mark A. 1992. "The Motives of Judges: Empirical Evidence From Antitrust Sentencing." *International Review of Law and Economics* 12:13–30.

Cohen, Michael D., James G. March, and Johan P. Olsen. 1972. "A Garbage Can Model of Organizational Choice." *Administrative Science Quarterly* 17:1–25.

Cohen, Richard. 1991. "What's Thomas Doing in People Magazine?" *Washington Post,* November 12, A21.

Coleman, James S., and Thomas J. Fararo, eds. 1992. *Rational Choice: Advocacy and Critique.* Newbury Park, Calif.: Sage Publications.

Comparato, Scott. 1996. "The Continued Struggle for Judicial Supremacy: Franklin Roosevelt and the Court-Packing Plan." Paper presented at the annual meeting of the Midwest Political Science Association, Chicago, April 18–20.

Conley, John M., and William M. O'Barr. 1990. *Rules Versus Relationships: The Ethnography of Legal Discourse.* Chicago: University of Chicago Press.

Conover, Pamela Johnston, and Stanley Feldman. 1984. *American Journal of Political Science* 28:95–126.

Cook, Beverly B. 1977. "Public Opinion and Federal Judicial Policy." *American Journal of Political Science* 21:567–600.

Cook, Beverly B. 1979. "Sentencing Problems and Internal Court Reform." In *The Study of Criminal Courts: Political Perspectives,* ed. Peter F. Nardulli, 227–71. Cambridge, Mass.: Ballinger Publishing Co.

Cook, Beverly Blair. 1995. "Justice Brennan and the Institutionalization of Dissent Assignment." *Judicature* 79:17–23.

Coombs, Clyde H. 1964. *A Theory of Data.* New York: John Wiley and Sons.

Cooper, Phillip J. 1995. *Battles on the Bench: Conflict Inside the Supreme Court.* Lawrence: University Press of Kansas.

Coursol, Allan, and Edwin E. Wagner. 1986. "Effect of Positive Findings on Submission and Acceptance Rates: A Note on Meta-Analysis Bias." *Professional Psychology* 17:136–37.

Curtis, Charles P. 1959. *Law as Large as Life.* New York: Simon and Schuster.

Dahl, Robert. 1957. "Decision-Making in a Democracy: The Supreme Court as a National Policy-Maker." *Journal of Public Law* 6:279–95.

Dalton, Clare. 1985. "An Essay in the Deconstruction of Contract Doctrine." *Yale Law Journal* 94:997–1114.

Dalton, Russell J., and Martin P. Wattenberg. 1993. "The Not So Simple Act of Voting." In *Political Science: The State of the Discipline: II,* ed. Ada W. Finifter, 193–218. Washington, D.C.: American Political Science Association.

D'Amato, Anthony. 1989. "Aspects of Deconstruction: The 'Easy Case' of the Under-Aged President." *Northwestern University Law Review* 84: 250–56.

Danelski, David J. 1966. "Values as Variables in Judicial Decision-Making: Notes Toward a Theory." *Vanderbilt Law Review* 19:721–40.

Danelski, David J. 1968. "The Influence of the Chief Justice in the Decisional Process of the Supreme Court." In *The Federal Judicial System: Readings in Process and Behavior,* ed. Thomas P. Jahnige and Sheldon Goldman, 147–60. New York: Holt, Rinehart and Winston.

Danelski, David J. 1970. "Legislative and Judicial Decision-Making: The Case of Harold H. Burton." In *Political Decision-Making,* ed. S. Sidney Ulmer, 121–46. New York: Van Nostrand Reinhold.

Danelski, David J. 1986. "Causes and Consequences of Conflict and Its Resolution in the Supreme Court." In *Judicial Conflict and Consensus,* ed. Sheldon Goldman and Charles M. Lamb, 21–49. Lexington: University of Kentucky Press.

Dash, Leon. 1975. "Sentences Tied to 'Gut Reaction'." *Washington Post,* June 26, D5.

Davies, Thomas Y. 1981. "Gresham's Law Revisited: Expedited Processing Techniques and the Allocation of Appellate Resources." *Justice System Journal* 6:372–404.

Davies, Thomas Y. 1982. "Affirmed: A Study of Criminal Appeals and Decision-Making Norms in a California Court of Appeal." *American Bar Foundation Research Journal* 1982:543–648.

Davis, Richard. 1994. *Decisions and Images: The Supreme Court and the Press.* Englewood Cliffs, N.J.: Prentice-Hall.

Davis, Sue. 1990. "Power on the Court: Chief Justice Rehnquist's Opinion Assignments." *Judicature* 74:66–72.

Davis, Sue. 1992. "Rehnquist and State Courts: Federalism Revisited." *Western Political Quarterly* 45:773–82.

Dawes, Robyn M. 1988. *Rational Choice in an Uncertain World.* Fort Worth, Texas: Harcourt Brace.

De Long, J. Bradford, and Kevin Lang. 1992. "Are All Economic Hypotheses False?" *Journal of Political Economy* 100:1257–72.

Dennis, Jack. 1991. "The Study of Voting Behavior." In *Political Science: Looking to the Future,* vol. 3, ed. William Crotty, 51–89. Evanston, Ill.: Northwestern University Press.

Denzau, Arthur T., and Robert J. Mackay. 1983. "Gatekeeping and Monopoly Power of Committees: An Analysis of Sincere and Sophisticated Behavior." *American Journal of Political Science* 27:740–61.

Denzau, Arthur, William Riker, and Kenneth Shepsle. 1985. "Farquharson and Fenno: Sophisticated Voting and Home Style." *American Political Science Review* 79:1117–34.

De Palma, André, Gordon M. Myers, and Yorgos Y. Papageorgiou. 1994. "Rational Choice Under an Imperfect Ability to Choose." *American Economic Review* 84:419–40.

Diamond, Shari Seidman, and Hans Zeisel. 1975. "Sentencing Councils: A Study of Sentence Disparity and Its Reduction." *University of Chicago Law Review* 43:109–49.

Dickersin, K., S. Chan, T. C. Chalmers, H. S. Sacks, and H. Smith Jr. 1987.

"Publication Bias and Clinical Trials." *Controlled Clinical Trials* 8: 343–53.

Ditto, Peter H., and David F. Lopez. 1992. "Motivated Skepticism: Use of Differential Decision Criteria for Preferred and Nonpreferred Conclusions." *Journal of Personality and Social Psychology* 63:568–84.

Dixon, Jo. 1995. "The Organizational Context of Criminal Sentencing." *American Journal of Sociology* 100:1157–98.

Dodd, Lawrence C. 1977. "Congress and the Quest for Power." In *Congress Reconsidered,* ed. Lawrence C. Dodd and Bruce I. Oppenheimer, 269–307. New York: Praeger.

Dodd, Lawrence C. 1986. "A Theory of Congressional Cycles: Solving the Puzzle of Change." In *Congress and Policy Change,* ed. Gerald C. Wright Jr., Leroy N. Rieselbach, and Lawrence C. Dodd, 3–44. New York: Agathon Press.

Dolbeare, Kenneth M. 1967. *Trial Courts in Urban Politics: State Court Policy Impact and Functions in a Local Political System.* New York: John Wiley and Sons.

Donley, Richard E., and David G. Winter. 1970. "Measuring the Motives of Public Officials at a Distance: An Exploratory Study of American Presidents." *Behavioral Science* 15:227–36.

Dorff, Robert H., and Saul Brenner. 1992. "Conformity Voting on the United States Supreme Court." *Journal of Politics* 54:762–75.

Dorsen, Norman. 1993. "John Marshall Harlan and the Warren Court." In *The Warren Court in Historical and Political Perspective,* ed. Mark Tushnet, 109–22. Charlottesville: University Press of Virginia.

Douglas, William O.; ed. Philip E. Urofsky. 1995. "The Diary of Wm. O. Douglas." *Journal of Supreme Court History* 1995:80–112.

Downing, James W., Charles M. Judd, and Markus Brauer. 1992. "Effects of Repeated Expressions on Attitude Extremity." *Journal of Personality and Social Psychology* 63:17–29.

Downs, Anthony. 1957. *An Economic Theory of Democracy.* New York: Harper and Row.

Dubois, Philip L. 1980. *From Bench to Ballot: Judicial Elections and the Quest for Accountability.* Austin: University of Texas Press.

Dubois, Philip L. 1983. "The Influence of Selection System and Region on the Characteristics of a Trial Court Bench: The Case of California." *Justice System Journal* 8:59–87.

Dubois, Philip L. 1988. "The Illusion of Judicial Consensus Revisited: Partisan Conflict on an Intermediate Court of Appeals." *American Journal of Political Science* 32:946–67.

Ducat, Craig R., and Robert L. Dudley. 1987. "Dimensions Underlying Economic Policymaking in the Early and Later Burger Courts." *Journal of Politics* 49:521–39.

Dworkin, Ronald. 1975. "Hard Cases." *Harvard Law Review* 88:1057–1109.

Eagly, Alice H., and Shelly Chaiken. 1993. *The Psychology of Attitudes.* Fort Worth, Texas: Harcourt Brace Jovanovich.

Easterbrook, Frank H. 1982. "Ways of Criticizing the Court." *Harvard Law Review* 95:802–32.

Easterbrook, Frank H. 1990. "What's So Special About Judges?" *University of Colorado Law Review* 61:773–82.

Eckstein, Harry. 1991. "Rationality and Frustration in Political Behavior." In *The Economic Approach to Politics: A Critical Reassessment of the Theory of Rational Action,* ed. Kristen Renwick Monroe, 74–93. New York: HarperCollins.

Edwards, Harry T. 1991. "The Judicial Function and the Elusive Goal of Principled Decisionmaking." *Wisconsin Law Review* 1991:837–65.

Eisenberg, Theodore. 1990. "Testing the Selection Effect: A New Theoretical Framework with Empirical Tests." *Journal of Legal Studies* 19:337–58.

Eisenstein, James, Roy B. Flemming, and Peter F. Nardulli. 1988. *The Contours of Justice: Communities and Their Courts.* New York: Little, Brown.

Eisenstein, James, and Herbert Jacob. 1977. *Felony Justice: An Organizational Analysis of Criminal Courts.* Boston: Little, Brown.

Eisler, Kim Isaac. 1993. *A Justice for All: William J. Brennan, Jr., and the Decisions That Transformed America.* New York: Simon and Schuster.

Elder, Harold W. 1987. "Property Rights Structures and Criminal Courts: An Analysis of State Criminal Courts." *International Review of Law and Economics* 7:21–32.

Ellsberg, Daniel. 1961. "Risk, Ambiguity, and the Savage Axioms." *Quarterly Journal of Economics* 75:643–69.

Elster, Jon. 1983a. *Explaining Technical Change.* Cambridge, England: Cambridge University Press.

Elster, Jon. 1983b. *Sour Grapes: Studies in the Subversion of Rationality.* Cambridge, England: Cambridge University Press.

Elster, Jon. 1989. *Nuts and Bolts for the Social Sciences.* Cambridge, England: Cambridge University Press.

Emmert, Craig F., and Carol Ann Traut. 1994. "The California Supreme Court and the Death Penalty." *American Politics Quarterly* 22:41–61.

Enelow, James M. 1981. "Saving Amendments, Killer Amendments, and an Expected Utility Theory of Sophisticated Voting." *Journal of Politics* 43:1062–89.

Enelow, James M., and David Koehler. 1980. "The Amendment in Legislative Strategy: Sophisticated Voting in the U.S. Congress." *Journal of Politics* 42:396–413.

Epstein, Lee. 1993. "Interest Group Litigation During the Rehnquist Court Era." *Journal of Law and Politics* 9:639–717.

Epstein, Lee, Valerie Hoekstra, Jeffrey A. Segal, and Harold J. Spaeth. 1995. "Do Sincere Political Preferences Change? A Longitudinal Study of U.S. Supreme Court Justices." Paper presented at the annual meeting of the Midwest Political Science Association, Chicago, April 6–8.

Epstein, Lee, and Jack Knight. 1995. "Documenting Strategic Interactions on the U.S. Supreme Court." Paper presented at the annual meeting of the American Political Science Association, Chicago, August 31–September 3.

Epstein, Lee, and Jack Knight. 1998. *The Choices Justices Make.* Washington, D.C.: CQ Press.

Epstein, Lee, and Joseph F. Kobylka. 1992. *The Supreme Court and Legal*

Change: Abortion and the Death Penalty. Chapel Hill: University of North Carolina Press.

Epstein, Lee, and Carol Mershon. 1996. "Measuring Political Preferences." *American Journal of Political Science* 40:261–94.

Epstein, Lee, and C. K. Rowland. 1991. "Debunking the Myth of Interest Group Invincibility in the Courts." *American Political Science Review* 85:205–17.

Epstein, Lee, Jeffrey A. Segal, Harold J. Spaeth, and Thomas G. Walker. 1994. *The Supreme Court Compendium: Data, Decisions, and Developments.* Washington, D.C.: CQ Press.

Epstein, Lee, and Thomas G. Walker. 1995. "The Role of the Supreme Court in American Society: Playing the Reconstruction Game." In *Contemplating Courts,* ed. Lee Epstein, 315–46. Washington, D.C.: CQ Press.

Epstein, Richard A. 1990. "The Independence of Judges: The Uses and Limitations of Public Choice Theory." *Brigham Young University Law Review* 1990:827–55.

Eskridge, William N., Jr. 1988. "Politics Without Romance: Implications of Public Choice Theory for Statutory Interpretation." *Virginia Law Review* 74:275–338.

Eskridge, William N., Jr. 1990. "The New Textualism." *UCLA Law Review* 37:621–91.

Eskridge, William N., Jr. 1991a. "Reneging on History? Playing the Court/Congress/President Civil Rights Game." *California Law Review* 79:613–84.

Eskridge, William N., Jr. 1991b. "Overriding Supreme Court Statutory Interpretation Decisions." *Yale Law Journal* 101:331–455.

Eskridge, William N., Jr., and Philip P. Frickey. 1994. "Foreword: Law as Equilibrium." *Harvard Law Review* 108:26–108.

Esler, Michael. 1994. "Progress and Rationality in Judicial Behavioralism." Paper presented at the annual meeting of the American Political Science Association, New York, September 1–4.

Esler, Michael, and John Stookey. 1995. "Situational Analysis in Judicial Research." Paper presented at the annual meeting of the Midwest Political Science Association, Chicago, April 6–8.

Etheredge, Lloyd S. 1985. *Can Governments Learn? American Foreign Policy and Central American Revolutions.* New York: Pergamon Press.

Farber, Daniel A., and Philip P. Frickey. 1992. "Foreword: Positive Political Theory in the Nineties." *Georgetown Law Journal* 80:457–76.

Farquharson, Robin. 1969. *Theory of Voting.* New Haven, Conn.: Yale University Press.

Farr, James. 1985. "Situational Analysis: Explanation in Political Science." *Journal of Politics* 47:1085–1107.

Fazio, Russell H. 1986. "How Do Attitudes Guide Behavior?" In *Handbook of Motivation and Cognition: Foundations of Social Behavior,* ed. Richard M. Sorrentino and E. Tory Higgins, 204–43. New York: John Wiley and Sons.

Feeley, Malcolm M. 1979. *The Process is the Punishment: Handling Cases in a Lower Court.* New York: Russell Sage Foundation.

Feige, Edgar L. 1975. "The Consequences of Journal Editorial Policies and a Suggestion for Revision." *Journal of Political Economy* 83:1291–95.

Felitti, Eve M. 1995. "The Honorable Jacqueline Taber: An Oral History." *Western Legal History* 8:91–113.

Fenno, Richard F. 1973. *Congressmen in Committees.* Boston: Little, Brown.

Ferejohn, John A. 1991. "Rationality and Interpretation: Parliamentary Elections in Early Stuart England." In *The Economic Approach to Politics: A Critical Reassessment of the Theory of Rational Action,* ed. Kristen Renwick Monroe, 279–305. New York: HarperCollins.

Ferejohn, John A. 1995. "Foreword." In *Positive Theories of Congressional Institutions,* ed. Kenneth A. Shepsle and Barry R. Weingast, ix–xiii. Ann Arbor: University of Michigan Press.

Ferejohn, John A., and Morris P. Fiorina. 1975. "Purposive Models of Legislative Behavior." *American Economic Association Papers and Proceedings* 65:407–14.

Ferejohn, John, and Debra Satz. 1995. "Unification, Universalism, and Rational Choice Theory." *Critical Review* 9:71–84.

Ferejohn, John A., and Barry R. Weingast. 1992a. "Limitation of Statutes: Strategic Statutory Interpretation." *Georgetown Law Journal* 80:565–82.

Ferejohn, John A., and Barry R. Weingast. 1992b. "A Positive Theory of Statutory Interpretation." *International Review of Law and Economics* 12:263–79.

Fiorina, Morris P. 1989. *Congress: Keystone of the Washington Establishment,* 2d ed. New Haven, Conn.: Yale University Press.

Fiorina, Morris P. 1995a. "Afterword (But Undoubtedly Not the Last Word)." In *Positive Theories of Congressional Institutions,* ed. Kenneth A. Shepsle and Barry R. Weingast, 303–12. Ann Arbor: University of Michigan Press.

Fiorina, Morris P. 1995b. "Rational Choice, Empirical Contributions, and the Scientific Enterprise." *Critical Review* 9:85–94.

Fishbein, M. 1980. "A Theory of Reasoned Action: Some Applications and Implications." In *Nebraska Symposium on Motivation 1979,* ed. Monte M. Page, 65–116. Lincoln: University of Nebraska Press.

Fisher, Marc. 1995. "The Private World of Justice Thomas." *Washington Post,* September 11, B1, B4.

Fisher, William W., III, Morton J. Horwitz, and Thomas A. Reed, eds. 1993. *American Legal Realism.* New York: Oxford University Press.

Fiske, Susan T. 1993. "Social Cognition and Social Perception." *Annual Review of Psychology* 44:155–94.

Fiske, Susan T., and Patricia W. Linville. 1980. "What Does the Schema Concept Buy Us?" *Personality and Social Psychology Bulletin* 6:543–57.

Fiske, Susan T., and Shelley E. Taylor. 1991. *Social Cognition,* 2d ed. New York: McGraw-Hill.

Flango, Victor E., and Craig R. Ducat. 1977. "Toward an Integration of Public Law and Judicial Behavior." *Journal of Politics* 39:41–72.

Flango, Victor E., Craig R. Ducat, and R. Neal McKnight. 1986. "Measuring Leadership Through Opinion Assignment in Two State Supreme Courts." In *Judicial Conflict and Consensus,* ed. Sheldon Goldman and Charles M. Lamb, 215–39. Lexington: University of Kentucky Press.

Flango, Victor Eugene, Lettie McSpadden Wenner, and Manfred W. Wenner. 1975. "The Concept of Judicial Role: A Methodological Note." *American Journal of Political Science* 19:277–89.

Flemming, Roy B. 1982. *Punishment Before Trial: An Organizational Perspective of Felony Bail Processes.* New York: Longman.

Flemming, Roy B., Peter F. Nardulli, and James Eisenstein. 1992. *The Craft of Justice: Politics and Work in Criminal Court Communities.* Philadelphia: University of Pennsylvania Press.

Flemming, Roy B., and B. Dan Wood. 1997. "The Public and the Supreme Court: Individual Justice Responsiveness to American Public Moods." *American Journal of Political Science* 41:468–98.

Fowler, Linda L. 1993. *Candidates, Congress, and the American Democracy.* Ann Arbor: University of Michigan Press.

Fowler, Linda L., and Robert D. McClure. 1989. *Political Ambition: Who Decides to Run for Congress.* New Haven, Conn.: Yale University Press.

Frank, Jerome. 1949. *Courts on Trial: Myth and Reality in American Justice.* Princeton, N.J.: Princeton University Press.

Frank, John P. 1949. *Mr. Justice Black: The Man and His Opinions.* New York: Alfred A. Knopf.

Frank, John P. 1970. "Conflict of Interest and U.S. Supreme Court Justices." *American Journal of Comparative Law* 18:744–61.

Frank, Robert H. 1985. *Choosing the Right Pond: Human Behavior and the Quest for Status.* New York: Oxford University Press.

Frank, Robert H. 1987. "If *Homo Economicus* Could Choose His Own Utility Function, Would He Want One With a Conscience?" *American Economic Review* 77:593–604.

Franklin, Kurt A., and David A. Weldy. 1993. "Dark of the Night Legislation Takes Aim at Forum Selection Clauses: Statutory Revisions in Reaction to *Carnival Cruise Lines, Inc. v. Shute.*" *University of San Francisco Maritime Law Journal* 6:259–71.

Frase, Richard S. 1995. "State Sentencing Guidelines: Still Going Strong." *Judicature* 78:173–79.

Freedman, Dan. 1995. "High Court Joins March Right." *San Francisco Examiner,* July 2, A–8.

Freedman, David A. 1983. "A Note on Screening Regression Equations." *American Statistician* 37:152–55.

Frese, Michael, and John Sabini, eds. 1985. *Goal Directed Behavior: The Concept of Action in Psychology.* Hillsdale, N.J.: Lawrence Erlbaum Associates.

Fried, Charles. 1993. "Impudence." In *The Supreme Court Review 1992,* ed. Dennis J. Hutchinson, David A. Strauss, and Geoffrey R. Stone, 155–94. Chicago: University of Chicago Press.

Friedman, Jeffrey. 1995. "Economic Approaches to Politics." *Critical Review* 9:1–24.

Friedman, Jeffrey, ed. 1996. *The Rational Choice Controversy: Economic Models of Politics Reconsidered.* New Haven, Conn.: Yale University Press.

Friedman, Milton. 1953. *Essays in Positive Economics.* Chicago: University of Chicago Press.

Fuld, Stanley H. 1953. "A Judge Looks at the Law Review." *New York University Law Review* 28:915–21.

Galanter, Marc, Frank S. Palen, and John M. Thomas. 1979. "The Crusading Judge: Judicial Activism in Trial Courts." *Southern California Law Review* 52:699–741.

Gardner, Roy. 1995. *Games for Business and Economics.* New York: John Wiley and Sons.

Gates, John B., and Charles A. Johnson, eds. 1991. *The American Courts: A Critical Assessment.* Washington, D.C.: CQ Press.

Gates, John B., and Glenn A. Phelps. 1996. "Intentionalism in Constitutional Opinions." *Political Research Quarterly* 49:245–61.

Gely, Rafael, and Pablo T. Spiller. 1990. "A Rational Choice Theory of Supreme Court Statutory Decisions with Applications to the *State Farm* and *Grove City* Cases." *Journal of Law, Economics, and Organization* 6:263–300.

Gely, Rafael, and Pablo T. Spiller. 1992. "The Political Economy of Supreme Court Constitutional Decisions: The Case of Roosevelt's Court-Packing Plan." *International Review of Law and Economics* 12:45–67.

George, Tracey E., and Lee Epstein. 1992. "On the Nature of Supreme Court Decision Making." *American Political Science Review* 86:323–37.

Gerber, Elisabeth R., and John E. Jackson. 1993. "Endogenous Preferences and the Study of Institutions." *American Political Science Review* 87:639–56.

Gerhart, Eugene C. 1958. *America's Advocate: Robert H. Jackson.* Indianapolis: Bobbs-Merrill.

Gibson, James L. 1978a. "Decision Making Across Institutions: Legislators and Lower Court Judges in California." Paper presented at the annual meeting of the Midwest Political Science Association, Chicago.

Gibson, James L. 1978b. "Judges' Role Orientations, Attitudes, and Decisions: An Interactive Model." *American Political Science Review* 72: 911–24.

Gibson, James L. 1979. "Discriminant Functions, Role Orientations and Judicial Behavior: Theoretical and Methodological Linkages." *Journal of Politics* 39:984–1007.

Gibson, James L. 1980. "Environmental Constraints on the Behavior of Judges: A Representational Model of Judicial Decision Making." *Law and Society Review* 14:343–70.

Gibson, James L. 1981a. "Personality and Elite Political Behavior: The Influence of Self Esteem on Judicial Decision Making." *Journal of Politics* 43:104–25.

Gibson, James L. 1981b. "The Role Concept in Judicial Research." *Law and Policy Quarterly* 3:291–311.

Gibson, James L. 1983. "From Simplicity to Complexity: The Development of Theory in the Study of Judicial Behavior." *Political Behavior* 5:7–49.

Gibson, James L. 1986. "The Social Science of Judicial Politics." In *Political Science: The Science of Politics,* ed. Herbert F. Weisberg, 141–66. New York: Agathon Press.

Gibson, James L. 1991. "Decision Making in Appellate Courts." In *The*

American Courts: A Critical Assessment, ed. John B. Gates and Charles A. Johnson, 255–78. Washington, D.C.: CQ Press.

Giles, Micheal W. 1977. "Equivalent Versus Minimum Winning Opinion Coalition Size: A Test of Two Hypotheses." *American Journal of Political Science* 21:405–8.

Giles, Micheal W., and Thomas G. Walker. 1975. "Judicial Policy-Making and Southern School Segregation." *Journal of Politics* 37:917–36.

Gillman, Howard. 1993. *The Constitution Besieged: The Rise and Demise of Lochner Era Police Powers Jurisprudence.* Durham, N.C.: Duke University Press.

Ginsburg, Ruth Bader. 1995. "Communicating and Commenting on the Court's Work." *Georgetown Law Journal* 83:2119–29.

Glazer, Amihai. 1993. "Political Equilibrium Under Group Identification." In *Information, Participation, and Choice: An Economic Theory of Democracy in Perspective,* 81–92. Ann Arbor: University of Michigan Press.

Glendon, Mary Ann. 1994. *A Nation Under Lawyers: How the Crisis in the Legal Profession is Transforming American Society.* New York: Farrar, Straus and Giroux.

Glennon, Robert Jerome. 1985. *The Iconoclast as Reformer: Jerome Frank's Impact on American Law.* Ithaca, N.Y.: Cornell University Press.

Glick, Henry R. 1971. *Supreme Courts in State Politics.* New York: Basic Books.

Glick, Henry R. 1991. "Policy Making and State Supreme Courts." In *The American Courts: A Critical Assessment,* ed. John B. Gates and Charles A. Johnson, 87–118. Washington, D.C.: CQ Press.

Glick, Henry R. 1992. *The Right to Die: Policy Innovation and Its Consequences.* New York: Columbia University Press.

Glick, Henry R. 1993. *Courts, Politics, and Justice,* 3d ed. New York: McGraw-Hill.

Glick, Henry R., and Craig F. Emmert. 1986. "Stability and Change: Characteristics of State Supreme Court Judges." *Judicature* 70:107–12.

Glick, Henry R., and Craig F. Emmert. 1987. "Selection Systems and Judicial Characteristics: The Recruitment of State Supreme Court Judges." *Judicature* 70:228–35.

Glick, Henry Robert, and Kenneth N. Vines. 1969. "Law-Making in the State Judiciary: A Comparative Study of the Judicial Role in Four States." *Polity* 2:142–59.

Goldman, Sheldon. 1966. "Voting Behavior on the United States Courts of Appeals, 1961–1964." *American Political Science Review* 60:374–83.

Goldman, Sheldon. 1975. "Voting Behavior on the U.S. Courts of Appeals Revisited." *American Political Science Review* 69:491–506.

Goldman, Sheldon. 1991. "Federal Judicial Recruitment." In *The American Courts: A Critical Assessment,* ed. John B. Gates and Charles A. Johnson, 189–210. Washington, D.C.: CQ Press.

Goldman, Sheldon. 1995a. "Judicial Selection Under Clinton: A Midterm Examination." *Judicature* 78:276–91.

Goldman, Sheldon. 1995b. Personal communication with author, October 16.

Goldman, Sheldon, and Thomas P. Jahnige. 1985. *The Federal Courts as a Political System,* 3d ed. New York: Harper and Row.

Gordon, Jeffrey N. 1991. "Corporations, Markets, and Courts." *Columbia Law Review* 91:1931–88.

Gorton, Peter A. 1974. "The Fee System Courts: Financial Interest of Judges and Due Process." *Washington and Lee Law Review* 31:474–93.

Goshko, John M., and Nancy Reckler. 1996. "Controversial Drug Ruling is Reversed." *Washington Post,* April 2, A1, A5.

Gould, Stephen Jay. 1989. *Wonderful Life: The Burgess Shale and the Nature of History.* New York: W. W. Norton.

Goulden, Joseph C. 1974. *The Benchwarmers: The Private World of the Powerful Federal Judges.* New York: Weybright and Talley.

Graham, Jean Ann, Michael Argyle, and Adrian Furnham. 1980. "The Goal Structure of Situations." *European Journal of Social Psychology* 10: 345–66.

Green, Donald P., and Ian Shapiro. 1994. *Pathologies of Rational Choice Theory: A Critique of Applications in Political Science.* New Haven, Conn.: Yale University Press.

Green, Donald P., and Ian Shapiro. 1995. "Pathologies Revisited: Reflections on Our Critics." *Critical Review* 9:235–76.

Greenberg, Paul E., and James A. Haley. 1986. "The Role of the Compensation Structure in Enhancing Judicial Quality." *Journal of Legal Studies* 15:417–26.

Greenwald, Anthony G. 1975. "Consequences of Prejudice Against the Null Hypothesis." *Psychological Bulletin* 82:1–20.

Gressman, Eugene. 1964. "Much Ado About Certiorari." *Georgetown Law Review* 52:742–66.

Griset, Pamala. 1991. *Determinate Sentencing: The Promise and the Reality of Retributive Justice.* Albany: State University of New York Press.

Grofman, Bernard. 1993. "On the Gentle Art of Rational Choice Bashing." In *Information, Participation, and Choice:* An Economic Theory of Democracy in Perspective, ed. Grofman, 239–42. Ann Arbor: University of Michigan Press.

Gross, Samuel R., and Kent D. Syverud. 1991. "Getting to No: A Study of Settlement Negotiations and the Selection of Cases for Trial." *Michigan Law Review* 90:319–93.

Grossman, Joel B. 1962. "Role Playing and Analysis of Judicial Behavior: The Case of Mr. Justice Frankfurter." *Journal of Public Law* 11:285–309.

Grossman, Joel B. 1968. "Dissenting Blocs on the Warren Court: A Study in Judicial Role Behavior." *Journal of Politics* 30:1068–90.

Grossman, Joel B., and Joseph Tanenhaus. 1969. "Toward a Renascence of Public Law." In *Frontiers of Judicial Research,* ed. Joel B. Grossman and Joseph Tanenhaus, 3–25. New York: John Wiley and Sons.

Gruenfeld, Deborah H. 1995. "Status, Ideology, and Integrative Complexity on the U.S. Supreme Court: Rethinking the Politics of Political Decision Making." *Journal of Personality and Social Psychology* 68:5–20.

Gruhl, John. 1982. "Patterns of Compliance with U.S. Supreme Court Rulings: The Case of Libel in Federal Courts of Appeals and State Supreme Courts." *Publius* 12:109–26.

Gryski, Gerard S., and Eleanor C. Main. 1986. "Social Backgrounds as Predictors of Votes on State Courts of Last Resort: The Case of Sex Discrimination." *Western Political Quarterly* 39:528–37.

Haar, Charles M. 1996. *Suburbs Under Siege: Race, Space, and Audacious Judges.* Princeton, N.J.: Princeton University Press.

Hagan, John, and Kristin Bumiller. 1983. "Making Sense of Sentencing: A Review and Critique of Sentencing Research." In *Research on Sentencing: The Search for Reform,* ed. Alfred Blumstein, Jacqueline Cohen, Susan E. Martin, and Michael H. Tonry, vol. 2, 1–54. Washington, D.C.: National Academy Press.

Hagle, Timothy M., and Harold J. Spaeth. 1991. "Voting Fluidity and the Attitudinal Model of Supreme Court Decision Making." *Western Political Quarterly* 44:119–28.

Hagle, Timothy M., and Harold J. Spaeth. 1992a. "The Emergence of a New Ideology: The Business Decisions of the Burger Court." *Journal of Politics* 54 (February): 120–34.

Hagle, Timothy M., and Harold J. Spaeth. 1992b. "A Validity Test for Inferring Judicial Attitudes from Individual Voting Behavior." Paper presented at the annual meeting of the American Political Science Association, Chicago, September 3–6.

Hagle, Timothy M., and Harold J. Spaeth. 1993. "Ideological Patterns in the Justices' Voting in the Burger Court's Business Cases." *Journal of Politics* 55:492–505.

Haines, Charles Grove. 1922. "General Observations on the Effects of Personal, Political, and Economic Influences in the Decisions of Judges." *Illinois Law Review* 17:96–116.

Hall, Melinda Gann. 1987. "Constituent Influence in State Supreme Courts: Conceptual Notes and a Case Study." *Journal of Politics* 49:1117–25.

Hall, Melinda Gann. 1992. "Electoral Politics and Strategic Voting in State Supreme Courts." *Journal of Politics* 54:427–46.

Hall, Melinda Gann. 1995. "Justices as Representatives: Elections and Judicial Politics in the American States." *American Politics Quarterly* 23: 485–503.

Hall, Melinda Gann, and Paul Brace. 1989. "Order in the Courts: A Neo-Institutional Approach to Judicial Consensus." *Western Political Quarterly* 42:391–407.

Hall, Melinda Gann, and Paul Brace. 1996. "Justices' Responses to Case Facts: An Interactive Model." *American Politics Quarterly* 24:237–61.

Halpern, Stephen C., and Charles M. Lamb, eds. 1982. *Supreme Court Activism and Restraint.* Lexington, Mass.: Lexington Books.

Halpern, Stephen C., and Kenneth N. Vines. 1977. "Institutional Disunity, the Judges' Bill and the Role of the Supreme Court." *Western Political Quarterly* 30:471–83.

Handberg, Roger. 1991. "The Elements of Judicial Strategy: Judicial Rhetoric and Behavior." Paper presented at the annual meeting of the American Political Science Association, Washington, D.C., August 29–September 1.

Hansen, John Mark. 1991. *Gaining Access: Congress and the Farm Lobby, 1919–1981.* Chicago: University of Chicago Press.

Hansen, Wendy L., Renée J. Johnson, and Isaac Unah. 1995. "Specialized

Courts, Bureaucratic Agencies, and the Politics of U.S. Trade Policy." *American Journal of Political Science* 39:529–57.

Harsanyi, John C. 1969. "Rational-Choice Models of Political Behavior vs. Functionalist and Conformist Theories." *World Politics* 21:513–38.

Hausegger, Lori, and Lawrence Baum. 1996. "Inviting Congressional Action: A Study of Supreme Court Motivations in Statutory Interpretation." Paper presented at the annual meeting of the American Political Science Association, San Francisco, August 29–September 1.

Hausegger, Lori, and Lawrence Baum. Forthcoming. "Behind the Scenes: The Supreme Court and Congress in Statutory Interpretation." In *Great Theater: The American Congress in Action,* ed. Herbert F. Weisberg and Samuel C. Patterson. New York: Cambridge University Press.

Haynie, Stacia L. 1992. "Leadership and Consensus on the U.S. Supreme Court." *Journal of Politics* 54:1158–69.

Heckman, James J. 1979. "Sample Selection Bias as a Specification Error." *Econometrica* 47:153–61.

Hedges, Larry V., and Ingram Olkin. 1985. *Statistical Methods for Meta-Analysis.* Orlando, Fla.: Academic Press.

Heinzelmann, Fred. 1985. "Mandatory Confinement as a Response to Community Concerns About Drunk Driving." *Justice System Journal* 10: 265–78.

Hempel, Carl G., and Paul Oppenheim. 1948. "Studies in the Logic of Explanation." *Philosophy of Science* 15:135–75.

Hendry, David F. 1980. "Econometrics—Alchemy or Science?" *Economica* 47:387–406.

Henschen, Beth M. 1983. "Statutory Interpretations of the Supreme Court: Congressional Response." *American Politics Quarterly* 11:441–58.

Henschen, Beth M., and Edward I. Sidlow. 1989. "The Supreme Court and the Congressional Agenda-Setting Process." *Journal of Law and Politics* 5:685–724.

Hensley, Thomas R., and Ashlyn K. Kuersten. 1995. "Studying the Studies: An Assessment of Judicial Politics Research in Four Major Political Science Journals, 1960–1994." Paper presented at the annual meeting of the Southern Political Science Association, Tampa, November 1–4.

Hermann, Margaret G., ed. 1986. *Political Psychology: Contemporary Problems and Issues.* San Francisco: Jossey-Bass.

Hermann, Margaret G. 1988. "The Role of Leaders and Leadership in the Making of American Foreign Policy." In *The Domestic Sources of American Foreign Policy: Insights and Evidence,* ed. Charles W. Kegley Jr., and Eugene R. Wittkopf, 266–84. New York: St. Martin's Press.

Heumann, Milton. 1978. *Plea Bargaining: The Experiences of Prosecutors, Judges, and Defense Attorneys.* Chicago: University of Chicago Press.

Hibbing, John R. 1991. *Congressional Careers: Contours of Life in the U.S. House of Representatives.* Chapel Hill: University of North Carolina Press.

Higgins, Richard S., and Paul H. Rubin. 1980. "Judicial Discretion." *Journal of Legal Studies* 9:129–38.

Hirsch, H. N. 1981. *The Enigma of Felix Frankfurter.* New York: Basic Books.

Hogarth, Robin M., and Melvin W. Reder, eds. 1987a. *Rational Choice: The*

Contrast Between Economics and Psychology. Chicago: University of Chicago Press.

Hogarth, Robin M., and Melvin W. Reder. 1987b. "Introduction." In *Rational Choice: The Contrast Between Economics and Psychology,* ed. Hogarth and Reder, 1–23. Chicago: University of Chicago Press.

Holding, Reynolds. 1992. "Blackmun Says Court Direction Disappointing." *San Francisco Chronicle,* June 10, A12.

Howard, J. Woodford, Jr. 1968. "On the Fluidity of Judicial Choice." *American Political Science Review* 62:43–56.

Howard, J. Woodford, Jr. 1971. "Judicial Biography and the Behavioral Persuasion." *American Political Science Review* 65:704–15.

Howard, J. Woodford, Jr. 1977. "Role Perceptions and Behavior in Three U.S. Courts of Appeals." *Journal of Politics* 39:916–38.

Howard, J. Woodford, Jr. 1981. *Courts of Appeals in the Federal Judicial System: A Study of the Second, Fifth, and District of Columbia Circuits.* Princeton, N.J.: Princeton University Press.

Huckfeldt, Robert, and John Sprague. 1995. *Citizens, Politics, and Social Communication.* New York: Cambridge University Press.

Hughes, Charles Evans. 1928. *The Supreme Court of the United States.* New York: Columbia University Press.

Ignagni, Joseph A. 1994. "Explaining and Predicting Supreme Court Decision Making: The Burger Court's Establishment Clause Decisions." *Journal of Church and State* 36:301–27.

Ignagni, Joseph, and James Meernik. 1994. "Explaining Congressional Attempts to Reverse Supreme Court Decisions." *Political Research Quarterly* 47:353–71.

Iyengar, Satish, and Joel B. Greenhouse. 1988. "Selection Models and the File Drawer Problem." *Statistical Science* 3:109–35.

Jackson, Donald Dale. 1974. *Judges.* New York: Atheneum.

Jackson, Donald W., and James W. Riddlesperger Jr. 1991. "Money and Politics in Judicial Elections: The 1988 Election of the Chief Justice of the Texas Supreme Court." *Judicature* 74:184–89.

Jacob, Herbert. 1962. "Initial Recruitment of Elected Officials in the U.S.—A Model." *Journal of Politics* 24:703–16.

Jacob, Herbert. 1991. "Decision Making in Trial Courts." In *The American Courts: A Critical Assessment,* ed. John B. Gates and Charles A. Johnson, 213–33. Washington, D.C.: CQ Press.

James, Dorothy B. 1968. "Role Theory and the Supreme Court." *Journal of Politics* 30:160–86.

Jaros, Dean, and Bradley C. Canon. 1971. "Dissent on State Supreme Courts: The Differential Significance of Characteristics of Judges." *Midwest Journal of Political Science* 15:322–46.

Jeffries, John C., Jr. 1994. *Justice Lewis F. Powell, Jr.* New York: Charles Scribner's Sons.

Johnson, Charles A. 1977. "The Shapley-Shubik Power Index and the Supreme Court: A Few Empirical Notes." *Jurimetrics Journal* 18:40–45.

Johnson, Charles A. 1979. "Lower Court Reactions to Supreme Court Decisions: A Quantitative Examination." *American Journal of Political Science* 23:792–804.

Johnson, Charles A. 1987. "Law, Politics, and Judicial Decision Making: Lower Federal Court Uses of Supreme Court Decisions." *Law and Society Review* 21:325–40.

Johnson, Charles A., ed. 1990. "Strategies for Judicial Research: Soaking and Poking in the Judiciary." *Judicature* 73:192–203.

Johnson, Charles A., and Bradley C. Canon. 1984. *Judicial Policies: Implementation and Impact.* Washington, D.C.: CQ Press.

Johnston, David. 1991. "Human Agency and Rational Action." In *The Economic Approach to Politics: A Critical Reassessment of the Theory of Rational Action,* ed. Kristen Renwick Monroe, 94–112. New York: HarperCollins.

Judicial Council of California. 1994. *1994 Annual Report.* San Francisco: Administrative Office of the California Courts.

Kahn, Ronald. 1994. *The Supreme Court and Constitutional Theory, 1953–1993.* Lawrence: University Press of Kansas.

Kahneman, Daniel, Paul Slovic, and Amos Tversky. 1982. *Judgment Under Uncertainty: Heuristics and Biases.* New York: Cambridge University Press.

Kahneman, Daniel, and Richard Thaler. 1991. "Economic Analysis and the Psychology of Utility: Applications to Compensation Policy." *American Economic Association Papers and Proceedings* 81:341–46.

Kahneman, Daniel, and Amos Tversky. 1979. "Prospect Theory: An Analysis of Decision Under Risk." *Econometrica* 47:263–91.

Kahneman, Daniel, and Amos Tversky. 1984. "Choices, Values, and Frames." *American Psychologist* 39:341–50.

Kahneman, Daniel, and Carol Varey. 1991. "Notes on the Psychology of Utility." In *Interpersonal Comparisons of Well-Being,* ed. Jon Elster and John E. Roemer, 127–63. New York: Cambridge University Press.

Kalman, Laura. 1990. *Abe Fortas: A Biography.* New Haven, Conn.: Yale University Press.

Kaplan, David A. 1990. "Campaigning for the High Court." *Newsweek,* July 2, 61.

Kavka, Gregory S. 1991. "Rational Maximizing in Economic Theories of Politics." In *The Economic Approach to Politics: A Critical Reassessment of the Theory of Rational Action,* ed. Kristen Renwick Monroe, 371–85. New York: HarperCollins.

Kazee, Thomas A., ed. 1994. *Who Runs for Congress? Ambition, Context, and Candidate Emergence.* Washington, D.C.: CQ Press.

Kelley, Stanley, Jr. 1995. "The Promise and Limitations of Rational Choice Theory." *Critical Theory* 9:95–106.

Kelly, Michael J. 1994. *Lives of Lawyers: Journeys in the Organizations of Practice.* Ann Arbor: University of Michigan Press.

Kenrick, Douglas T., and David C. Funder. 1988. "Profiting from Controversy: Lessons From the Person-Situation Debate." *American Psychologist* 43:23–34.

Kessler, Daniel, Thomas Meites, and Geoffrey Miller. 1996. "Explaining Deviations From the Fifty-Percent Rule: A Multimodal Approach to the Selection of Cases for Litigation." *Journal of Legal Studies* 25:233–59.

Kester, John G. 1983. "The Law Clerk Explosion." *Litigation* 9 (Spring): 20–24, 61–62.

Keynes, Edward, with Randall K. Miller. 1989. *The Court vs. Congress: Prayer, Busing, and Abortion.* Durham, N.C.: Duke University Press.

Kilwein, John C., and Richard A. Brisbin Jr. 1997. "Policy Convergence in a Federal Judicial System: The Application of Intensified Scrutiny Doctrines by State Supreme Courts." *American Journal of Political Science* 41:122–48.

Kinder, Donald R. 1993. "Rational and Not-So-Rational Processes in Judgment and Choice." In *Experimental Foundations of Political Science,* ed. Donald R. Kinder and Thomas R. Palfrey, 119–27. Ann Arbor: University of Michigan Press.

Kinder, Donald R., and Janet A. Weiss. 1978. "In Lieu of Rationality: Psychological Perspectives on Foreign Policy Decision Making." *Journal of Conflict Resolution* 22:707–35.

King, Gary, Robert O. Keohane, and Sidney Verba. 1994. *Designing Social Inquiry: Scientific Inference in Qualitative Research.* Princeton, N.J.: Princeton University Press.

King, Kimi Lynn, and Casi Gail Davis. 1995. "Judicial Neutrality or Politics as Usual?: Judicial Decision-Making in School Desegregation and Housing Discrimination Cases, 1968–1989." Paper presented at the annual meeting of the Midwest Political Science Association, Chicago, April 6–8.

Kingdon, John W. 1995. *Agendas, Alternatives, and Public Policies,* 2d ed. New York: HarperCollins.

Kirk, Jerome, and Marc L. Miller. 1986. *Reliability and Validity in Qualitative Research.* Beverly Hills, Calif.: Sage Publications.

Klein, David. 1996a. "The Adoption and Rejection of Legal Doctrines: Explaining the Choices of Federal Appellate Court Judges." Ph.D. dissertation, Ohio State University.

Klein, David. 1996b. "Explaining the Adoption and Rejection of Legal Doctrines in the U.S. Courts of Appeals." Paper presented at the Conference on the Scientific Study of Judicial Politics, St. Louis, November 15–16.

Klein, Stephen, Joan Petersilia, and Susan Turner. 1990. "Race and Imprisonment Decisions in California." *Science* 247:812–16.

Klein, William M., and Ziva Kunda. 1992. "Motivated Person Perception: Constructing Justifications for Desired Beliefs." *Journal of Experimental Social Psychology* 28:145–68.

Klepper, Steven, Daniel Nagin, and Luke-Jon Tierney. 1983. "Discrimination in the Criminal Justice System: A Critical Appraisal of the Literature." In *Research on Sentencing: The Search for Reform,* ed. Alfred Blumstein, Jacqueline Cohen, Susan E. Martin, and Michael H. Tonry, vol. 2, 55–128. Washington, D.C.: National Academy Press.

Kluger, Richard. 1976. *Simple Justice: The History of Brown v. Board of Education and Black America's Struggle for Equality.* New York: Alfred A. Knopf.

Knight, Jack. 1994. (Comments on *The Supreme Court and the Attitudinal Model.) Law and Courts* 4 (Spring): 5–6.

Knight, Jack, and Lee Epstein. 1996a. "The Norm of *Stare Decisis.*" *American Journal of Political Science* 40:1018–35.

Knight, Jack, and Lee Epstein. 1996b. "On the Struggle for Judicial Supremacy." *Law and Society Review* 30:87–120.

Kobylka, Joseph F. 1992. "The Judicial Odyssey of Harry Blackmun: The Determinants of Individual-Level Change on the U.S. Supreme Court." Paper presented at the annual meeting of the Midwest Political Science Association, Chicago, April 9–11.

Kobylka, Joseph F. 1995. "The Mysterious Case of Establishment Clause Litigation: How Organized Litigants Foiled Legal Change." In *Contemplating Courts,* ed. Lee Epstein, 93–128. Washington, D.C.: CQ Press.

Koford, Kenneth. 1989. "Dimensions in Congressional Voting." *American Political Science Review* 83:949–62.

Koh, Harold Hongju. 1994. "A Tribute to Justice Harry A. Blackmun." *Harvard Law Review* 108:20–22.

Kornhauser, Lewis A. 1992. "Modeling Collegial Courts I: Path-Dependence." *International Review of Law and Economics* 12:169–85.

Kornhauser, Lewis A., and Lawrence G. Sager. 1993. "The One and the Many: Adjudication in Collegial Courts." *California Law Review* 81: 1–59.

Kort, Fred. 1963a. "Content Analysis of Judicial Opinions and Rules of Law." In *Judicial Decision-Making,* ed. Glendon Schubert, 133–97. New York: Free Press.

Kort, Fred. 1963b. "Simultaneous Equations and Boolean Algebra in the Analysis of Judicial Decisions." *Law and Contemporary Problems* 28: 143–63.

Kort, Fred. 1966. "Quantitative Analysis of Fact-Patterns in Cases and Their Impact on Judicial Decisions." *Harvard Law Review* 79:1595–1603.

Kort, Fred. 1973. "Regression Analysis and Discriminant Analysis: An Application of R. A. Fisher's Theory to Data in Political Science." *American Political Science Review* 67:555–59.

Kozinski, Alex. 1991. "My Pizza With Nino." *Cardozo Law Review* 12: 1583–91.

Kozinski, Alex. 1997. "Tinkering With Death." *New Yorker,* February 10, 48–53.

Krehbiel, Keith. 1987. "Sophisticated Committees and Structure-Induced Equilibria in Congress." In *Congress: Structure and Policy,* ed. Mathew D. McCubbins and Terry Sullivan, 376–402. New York: Cambridge University Press.

Krehbiel, Keith. 1991. *Information and Legislative Organization.* Ann Arbor: University of Michigan Press.

Krehbiel, Keith, and Douglas Rivers. 1990. "Sophisticated Voting in Congress: A Reconsideration." *Journal of Politics* 52:548–78.

Kreps, David M. 1990. *Game Theory and Economic Modeling.* Oxford: Clarendon Press.

Kressel, Neil J., ed. 1993. *Political Psychology: Classic and Contemporary Readings.* New York: Paragon House.

Krislov, Samuel. 1963. "Power and Coalition in a Nine-Man Body." *American Behavioral Scientist* 6:24–26.

Kritzer, Herbert M. 1978. "Political Correlates of the Behavior of Federal District Judges: A 'Best Case' Analysis." *Journal of Politics* 40:25–58.

Kritzer, Herbert M. 1994. "Interpretation and Validity Assessment in Qualitative Research: The Case of H. W. Perry's *Deciding to Decide.*" *Law and Social Inquiry* 19:687–724.

Kritzer, Herbert M. 1996. "The Data Puzzle: The Nature of Interpretation in Quantitative Research." *American Journal of Political Science* 40:1–32.

Krol, John F., and Saul Brenner. 1990. "Strategies in Certiorari Voting on the United States Supreme Court: A Reevaluation." *Western Political Quarterly* 43:335–42.

Kuklinski, James H., Robert C. Luskin, and John Bolland. 1991. "Where is the Schema? Going Beyond the 'S' Word in Political Psychology." *American Political Science Review* 85:1341–56.

Kuklinski, James, and John Stanga. 1979. "Political Participation and Governmental Responsiveness: The Behavior of California Superior Courts." *American Political Science Review* 73:1090–99.

Kunda, Ziva. 1990. "The Case for Motivated Reasoning." *Psychological Bulletin* 108:480–98.

Kunen, James S. 1983. *"How Can You Defend Those People?" The Making of a Criminal Lawyer.* New York: Random House.

Kuran, Timur. 1995. *Private Truths, Public Lies: The Social Consequences of Preference Falsification.* Cambridge, Mass.: Harvard University Press.

Labovitz, Sanford. 1968. "Criteria for Selecting a Significance Level: A Note on the Sacredness of .05." *American Sociologist* 3:220–22.

Lalman, David, Joe Oppenheimer, and Piotr Swistak. 1993. "Formal Rational Choice Theory: A Cumulative Science of Politics." In *Political Science: The State of the Discipline II,* ed. Ada W. Finifter, 77–104. Washington, D.C.: American Political Science Association.

Lamb, Charles M., and Stephen C. Halpern, eds. 1991. *The Burger Court: Political and Judicial Profiles.* Urbana: University of Illinois Press.

Landes, William M., and Richard A. Posner. 1975. "The Independent Judiciary in an Interest-Group Perspective." *Journal of Law and Economics* 18:875–901.

Lane, Ruth. 1990. "Concrete Theory: An Emerging Political Method." *American Political Science Review* 84:927–41.

Langbein, John H. 1979. "Understanding the Short History of Plea Bargaining." *Law and Society Review* 13:261–72.

Lasswell, Harold Dwight. 1948. *Power and Personality.* New York: Norton.

Lave, Charles A., and James G. March. 1975. *An Introduction to Models in the Social Sciences.* New York: Harper and Row.

Lawler, James J., and William M. Parle. 1989. "Expansion of the Public Trust Doctrine in Environmental Law: An Examination of Judicial Policy Making by State Supreme Courts." *Social Science Quarterly* 70:134–48.

Lawlor, Reed C. 1963. "Foundations of Logical Legal Decision Making." *Modern Uses of Logic in Law,* 98–114.

Lawrence, Susan E. 1990. *The Poor in Court: The Legal Services Program and Supreme Court Decision Making.* Princeton, N.J.: Princeton University Press.

Leamer, Edward E. 1974. "False Models and Post-Data Model Construction." *Journal of the American Statistical Association* 69:122–31.

Leamer, Edward E. 1978. *Specification Searches: Ad Hoc Inference with Nonexperimental Data.* New York: John Wiley and Sons.

Leamer, Edward E. 1983. "Let's Take the Con Out of Econometrics." *American Economic Review* 73:31–43.

Levin, Martin A. 1977. *Urban Politics and the Criminal Courts.* Chicago: University of Chicago Press.

Lewin, Nathan. 1973. "Helping the Court With Its Work." *New Republic* 168 (March 3): 15–19.

Lewis, Michael. 1990. "The Development of Intentionality and the Role of Consciousness." *Psychological Inquiry* 1:231–47.

Lichtenstein, Sarah, and Paul Slovic. 1971. "Reversals of Preference Between Bids and Choices in Gambling Decisions." *Journal of Experimental Psychology* 89:46–55.

Liess, Elizabeth A. 1993. "Censoring Legislative History: Justice Scalia on the Use of Legislative History in Statutory Interpretation." *Nebraska Law Review* 72:568–85.

Light, Richard J., and David B. Pillemer. 1984. *Summing Up: The Science of Reviewing Research.* Cambridge, Mass.: Harvard University Press.

Lindquist, Stefanie A., and Donald R. Songer. 1994. "Supreme Court Decision Making in the Outcome and Jurisprudential Modes: A Reconsideration of Legal and Extra-Legal Effects." Paper presented at the annual meeting of the American Political Science Association, New York, N.Y., September 1–4.

Link, Michael W. 1995. "Tracking Public Mood in the Supreme Court: Cross-Time Analyses of Criminal Procedure and Civil Rights Cases." *Political Research Quarterly* 48:61–78.

Lipsky, Michael. 1980. *Street-Level Bureaucracy: Dilemmas of the Individual in Public Services.* New York: Russell Sage Foundation.

Lloyd, Randall D. 1995. "Separating Partisanship from Party in Judicial Research: Reapportionment in the U.S. District Courts." *American Political Science Review* 89:413–20.

Lodge, Milton, and Kathleen M. McGraw, eds. 1995. *Political Judgment: Structure and Process.* Ann Arbor: University of Michigan Press.

Lodge, Milton, and Kathleen M. McGraw; Pamela J. Conover and Stanley Feldman; and Arthur H. Miller. 1991. "Where Is the Schema? Critiques." *American Political Science Review* 85:1357–80.

Loewenstein, George, and Jon Elster, eds. 1992. *Choice Over Time.* New York: Russell Sage Foundation.

Loomis, Burdett A. 1994. "The Motivations of Legislators." In *Encyclopedia of the American Legislative System,* ed. Joel H. Silbey, 343–52. New York: Charles Scribner's Sons.

Lopes, Lola L. 1994. "Psychology and Economics: Perspectives on Risk, Cooperation, and the Marketplace." *Annual Review of Psychology* 45: 197–227.

Louthan, William C. 1991. *The United States Supreme Court: Lawmaking in the Third Branch of Government.* Englewood Cliffs, N.J.: Prentice-Hall.

Lovell, Michael C. 1983. "Data Mining." *Review of Economics and Statistics* 65:1–12.

Lynch, David. 1994. "The Impropriety of Plea Agreements: A Tale of Two Counties." *Law and Social Inquiry* 19:115–33.

Lyons, David. 1984. "Justification and Judicial Responsibility." *California Law Review* 72:178–99.

Macey, Jonathan R. 1989. "The Internal and External Costs and Benefits of Stare Decisis." *Chicago-Kent Law Review* 65:93–113.

Macey, Jonathan R. 1994. "Judicial Preferences, Public Choice, and the Rules of Procedure." *Journal of Legal Studies* 23:627–46.

Macey, Jonathan R., and Geoffrey P. Miller. 1992. "The Canons of Statutory Construction and Judicial Preferences." *Vanderbilt Law Review* 45: 647–72.

Maher, Charles. 1985. "Engine, Engine Number 9 . . ." *California Lawyer,* February, 38–43, 66–67.

Main, Eleanor C., and Thomas G. Walker. 1973. "Choice Shifts and Extreme Behavior: Judicial Review in the Federal Courts." *Journal of Social Psychology* 91:215–21.

Maltz, Earl M. 1980. "Some Thoughts on the Death of Stare Decisis in Constitutional Law." *Wisconsin Law Review* 1980:467–96.

Maltzman, Forrest, and Paul J. Wahlbeck. 1995. "Hail to the Chief: Opinion Assignment on the Supreme Court." Paper presented at the annual meeting of the American Political Science Association, Chicago, August 31–September 3.

Maltzman, Forrest, and Paul J. Wahlbeck. 1996a. "May It Please the Chief? Opinion Assignments in the Rehnquist Court." *American Journal of Political Science* 40:421–43.

Maltzman, Forrest, and Paul J. Wahlbeck. 1996b. "Strategic Policy Considerations and Voting Fluidity on the Burger Court." *American Political Science Review* 90:581–92.

Mann, Jim. 1983. "Season of Lost Causes." *American Lawyer,* November, 112–13.

Mansbridge, Jane J., ed. 1990. *Beyond Self-Interest.* Chicago: University of Chicago Press.

March, James G. 1956. "Sociological Jurisprudence Revisited, A Review (More or Less) of Max Gluckman." *Stanford Law Review* 8:499–534.

March, James G. 1978. "Bounded Rationality, Ambiguity, and the Engineering of Choice." *Bell Journal of Economics* 9:587–608.

Marcus, Ruth. 1986. "Alumni Brennan, Blackmun Greet Harvard Law Freshmen." *Washington Post,* September 6, 2.

Marini, Margaret Mooney. 1992. "The Role of Models of Purposive Action in Sociology." In *Rational Choice Theory: Advocacy and Critique,* ed. James S. Coleman and Thomas J. Fararo, 21–48. Newbury Park, Calif.: Sage Publications.

Marks, Brian A. 1989. "A Model of Judicial Influence on Congressional Policymaking: Grove City College v. Bell." Ph.D. dissertation, Washington University.

Markus, Hazel, and R. B. Zajonc. 1985. "The Cognitive Perspective in Social

Psychology." In *Handbook of Social Psychology,* 3d ed., vol. 1, ed. Gardner Lindzey and Elliot Aronson, 137–230. New York: Random House.

Marshall, Thomas. 1989. *Public Opinion and the Supreme Court.* New York: Longman.

Marshall, Thomas R., and Joseph A. Ignagni. 1995. "An Analysis of the U.S. Supreme Court's Women's Rights Cases and Public Opinion." Paper presented at the annual meeting of the Western Political Science Association, Portland, Oregon, March 15–18.

Marvell, Thomas B. 1978. *Appellate Courts and Lawyers: Information Gathering in the Adversary System.* Westport, Conn.: Greenwood Press.

Maslow, Abraham H. 1970. *Motivation and Personality,* 2d ed. New York: Harper and Row.

Mason, Alpheus Thomas. 1979. *The Supreme Court From Taft to Burger.* Baton Rouge: Louisiana State University Press.

Mather, Lynn M. 1979. *Plea-Bargaining or Trial? The Process of Criminal Case Disposition.* Lexington, Mass.: Lexington Books.

Mather, Lynn M. 1995. "The Fired Football Coach (Or, How Trial Courts Make Policy)." In *Contemplating Courts,* ed. Lee Epstein, 170–202. Washington, D.C.: CQ Press.

Mauro, Tony. 1992a. "For the Justices, A Season of Soft Ethics." *Legal Times,* September 28, 10–13.

Mauro, Tony. 1992b. "The Highs and Lows of the 1992 Court." *Legal Times,* December 28, 12, 14.

Mauro, Tony. 1994. "Lessons in Passion for Stephen Breyer." *Legal Times,* June 6, 8–9.

Mauro, Tony. 1995. "The Long-Lost Brennan Biography." *Legal Times,* April 10, 10–11.

Mayer, Thomas. 1975. "Selecting Economic Hypotheses by Goodness of Fit." *Economic Journal* 85:877–83.

Mayhew, David R. 1974. *Congress: The Electoral Connection.* New Haven, Conn.: Yale University Press.

McClintock, Charles G., and Wim B. G. Liebrand. 1988. "Role of Interdependence Structure, Individual Value Orientation, and Another's Strategy in Social Decision Making: A Transformational Analysis." *Journal of Personality and Social Psychology* 55:396–409.

McCloskey, Robert G. 1960. *The American Supreme Court.* Chicago: University of Chicago Press.

McCloskey, Robert G.; revised by Sanford Levinson. 1994. *The American Supreme Court,* 2d ed. Chicago: University of Chicago Press.

McCoy, Candace. 1993. *Politics and Plea Bargaining: Victims' Rights in California.* Philadelphia: University of Pennsylvania Press.

McCrone, Donald J. 1977. "Identifying Voting Strategies From Roll Call Votes: A Method and an Application." *Legislative Studies Quarterly* 2:177–91.

McDowell, Gary L. 1985. *The Constitution and Contemporary Constitutional Theory.* Cumberland, Va.: Center for Judicial Studies.

McGraw, Kathleen M., and Milton Lodge. 1995. "Introduction." In *Political Judgment: Structure and Process,* ed. Lodge and McGraw, 1–13. Ann Arbor: University of Michigan Press.

McGuire, Kevin T. 1990. "Obscenity, Libertarian Values, and Decision Making in the Supreme Court." *American Politics Quarterly* 18:47–67.

McGuire, Kevin T. 1996. "Explaining Executive Success in the U.S. Supreme Court." Paper presented at the Conference on the Scientific Study of Judicial Politics, St. Louis, November 15–16.

McGuire, Kevin T., and Gregory A. Caldeira. 1993. "Lawyers, Organized Interests, and the Law of Obscenity: Agenda Setting in the Supreme Court." *American Political Science Review* 87:717–26.

McIntosh, Wayne V., and Cynthia L. Cates. Forthcoming. *Judicial Entrepreneurship: The Role of the Judge in the Marketplace of Ideas.* Westport, Conn.: Greenwood Press.

McLauchlan, William P. 1972. "Research Note: Ideology and Conflict in Supreme Court Opinion Assignment." *Western Political Quarterly* 25:16–27.

McNollgast. 1995. "Politics and the Courts: A Positive Theory of Judicial Doctrine and the Rule of Law." *Southern California Law Review* 68:1631–89.

Meernik, James, and Joseph Ignagni. 1997. "Judicial Review and Coordinate Construction of the Constitution." *American Journal of Political Science* 41:447–67.

Melnick, R. Shep. 1994. *Between the Lines: Interpreting Welfare Rights.* Washington, D.C.: Brookings Institution.

Mendelson, Wallace. 1991. "Justice John Marshall Harlan: *Non sub Homine* . . ." In *The Burger Court: Political and Judicial Profiles,* ed. Charles M. Lamb and Stephen C. Halpern, 193–211. Urbana: University of Illinois Press.

Mero, Neal P., and Stephan J. Motowidlo. 1995. "Effects of Rater Accountability on the Accuracy and the Favorability of Performance Ratings." *Journal of Applied Psychology* 80:517–24.

Mileski, Maureen. 1971. "Courtroom Encounters: An Observation Study of a Lower Criminal Court." *Law and Society Review* 5:473–538.

Miller, Mark C. 1992. "Congressional Committees and the Federal Courts: A Neo-Institutional Perspective." *Western Political Quarterly* 45:949–70.

Miller, Mark C. 1995. *The High Priests of American Politics: The Role of Lawyers in American Political Institutions.* Knoxville: University of Tennessee Press.

Mishler, William, and Reginald S. Sheehan. 1993. "The Supreme Court as a Countermajoritarian Institution? The Impact of Public Opinion on Supreme Court Decisions." *American Political Science Review* 87:87–101.

Mishler, William, and Reginald S. Sheehan. 1996. "Public Opinion, the Attitudinal Model, and Supreme Court Decision Making: A Micro-Analytic Perspective." *Journal of Politics* 58:169–200.

Mock, Carol. 1988. "Similarities of Inference in Functional and Rational Causal Models." Paper presented at the annual meeting of the American Political Science Association, Washington, D.C., September 1–4.

Mock, Carol, and Herbert F. Weisberg. 1992. "Political Innumeracy: Encounters with Coincidence, Improbability, and Chance." *American Journal of Political Science* 36:1023–46.

Moe, Terry M. 1979. "On the Scientific Status of Rational Models." *American Journal of Political Science* 23:215–43.

Mohr, Lawrence B. 1976. "Organizations, Decisions, and Courts." *Law and Society Review* 10:621–42.

Monroe, Kristen Renwick, ed. 1991a. *The Economic Approach to Politics: A Critical Reassessment of the Theory of Rational Action.* New York: HarperCollins.

Monroe, Kristen Renwick. 1991b. "The Theory of Rational Action: Origins and Usefulness for Political Science." In *The Economic Approach to Politics: A Critical Reassessment of the Theory of Rational Action,* ed. Monroe, 1–31. New York: HarperCollins.

Monroe, Kristen R., ed. 1995. "Special Issue: Political Economy and Political Psychology." *Political Psychology* 16:1–98.

Moore, Charles A., and Terance D. Miethe. 1986. "Regulated and Unregulated Sentencing Decisions: An Analysis of First-Year Practices Under Minnesota's Felony Sentencing Guidelines." *Law and Society Review* 20:253–77.

Morrow, James D. 1994. *Game Theory for Political Scientists.* Princeton, N.J.: Princeton University Press.

Mott, Rodney L. 1936. "Judicial Influence." *American Political Science Review* 30:295–315.

Moulton, Beatrice A. 1969. "The Persecution and Intimidation of the Low-Income Litigant as Performed by the Small Claims Court in California." *Stanford Law Review* 21:1657–84.

Mueller, Dennis C. 1986. "Rational Egoism Versus Adaptive Egoism as Fundamental Postulate for a Descriptive Theory of Human Behavior." *Public Choice* 51:3–23.

Murphy, Bruce Allen. 1988. *Fortas: The Rise and Ruin of a Supreme Court Justice.* New York: William Morrow and Company.

Murphy, Walter F. 1959. "Lower Court Checks on Supreme Court Power." *American Political Science Review* 53:1017–31.

Murphy, Walter F. 1962. *Congress and the Court.* Chicago: University of Chicago Press.

Murphy, Walter F. 1964. *Elements of Judicial Strategy.* Chicago: University of Chicago Press.

Murphy, Walter F., and Joseph Tanenhaus. 1972. *The Study of Public Law.* New York: Random House.

Murray, Henry A. 1938. *Explorations in Personality.* New York: Oxford University Press.

Myers, Laura B., and Sue Titus Reid. 1995. "The Importance of County Context in the Measurement of Sentence Disparity: The Search for Routinization." *Journal of Criminal Justice* 23:223–41.

Myers, Martha A. 1988. "Social Background and the Sentencing Behavior of Judges." *Criminology* 26:649–75.

Myers, Martha A., and Susette M. Talarico. 1986. "The Social Contexts of Racial Discrimination in Sentencing." *Social Problems* 33:236–51.

Myers, Martha A., and Susette M. Talarico. 1987. *The Social Contexts of Criminal Sentencing.* New York: Springer-Verlag.

Nagel, Ernest. 1961. *The Structure of Science: Problems in the Logic of Scientific Explanation.* New York: Harcourt, Brace and World.

Nagel, Stuart S. 1961. "Political Party Affiliation and Judges' Decisions." *American Political Science Review* 55:843–50.

Nagel, Stuart S. 1973. *Comparing Elected and Appointed Judicial Systems.* Beverly Hills, Calif.: Sage Publications.

Nardulli, Peter F., James Eisenstein, and Roy B. Flemming. 1988. *The Tenor of Justice: Criminal Courts and the Guilty Plea Process.* Urbana: University of Illinois Press.

Neubauer, David W. 1974. *Criminal Justice in Middle America.* Morristown, N.J.: General Learning Press.

Newman, Jon O. 1984. "Between Legal Realism and Neutral Principles: The Legitimacy of Institutional Values." *California Law Review* 72:200–216.

New York State Commission on Government Integrity. 1988. *Becoming a Judge: Report on the Failings of Judicial Elections in New York State.* New York: State Commission on Government Integrity.

Niemi, Richard G., and Herbert F. Weisberg, eds. 1993. *Controversies in Voting Behavior,* 3d ed. Washington, D.C.: CQ Press.

Nisbett, Richard, and Lee Ross. 1980. *Human Inference: Strategies and Shortcomings of Social Judgment.* Englewood Cliffs, N.J.: Prentice-Hall.

Niskanen, William A. 1971. *Bureaucracy and Representative Government.* Chicago: Aldine Atherton.

Niskanen, William A. 1994. *Bureaucracy and Public Economics.* Aldershot, England: Edward Elgar Publishing.

Noll, Roger G., and Barry R. Weingast. 1991. "Rational Actor Theory, Social Norms, and Policy Implementation: Applications to Administrative Processes and Bureaucratic Culture." In *The Economic Approach to Politics: A Critical Reassessment of the Theory of Rational Action,* ed. Kristen Renwick Monroe, 237–58. New York: HarperCollins.

Noonan, John T. 1992. "Should State Executions Run on Schedule?" *New York Times,* April 27, A17.

Norpoth, Helmut, and Jeffrey A. Segal. 1994. "Popular Influence on Supreme Court Decisions—Comment." *American Political Science Review* 88:711–16.

Note. 1966. "The Justice of the Peace in Virginia: A Neglected Aspect of the Judiciary." *Virginia Law Review* 52:151–88.

O'Brien, David M. 1993. *Storm Center: The Supreme Court in American Politics,* 3d ed. New York: W. W. Norton.

O'Connor, Karen. 1980. *Women's Organizations' Use of the Courts.* Lexington, Mass.: Lexington Books.

O'Connor, Karen. 1983. "The Amicus Curiae Role of the U.S. Solicitor General in Supreme Court Litigation." *Judicature* 66:256–64.

Olson, Susan M. 1984. *Clients and Lawyers: Securing the Rights of Disabled Persons.* Westport, Conn.: Greenwood Press.

Olson, Susan M. 1992. "Studying Federal District Courts Through Published Cases: A Research Note." *Justice System Journal* 15:782–800.

Ordeshook, Peter D. 1993. "The Development of Contemporary Political Theory." In *Political Economy: Institutions, Competition, and Represen-*

tation, ed. William A. Barnett, Melvin J. Hinich, and Norman J. Schofield, 71–104. New York: Cambridge University Press.

Pacelle, Richard L., Jr. 1991. *The Transformation of the Supreme Court's Agenda: From the New Deal to the Reagan Administration.* Boulder, Colo.: Westview Press.

Pacelle, Richard L., Jr., and Lawrence Baum. 1992. "Supreme Court Authority in the Judiciary: A Study of Remands." *American Politics Quarterly* 20:169–91.

Paddock, Richard C. 1992. "9th Circuit Judge Criticizes High Court Over Execution." *Los Angeles Times,* April 26, A1, A32.

Palmer, Barbara. 1995. "The Defensive Denial: Institutional Rules and Strategic Voting on the Supreme Court." Paper presented at the annual meeting of the Midwest Political Science Association, Chicago, April 6–8.

Palmer, Jan. 1982. "An Econometric Analysis of the U.S. Supreme Court's Certiorari Decisions." *Public Choice* 39:387–98.

Palmer, Jan. 1990. *The Vinson Court Era: The Supreme Court's Conference Votes.* New York: AMS Press.

Panning, William H. 1985. "Formal Models of Legislative Processes." In *Handbook of Legislative Research,* ed. Gerhard Loewenberg, Samuel C. Patterson, and Malcolm E. Jewell, 669–97. Cambridge, Mass.: Harvard University Press.

Parker, Glenn R. 1992. *Institutional Change, Discretion, and the Making of Modern Congress: An Economic Interpretation.* Ann Arbor: University of Michigan Press.

Paschal, Richard A. 1991. "The Continuing Colloquy: Congress and the Finality of the Supreme Court." *Journal of Law and Politics* 8:143–226.

Patry, Jean-Luc. 1989. "Contradictory Goals, Different Expectations: Towards an Explanation of Cross-Situational Specificity in Social Behavior." *Psychological Reports* 65:1331–39.

Paulson, Darryl, and Paul Hawkes. 1984. "Desegregating the University of Florida Law School: Virgil Hawkins vs The Florida Board of Control." *Florida State University Law Review* 12:59–71.

Payne, James L., and Oliver H. Woshinsky. 1972. "Incentives for Political Participation." *World Politics* 24:518–46.

Payne, James L., Oliver H. Woshinsky, Eric P. Veblen, William H. Coogan, and Gene E. Bigler. 1984. *The Motivation of Politicians.* Chicago: Nelson-Hall.

Peltason, J. W. 1961. *Fifty-Eight Lonely Men: Southern Federal Judges and School Desegregation.* New York: Harcourt Brace.

Peltzman, Sam. 1984. "Constituent Interest and Congressional Voting." *Journal of Law and Economics* 27:181–210.

Pennington, Nancy, and Reid Hastie. 1986. "Evidence Evaluation in Complex Decision Making." *Journal of Personality and Social Psychology* 51:242–58.

Pennington, Nancy, and Reid Hastie. 1991. "A Cognitive Theory of Juror Decision Making: The Story Model." *Cardozo Law Review* 13:519–57.

Pennington, Nancy, and Reid Hastie. 1992. "Explaining the Evidence: Tests of the Story Model for Juror Decision Making." *Journal of Personality and Social Psychology* 62:189–206.

Perrow, Charles. 1984. *Normal Accidents: Living With High-Risk Technologies.* New York: Basic Books.

Perry, H. W., Jr. 1991. *Deciding to Decide: Agenda Setting in the United States Supreme Court.* Cambridge, Mass.: Harvard University Press.

Pervin, Lawrence A. 1983. "The Stasis and Flow of Behavior: Toward a Theory of Goals." In *Nebraska Symposium on Motivation 1982,* ed. Monte M. Page, 9–53. Lincoln: University of Nebraska Press.

Pervin, Lawrence A. 1985. "Personality: Current Controversies, Issues, and Directions." *Annual Review of Psychology* 36:83–114.

Pervin, Lawrence A., ed. 1989. *Goal Concepts in Personality and Social Psychology.* Hillsdale, N.J.: Lawrence Erlbaum Associates.

Petrick, Michael J. 1968. "The Supreme Court and Authority Acceptance." *Western Political Quarterly* 21:5–19.

Petty, Richard E., and Jon A. Krosnick, eds. 1995. *Attitude Strength: Antecedents and Consequences.* Hillsdale, N.J.: Lawrence Erlbaum Associates.

Petty, Richard E., Joseph R. Priester, and Duane T. Wegener. 1994. "Cognitive Processes in Attitude Change." In *Handbook of Social Cognition,* 2d ed., vol. 2, 69–142. Hillsdale, N.J.: Lawrence Erlbaum Associates.

Phelps, Glenn A., and John B. Gates. 1991. "The Myth of Jurisprudence: Interpretive Theory in the Constitutional Opinions of Justices Rehnquist and Brennan." *Santa Clara Law Review* 31:567–96.

Pickerill, J. Mitchell. 1996. "The Unanimously Ignored Issue of Unanimity and the Attitudinal Model." Paper presented at the annual meeting of the Midwest Political Science Association, Chicago, April 18–20.

Pinello, Daniel R. 1995. *The Impact of Judicial-Selection Method on State-Supreme-Court Policy: Innovation, Reaction and Atrophy.* Westport, Ct.: Greenwood Press.

Plott, Charles R. 1987. "Rational Choice in Experimental Markets." In *Rational Choice: The Contrast Between Economics and Psychology,* ed. Robin M. Hogarth and Melvin W. Reder, 117–43. Chicago: University of Chicago Press.

Poole, Keith T. 1988. "Recent Developments in Analytic Models of Voting in the U.S. Congress." *Legislative Studies Quarterly* 13:117–33.

Poole, Keith, and R. Steven Daniels. 1985. "Ideology, Party, and Voting in the U.S. Congress, 1959–1980." *American Political Science Review* 79 (June): 373–99.

Poole, Keith, and Howard Rosenthal. 1987. "The Unidimensional Congress, 1919–1984." Typescript.

Posner, Richard A. 1985. *The Federal Courts: Crisis and Reform.* Cambridge, Mass.: Harvard University Press.

Posner, Richard A. 1986. *Economic Analysis of Law,* 3d ed. Boston: Little, Brown.

Posner, Richard A. 1990. *Cardozo: A Study in Reputation.* Chicago: University of Chicago Press.

Posner, Richard A. 1995. *Overcoming Law.* Cambridge, Mass.: Harvard University Press.

Poulton, E. C. 1994. *Behavioral Decision Theory: A New Approach.* New York: Cambridge University Press.

Powell, Lewis F., Jr. 1982. "Are the Federal Courts Becoming Bureaucracies?" *American Bar Association Journal* 68:1370–72.

Prewitt, Kenneth. 1970. *The Recruitment of Political Leaders: A Study of Citizen-Politicians.* Indianapolis: Bobbs-Merrill.

Priest, George L. 1980. "Selective Characteristics of Litigation." *Journal of Legal Studies* 9:399–421.

Priest, George L., and Benjamin Klein. 1984. "The Selection of Disputes for Litigation." *Journal of Legal Studies* 13:1–55.

Pritchett, C. Herman. 1941. "Division of Opinion Among Justices of the U.S. Supreme Court, 1939–1941." *American Political Science Review* 35: 890–98.

Pritchett, C. Herman. 1948. *The Roosevelt Court: A Study in Judicial Politics and Values 1937–1947.* New York: Macmillan.

Pritchett, C. Herman. 1954. *Civil Liberties and the Vinson Court.* Chicago: University of Chicago Press.

Pritchett, C. Herman. 1961. *Congress Versus the Supreme Court, 1957–1960.* Minneapolis: University of Minnesota Press.

Pritchett, C. Herman. 1968. "Public Law and Judicial Behavior." *Journal of Politics* 30:480–509.

Pritchett, C. Herman. 1969. "The Development of Judicial Research." In *Frontiers of Judicial Research,* ed. Joel B. Grossman and Joseph Tanenhaus, 27–42. New York: John Wiley and Sons.

Provine, Doris Marie. 1980. *Case Selection in the United States Supreme Court.* Chicago: University of Chicago Press.

Provine, Doris Marie. 1986. *Judging Credentials: Nonlawyer Judges and the Politics of Professionalism.* Chicago: University of Chicago Press.

Pruet, George W., Jr., and Henry R. Glick. 1986. "Social Environment, Public Opinion, and Judicial Policymaking." *American Politics Quarterly* 14:5–33.

Pruitt, Charles R., and James Q. Wilson. 1983. "A Longitudinal Study of the Effect of Race on Sentencing." *Law and Society Review* 17:613–35.

Puro, Steven. 1981. "The United States as *Amicus Curiae.*" In *Courts, Law, and Judicial Processes,* ed. S. Sidney Ulmer, 220–29. New York: Free Press.

Pyszczynski, Tom, and Jeff Greenberg. 1987. "Toward an Integration of Cognitive and Motivational Perspectives on Social Inference: A Biased Hypothesis-Testing Model." In *Advances in Experimental Social Psychology, vol. 20,* ed. Leonard Berkowitz, 297–340. San Diego: Academic Press.

Quattrone, George A., and Amos Tversky. 1988. "Contrasting Rational and Psychological Analyses of Political Choice." *American Political Science Review* 82:720–36.

Rathjen, Gregory James. 1974a. "Policy Goals, Strategic Choice, and Majority Opinion Assignments in the U.S. Supreme Court: A Replication." *Midwest Journal of Political Science* 18:713–24.

Rathjen, Gregory James. 1974b. "An Analysis of Separate Opinion Writing

Behavior as Dissonance Reduction." *American Politics Quarterly* 2: 393–411.

Reidinger, Paul. 1987. "The Politics of Judging." *American Bar Association Journal* 73:52–58.

Reinhardt, Stephen. 1992. "The Supreme Court, The Death Penalty, and the Harris Case." *Yale Law Journal* 102:205–23.

Rhode, Deborah L. 1992. "Letting the Law Catch Up." *Stanford Law Review* 44:1259–65.

Rieselbach, Leroy N. 1992. "Purposive Politicians Meet the Institutional Congress: A Review Essay." *Legislative Studies Quarterly* 17:95–111.

Riker, William H. 1962. *The Theory of Political Coalitions.* New Haven, Conn.: Yale University Press.

Riker, William H. 1995. "The Political Psychology of Rational Choice Theory." *Political Psychology* 16:23–44.

Robertson, David. 1994. *Sly and Able: A Political Biography of James F. Byrnes.* New York: W. W. Norton.

Rodell, Fred. 1962. "For Every Justice, Judicial Deference Is a Sometime Thing." *Georgetown Law Journal* 50:700–708.

Rodriguez, Daniel B. 1994. "The Positive Political Dimensions of Regulatory Reform." *Washington University Law Quarterly* 72:1–150.

Rogers, John M. 1990–91. "'I Vote This Way Because I'm Wrong': The Supreme Court Justice as Epimenides." *Kentucky Law Journal* 79: 439–75.

Rohde, David W. 1972a. "A Theory of the Formation of Opinion Coalitions in the U.S. Supreme Court." In *Probability Models of Collective Decision Making,* ed. Richard G. Niemi and Herbert F. Weisberg, 165–78. Columbus: Charles E. Merrill.

Rohde, David W. 1972b. "Policy Goals and Opinion Coalitions in the Supreme Court." *Midwest Journal of Political Science* 16:208–24.

Rohde, David W. 1972c. "Policy Goals, Strategic Choice and Majority Opinion Assignments in the U.S. Supreme Court." *American Journal of Political Science* 16:652–82.

Rohde, David W. 1979. "Risk-Bearing and Progressive Ambition: The Case of the U.S. House of Representatives." *American Journal of Political Science* 23:1–26.

Rohde, David W., and Harold J. Spaeth. 1976. *Supreme Court Decision Making.* San Francisco: W. H. Freeman.

Rohde, David W., and Harold J. Spaeth. 1989. "Ideology, Strategy, and Supreme Court Decisions: William Rehnquist as Chief Justice." *Judicature* 72:247–50.

Rosenberg, Gerald N. 1994. Comments on *The Supreme Court and the Attitudinal Model. Law and Courts* 4 (Spring): 6–8.

Rosenthal, Howard. 1992. "Response to Snyder's 'Committee Power, Structure-Induced Equilibria, and Roll Call Votes': The Unidimensional Congress Is Not the Result of Selective Gatekeeping." *American Journal of Political Science* 36:31–35.

Rosenthal, Robert. 1979. "The 'File Drawer Problem' and Tolerance for Null Results." *Psychological Bulletin* 86:638–41.

Rosenthal, Robert. 1991. *Meta-Analytic Procedures for Social Research,* rev. ed. Beverly Hills, Calif.: Sage Publications.

Ross, H. Laurence. 1976. "The Neutralization of Severe Penalties: Some Traffic Law Studies." *Law and Society Review* 10:405–13.

Ross, H. Laurence. 1980. *Settled Out of Court: The Social Process of Insurance Claims Adjustment,* rev. 2d ed. New York: Aldine Publishing.

Ross, H. Laurence. 1992. *Confronting Drunk Driving: Social Policy for Saving Lives.* New Haven, Conn.: Yale University Press.

Ross, H. Laurence, and James P. Foley. 1987. "Judicial Disobedience of the Mandate to Imprison Drunk Drivers." *Law and Society Review* 21:315–23.

Ross, Lee. 1977. "The Intuitive Psychologist and His Shortcomings: Distortions in the Attribution Process." In *Advances in Experimental Social Psychology,* vol 10., ed. Leonard Berkowitz, 173–220. New York: Academic Press.

Ross, Lee, and Richard F. Nisbett. 1991. *The Person and the Situation: Perspectives of Social Psychology.* New York: McGraw-Hill.

Rowland, C. K. 1991. "The Federal District Courts." In *The American Courts: A Critical Assessment,* ed. John B. Gates and Charles A. Johnson, 61–85. Washington, D.C.: CQ Press.

Rowland, C. K., and Robert A. Carp. 1983. "The Relative Effects of Maturation, Time Period, and Appointing President on District Judges' Policy Choices: A Cohort Analysis." *Political Behavior* 5:109–33.

Rowland, C. K., and Robert A. Carp. 1996. *Politics and Judgment in Federal District Courts.* Lawrence: University Press of Kansas.

Rudenstine, David. 1996. *The Day the Presses Stopped: A History of the Pentagon Papers Case.* Berkeley: University of California Press.

Rumble, Wilfrid E., Jr. 1968. *American Legal Realism: Skepticism, Reform, and the Judicial Process.* Ithaca, N.Y.: Cornell University Press.

Ryan, John Paul. 1980–81. "Adjudication and Sentencing in a Misdemeanor Court: the Outcome is the Punishment." *Law and Society Review* 15:79–108.

Ryan, John Paul, and James J. Alfini. 1979. "Trial Judges' Participation in Plea Bargaining: An Empirical Perspective." *Law and Society Review* 13:479–507.

Ryan, John Paul, Allan Ashman, Bruce D. Sales, and Sandra Shane-DuBow. 1980. *American Trial Judges: Their Work Styles and Performance.* New York: Free Press.

Safire, William. 1985. "Free Speech v. Scalia." *New York Times,* April 29, A17.

Salmon, Wesley C. 1990. *Four Decades of Scientific Explanation.* Minneapolis: University of Minnesota Press.

Salokar, Rebecca Mae. 1992. *The Solicitor General: The Politics of Law.* Philadelphia: Temple University Press.

Sanders, Francine. 1995. "*Brown v. Board of Education:* An Empirical Reexamination of Its Effects on Federal District Courts." *Law and Society Review* 29:731–56.

Sarat, Austin. 1977. "Judging in Trial Courts: An Exploratory Study." *Journal of Politics* 39:368–98.

Satter, Robert. 1990. *Doing Justice: A Trial Judge at Work.* New York: Simon and Schuster.

Satz, Debra, and John Ferejohn. 1994. "Rational Choice and Social Theory." *Journal of Philosophy* 91:71–87.

Savage, David G. 1992. *Turning Right: The Making of the Rehnquist Supreme Court.* New York: John Wiley and Sons.

Scalia, Antonin. 1994. "The Dissenting Opinion." *Journal of Supreme Court History* 1994:33–44.

Schauer, Frederick. 1991. "Statutory Construction and the Coordinating Function of Plain Meaning." In *The Supreme Court Review 1990,* ed. Gerhard Casper, Dennis J. Hutchinson, and David A. Strauss, 231–56. Chicago: University of Chicago Press.

Scheb, John M., II, Terry Bowen, and Gary Anderson. 1991. "Ideology, Role Orientations, and Behavior in the State Courts of Last Resort." *American Politics Quarterly* 19:324–35.

Scheb, John M., II, Thomas D. Ungs, and Allison L. Hayes. 1989. "Judicial Role Orientations, Attitudes and Decision Making: A Research Note." *Western Political Quarterly* 42:427–35.

Schick, Marvin. 1970. *Learned Hand's Court.* Baltimore, Md.: Johns Hopkins Press.

Schlesinger, Joseph A. 1966. *Ambition and Politics: Political Careers in the United States.* Chicago: Rand McNally.

Schmidhauser, John R. 1959. "The Justices of the Supreme Court: A Collective Portrait." *Midwest Journal of Political Science* 3:1–57.

Schmidhauser, John R. 1961. "Judicial Behavior and the Sectional Crisis of 1837–1860." *Journal of Politics* 23:615–40.

Schmidhauser, John R. 1962. "*Stare Decisis,* Dissent, and the Background of the Justices of the Supreme Court of the United States." *University of Toronto Law Review* 14:194–212.

Schmidhauser, John R. 1979. *Judges and Justices: The Federal Appellate Judiciary.* Boston: Little, Brown.

Schneider, Ronald, and Ralph Maughan. 1979. "Does the Appointment of Judges Lead to a More Conservative Bench? The Case of California." *Justice System Journal* 5:45–57.

Schofield, Norman. 1995. "Rational Choice and Political Economy." *Critical Review* 9:189–211.

Schooler, Carmi. 1968. "A Note of Extreme Caution on the Use of Guttman Scales." *American Journal of Sociology* 74:296–301.

Schubert, Glendon A. 1959. *Quantitative Analysis of Judicial Behavior.* Glencoe, Ill.: Free Press.

Schubert, Glendon. 1962a. "The 1960 Term of the Supreme Court: A Psychological Analysis." *American Political Science Review* 56 (March): 90–107.

Schubert, Glendon. 1962b. "Policy Without Law: An Extension of the Certiorari Game." *Stanford Law Review* 14:284–327.

Schubert, Glendon. 1963a. "Civilian Control and Stare Decisis in the Warren Court." In *Judicial Decision-Making,* ed. Glendon Schubert, 55–77.

Schubert, Glendon. 1963b. "Judicial Attitudes and Voting Behavior: The 1961 Term of the United States Supreme Court." *Law and Contemporary Problems* 28:100–142.

Schubert, Glendon, ed. 1964a. *Judicial Behavior: A Reader in Theory and Research.* Chicago: Rand McNally.

Schubert, Glendon. 1964b. "The Power of Organized Minorities in a Small Group." *Administrative Science Quarterly* 9:133–53.

Schubert, Glendon. 1965. *The Judicial Mind: The Attitudes and Ideologies of Supreme Court Justices, 1946–1963.* Evanston, Ill.: Northwestern University Press.

Schubert, Glendon. 1974. *The Judicial Mind Revisited: Psychometric Analysis of Supreme Court Ideology.* New York: Oxford University Press.

Schubert, Glendon. 1983. "Aging, Conservatism, and Judicial Behavior." *Micropolitics* 3:135–79.

Schwartz, Bernard. 1983. *Super Chief: Earl Warren and His Supreme Court— A Judicial Biography.* New York: New York University Press.

Schwartz, Bernard. 1985. *The Unpublished Opinions of the Warren Court.* New York: Oxford University Press.

Schwartz, Bernard. 1988. *The Unpublished Opinions of the Burger Court.* New York: Oxford University Press.

Schwartz, Bernard. 1990. *The Ascent of Pragmatism: The Burger Court in Action.* Reading, Mass.: Addison-Wesley.

Schwartz, Bernard. 1996a. *The Unpublished Opinions of the Rehnquist Court.* New York: Oxford University Press.

Schwartz, Bernard. 1996b. *Decision: How the Supreme Court Decides Cases.* New York: Oxford University Press.

Schwartz, Edward P. 1993. "Information, Agendas, and the Rule of Four: Nonmajoritarian Certiorari Rules for the Supreme Court." Occasional Paper 93–10, Center for American Political Studies, Harvard University.

Schwartz, Edward P., Pablo T. Spiller, and Santiago Urbiztondo. 1994. "A Positive Theory of Legislative Intent." *Law and Contemporary Problems* 57 (Winter–Spring): 51–74.

Schwartz, Thomas. 1987. "Votes, Strategies, and Institutions: An Introduction to the Theory of Collective Choice." In *Congress: Structure and Policy,* ed. Mathew D. McCubbins and Terry Sullivan, 318–45. New York: Cambridge University Press.

Schwarz, Michiel, and Michael Thompson. 1990. *Divided We Stand: Redefining Politics, Technology and Social Choice.* New York: Harvester Wheatsheaf.

Scigliano, Robert. 1971. *The Supreme Court and the Presidency.* New York: Free Press.

Seagle, William. 1943. "Book Review." *Virginia Law Review* 29:664–71.

Sears, David O. 1987. "Political Psychology." *Annual Review of Psychology* 38:229–55.

Segal, Jeffrey A. 1984. "Predicting Supreme Court Cases Probabilistically: The Search and Seizure Cases, 1962–1981." *American Political Science Review* 78:891–900.

Segal, Jeffrey A. 1985. "Measuring Change on the Supreme Court: Examining Alternative Models." *American Journal of Political Science* 29:461–79.

Segal, Jeffrey A. 1986. "Supreme Court Justices as Human Decision Makers: An Individual-Level Analysis of the Search and Seizure Cases." *Journal of Politics* 48:938–55.

Segal, Jeffrey A. 1988. "Amicus Curiae Briefs by the Solicitor General During the Warren and Burger Courts: A Research Note." *Western Political Quarterly* 41:135–44.

Segal, Jeffrey A. 1990. "Supreme Court Support for the Solicitor General: The Effect of Presidential Appointments." *Western Political Quarterly* 43:137–52.

Segal, Jeffrey A. 1991. "Courts, Executives, and Legislatures." In *The American Courts: A Critical Assessment,* ed. John B. Gates and Charles A. Johnson, 373–93. Washington, D.C.: CQ Press.

Segal, Jeffrey A. 1994. "Appellate Court Research." Paper presented at the Columbus Conference, Columbus, November 11–12.

Segal, Jeffrey A. 1995. "Marksist (and Neo-Marksist) Models of Supreme Court Decision Making: Separation-of-Powers Games in the Positive Theory of Law and Courts." Paper presented at the annual meeting of the American Political Science Association, Chicago, August 31–September 3.

Segal, Jeffrey A. 1996. Personal communications with author, April 28 and August 19.

Segal, Jeffrey A. 1997. "Separation-of-Powers Games in the Positive Theory of Congress and Courts." *American Political Science Review* 91:28–44.

Segal, Jeffrey A., Robert Boucher, and Charles M. Cameron. 1995. "A Policy-Based Model of Certiorari Voting on the U.S. Supreme Court." Paper presented at the annual meeting of the Midwest Political Science Association, Chicago, April 6–8.

Segal, Jeffrey A., and Albert Cover. 1989. "Ideological Values and the Votes of Supreme Court Justices." *American Political Science Review* 83:557–65.

Segal, Jeffrey A., Lee Epstein, Charles M. Cameron, and Harold J. Spaeth. 1995. "Ideological Values and the Votes of U.S. Supreme Court Justices Revisited." *Journal of Politics* 57:812–23.

Segal, Jeffrey A., and Cheryl D. Reedy. 1988. "The Supreme Court and Sex Discrimination: The Role of the Solicitor General." *Western Political Quarterly* 41:553–68.

Segal, Jeffrey A., and Harold J. Spaeth. 1990. "Rehnquist Court Disposition of Lower Court Decisions: Affirmation Not Reversal." *Judicature* 74:84–88.

Segal, Jeffrey A., and Harold J. Spaeth. 1993. *The Supreme Court and the Attitudinal Model.* New York: Cambridge University Press.

Segal, Jeffrey A., and Harold J. Spaeth. 1994. "The Authors Respond." *Law and Courts* 4 (Spring): 10–12.

Segal, Jeffrey A., and Harold J. Spaeth. 1996a. "The Influence of *Stare Decisis* on the Votes of U.S. Supreme Court Justices." *American Journal of Political Science* 40:971–1003.

Segal, Jeffrey A., and Harold J. Spaeth. 1996b. "Norms, Dragons, and *Stare Decisis:* A Response." *American Journal of Political Science* 40:1064–82.

Selvin, Hanan C., and Alan Stuart. 1966. "Data-Dredging Procedures in Survey Analysis." *American Statistician* (June): 20–23.

Sen, Amartya K. 1970. *Collective Choice and Social Welfare.* San Francisco: Holden-Day.

Sen, Amartya K. 1977. "Rational Fools: A Critique of the Behavioral Foundations of Economic Theory." *Philosophy and Public Affairs* 6:317–44.

Shapiro, Martin. 1965. "Stability and Change in Judicial Decision-Making: Incrementalism or Stare Decisis?" *Law in Transition Quarterly* 2:134–57.

Shapiro, Martin. 1968. *The Supreme Court and Administrative Agencies.* New York: Free Press.

Shapiro, Martin. 1993. "Public Law and Judicial Politics." In *Political Science: The State of the Discipline II,* ed. Ada W. Finifter, 365–81. Washington, D.C.: American Political Science Association.

Shapley, L. S., and Martin Shubik. 1954. "A Method for Evaluating the Distribution of Power in a Committee System." *American Political Science Review* 48:787–92.

Sheldon, Charles H. 1974. *The American Judicial Process: Models and Approaches.* New York: Dodd, Mead.

Sheldon, Charles H., and Nicholas P. Lovrich Jr. 1991. "State Judicial Recruitment." In *The American Courts: A Critical Assessment,* ed. John B. Gates and Charles A. Johnson, 161–88. Washington, D.C.: CQ Press.

Shepsle, Kenneth. 1979. "Institutional Arrangements and Equilibrium in Multidimensional Voting Models." *American Journal of Political Science* 23:27–59.

Shepsle, Kenneth A., and Barry R. Weingast, eds. 1995. *Positive Theories of Congressional Institutions.* Ann Arbor: University of Michigan Press.

Shively, W. Phillips. 1995. Review of *Designing Social Inquiry: Scientific Inference in Social Research. Journal of Politics* 57:1192–94.

Showers, Carolin, and Nancy Cantor. 1985. "Social Cognition: A Look at Motivated Strategies." *Annual Review of Psychology* 36:275–305.

Sickels, Robert J. 1965. "The Illusion of Judicial Consensus: Zoning Decisions in the Maryland Court of Appeals." *American Political Science Review* 59:100–104.

Simon, Herbert A. 1955. "A Behavioral Model of Rational Choice." *Quarterly Journal of Economics* 69:99–118.

Simon, Herbert A. 1983. *Reason in Human Affairs.* Stanford, Calif.: Stanford University Press.

Simon, Herbert A. 1985. "Human Nature in Politics: The Dialogue of Psychology with Political Science." *American Political Science Review* 79:293–304.

Simon, Herbert A. 1987. "Rationality in Psychology and Economics." In *Rational Choice: The Contrast Between Economics and Psychology,* ed. Robin M. Hogarth and Melvin W. Reder, 25–40. Chicago: University of Chicago Press.

Simon, Herbert A. 1995. "Rationality in Political Behavior." *Political Psychology* 16:45–61.

Simon, James F. 1980. *Independent Journey: The Life of William O. Douglas.* New York: Harper and Row.

Sinclair, Barbara. 1989. *The Transformation of the U.S. Senate.* Baltimore: Johns Hopkins Press.

Sinclair, Barbara. 1993. "Studying Presidential Leadership." In *Researching the Presidency,* ed. George C. Edwards III, John H. Kessel, and Bert A. Rockman, 203–32. Pittsburgh: University of Pittsburgh Press.

Slotnick, Elliot E. 1977. "Who Speaks for the Court? The View From the States." *Emory Law Journal* 26:107–47.

Slotnick, Elliot E. 1978. "The Chief Justice and Self-Assignment of Majority Opinions: A Research Note." *Western Political Quarterly* 31:219–25.

Slotnick, Elliot E. 1979. "Who Speaks for the Court? Majority Opinion Assignment From Taft to Burger." *American Journal of Political Science* 23:60–77.

Slotnick, Elliot E. 1983. "Federal Trial and Appellate Judges: How Do They Differ?" *Western Political Quarterly* 36:570–78.

Slotnick, Elliot E. 1984. "Judicial Selection Systems and Nomination Outcomes: Does the Process Make a Difference?" *American Politics Quarterly* 12:225–40.

Slotnick, Elliot E. 1991. "Judicial Politics." In *Political Science: Looking to the Future,* ed. William Crotty, vol. 4, 67–97.

Smith, Alexander B., and Abraham S. Blumberg. 1967. "The Problem of Objectivity in Judicial Decision-Making." *Social Forces* 46:96–105.

Smith, Christopher E. 1993. *Courts, Politics, and the Judicial Process.* Chicago: Nelson-Hall.

Smith, Christopher E. 1995. *Judicial Self-Interest: Federal Judges and Court Administration.* Westport, Conn.: Praeger.

Smith, Mary Lee. 1980. "Publication Bias and Meta-Analysis." *Evaluation in Education* 4:22–24.

Smith, Rogers M. 1988. "Political Jurisprudence, The 'New Institutionalism,' and the Future of Public Law." *American Political Science Review* 82:89–108.

Smith, Rogers M. 1995. "The Inherent Deceptiveness of Constitutional Discourse: A Diagnosis and Prescription." Paper presented at the annual meeting of the American Political Science Association, Chicago, August 31–September 3.

Smith, Steven S., and Christopher J. Deering. 1983. "Changing Motives for Committee Preferences of New Members of the U.S. House." *Legislative Studies Quarterly* 8:271–81.

Snyder, James M., Jr. 1992a. "Committee Power, Structure-Induced Equilibria, and Roll Call Votes." *American Journal of Political Science* 36:1–30.

Snyder, James M., Jr. 1992b. "Rejoinder to Rosenthal's 'The Unidimensional Congress is Not the Result of Selective Gatekeeping': Gatekeeping or Not, Sample Selection in the Roll Call Agenda Matters." *American Journal of Political Science* 36:36–39.

Snyder, Mark, and William Ickes. 1985. "Personality and Social Behavior." In *Handbook of Social Psychology,* 3d ed, vol. 2, ed. Gardner Lindzey and Elliot Aronson, 883–947. New York: Random House.

Solimine, Michael E., and James L. Walker. 1992. "The Next Word: Congressional Response to Supreme Court Statutory Decisions." *Temple Law Review* 65:425–58.

Solum, Lawrence B. 1987. "On the Indeterminacy Crisis: Critiquing Critical Dogma." *University of Chicago Law Review* 54:462–503.

Songer, Donald R. 1979. "Concern for Policy Outputs as a Cue for Supreme Court Decisions on Certiorari." *Journal of Politics* 41:1185–94.

Songer, Donald R. 1982. "Consensual and Nonconsensual Decisions in

Unanimous Opinions of the United States Courts of Appeals." *American Journal of Political Science* 26:225–39.

Songer, Donald R. 1987. "The Impact of the Supreme Court on Trends in Economic Policy Making in the United States Courts of Appeals." *Journal of Politics* 49:830–41.

Songer, Donald R. 1991. "The Circuit Courts of Appeals." In *The American Courts: A Critical Assessment,* ed. John B. Gates and Charles A. Johnson, 35–59. Washington, D.C.: CQ Press.

Songer, Donald R., Charles M. Cameron, and Jeffrey A. Segal. 1995. "An Empirical Test of the Rational Actor Theory of Litigation." *Journal of Politics* 57:1119–29.

Songer, Donald R., Sue Davis, and Susan Haire. 1994. "A Reappraisal of Diversification in the Federal Courts: Gender Effects in the Courts of Appeals." *Journal of Politics* 56:425–39.

Songer, Donald R., and Susan Haire. 1992. "Integrating Alternative Approaches to the Study of Judicial Voting: Obscenity Cases in the U.S. Courts of Appeals." *American Journal of Political Science* 36:963–82.

Songer, Donald R., and Stefanie A. Lindquist. 1996. "Not the Whole Story: The Impact of Justices' Values on Supreme Court Decision Making." *American Journal of Political Science* 40:1049–63.

Songer, Donald R., Jeffrey A. Segal, and Charles M. Cameron. 1994. "The Hierarchy of Justice: Testing a Principal-Agent Model of Supreme Court-Circuit Court Interactions." *American Journal of Political Science* 38:673–96.

Songer, Donald R., and Reginald S. Sheehan. 1990. "Supreme Court Impact on Compliance and Outcomes: *Miranda* and *New York Times* in the United States Courts of Appeals." *Western Political Quarterly* 43:297–316.

Sorauf, Frank J. 1976. *The Wall of Separation: The Constitutional Politics of Church and State.* Princeton, N.J.: Princeton University Press.

Sorrentino, Richard M., and E. Tory Higgins. 1986. "Motivation and Cognition: Warming Up to Synergism." In *Handbook of Motivation and Cognition: Foundations of Social Behavior,"* ed. Sorrentino and Higgins, 3–19. New York: John Wiley and Sons.

Spaeth, Harold J. 1962. "Judicial Power as a Variable Motivating Supreme Court Behavior." *Midwest Journal of Political Science* 6:54–82.

Spaeth, Harold J. 1963. "An Analysis of Judicial Attitudes in the Labor Relations Decisions of the Warren Court." *Journal of Politics* 25:290–311.

Spaeth, Harold J. 1964. "The Judicial Restraint of Mr. Justice Frankfurter: Myth or Reality?" *Midwest Journal of Political Science* 8:22–38.

Spaeth, Harold J. 1979. *Supreme Court Policy Making: Explanation and Prediction.* San Francisco: W. H. Freeman.

Spaeth, Harold J. 1989. "Consensus in the Unanimous Decisions of the U.S. Supreme Court." *Judicature* 72:274–81.

Spaeth, Harold J. 1995. "The Attitudinal Model." In *Contemplating Courts,* ed. Lee Epstein, 296–314. Washington, D.C.: CQ Press.

Spaeth, Harold J., and Michael F. Altfeld. 1986. "Felix Frankfurter, Judicial Activism, and Voting Conflict on the Warren Court." In *Judicial Conflict and Consensus,* ed. Sheldon Goldman and Charles M. Lamb, 87–114. Lexington: University of Kentucky Press.

Spaeth, Harold J., and Douglas R. Parker. 1969. "Effects of Attitude Toward Situation Upon Attitude Toward Object." *Journal of Psychology* 73:173–82.

Spaeth, Harold J., and David J. Peterson. 1971. "The Analysis and Interpretation of Dimensionality: The Case of Civil Liberties Decision Making." *Midwest Journal of Political Science* 15:415–41.

Spaeth, Harold J., and Stuart H. Teger. 1982. "Activism and Restraint: A Cloak for the Justices' Policy Preferences." In *Supreme Court Activism and Restraint,* ed. Stephen C. Halpern and Charles M. Lamb, 277–301. Lexington, Mass.: Lexington Books.

Spiller, Pablo T., and Rafael Gely. 1992. "Congressional Control or Judicial Independence: The Determinants of U.S. Supreme Court Labor-Relations Decisions, 1949–1988." *RAND Journal of Economics* 23:463–92.

Spiller, Pablo T., and Matthew L. Spitzer. 1992. "Judicial Choice of Legal Doctrines." *Journal of Law, Economics, and Organization* 8:8–46.

Spiller, Pablo T., and Matthew L. Spitzer. 1995. "Where Is the Sin in Sincere? Sophisticated Manipulation of Sincere Judicial Voters (With Application to Other Voting Environments)." *Journal of Law, Economics, and Organization* 11:32–63.

Spiller, Pablo T., and Emerson H. Tiller. 1996. "Invitations to Override: Congressional Reversals of Supreme Court Decisions." *International Review of Law and Economics* 16:503–21.

Squire, Peverill. 1988. "Politics and Personal Factors in Retirement from the United States Supreme Court." *Political Behavior* 10:180–90.

Starr, Kenneth W. 1993. "Trivial Pursuits at the Supreme Court." *Wall Street Journal,* October 6, A19.

Stevens, John Paul. 1982. "Some Thoughts on Judicial Restraint." *Judicature* 66:177–83.

Stewart, James B. 1984. "Judicial Mavericks." *Wall Street Journal,* December 19, 1, 18.

Stidham, Ronald, and Robert A. Carp. 1982. "Trial Courts' Responses to Supreme Court Policy Changes: Three Case Studies." *Law and Policy Quarterly* 4:215–34.

Stidham, Ronald, and Robert A. Carp. 1987. "Judges, Presidents, and Policy Choices: Exploring the Linkage." *Social Science Quarterly* 68:395–404.

Stigler, George J., and Gary S. Becker. 1977. "De Gustibus Non Est Disputandum." *American Economic Review* 67:76–90.

Stimson, James A., Michael B. MacKuen, and Robert S. Erikson. 1995. "Dynamic Representation." *American Political Science Review* 89: 543–65.

Stinchcombe, Arthur L. 1990. "Reason and Rationality." In *The Limits of Rationality,* ed. Karen Schweers Cook and Margaret Levi, 285–317. Chicago: University of Chicago Press.

Stouffer, Samuel A., Louis Guttman, Edward A. Suchman, Paul F. Lazarsfeld, Shirley A. Star, and John A. Clausen. 1950. *Measurement and Prediction.* Princeton, N.J.: Princeton University Press.

Stover, Robert V. 1989. *Making It and Breaking It: The Fate of Public Interest*

Commitment During Law School. Edited by Howard S. Erlanger. Urbana: University of Illinois Press.

Stow, Mary Lou, and Harold J. Spaeth. 1992. "Centralized Research Staff: Is There a Monster in the Judicial Closet?" *Judicature* 75:216–21.

Strauss, Peter L. 1987. "One Hundred Fifty Cases Per Year: Some Implications of the Supreme Court's Limited Resources for Judicial Review of Agency Action." *Columbia Law Review* 87:1093–1136.

Stumpf, Harry P. 1965. "Congressional Response to Supreme Court Rulings: The Interaction of Law and Politics." *Journal of Public Law* 14:377–95.

Sturley, Michael F. 1993. "Forum Selection Clauses in Cruise Line Tickets: An Update on Congressional Action 'Overruling' the Supreme Court." *Journal of Maritime Law and Commerce* 24:399–401.

Sudnow, David. 1965. "Normal Crimes: Sociological Features of the Penal Code in a Public Defender Office." *Social Problems* 12:255–76.

Swinford, Bill. 1991. "A Predictive Model of Decision Making in State Supreme Courts: The School Financing Cases." *American Politics Quarterly* 19:336–52.

Sylvan, Donald A., and James F. Voss, eds. Forthcoming. *Problem Representation in Foreign Policy Decision Making.* New York: Cambridge University Press.

Tanenhaus, Joseph. 1966. "The Cumulative Scaling of Judicial Decisions." *Harvard Law Review* 79:1583–94.

Tanenhaus, Joseph, Marvin Schick, Matthew Muraskin, and Daniel Rosen. 1963. "The Supreme Court's Certiorari Jurisdiction: Cue Theory." In *Judicial Decision Making,* ed. Glendon Schubert, 111–32. New York: Free Press.

Tarr, G. Alan. 1977. *Judicial Impact and State Supreme Courts.* Lexington, Mass.: D. C. Heath.

Tarr, G. Alan. 1994. *Judicial Process and Judicial Policymaking.* St. Paul, Minn.: West Publishing Co.

Tarr, G. Alan, and Mary Cornelia Aldis Porter. 1988. *State Supreme Courts in State and Nation.* New Haven, Conn.: Yale University Press.

Tate, C. Neal. 1981. "Personal Attribute Models of the Voting Behavior of U.S. Supreme Court Justices: Liberalism in Civil Liberties and Economic Decisions, 1946–1978." *American Political Science Review* 75:355–67.

Tate, C. Neal. 1983. "The Methodology of Judicial Behavior Research: A Review and Critique." *Political Behavior* 5:51–82.

Tate, C. Neal, and Roger Handberg. 1991. "Time Binding and Theory Building in Personal Attribute Models of Supreme Court Voting Behavior, 1916–88." *American Journal of Political Science* 35:460–80.

Taylor, Charles. 1964. *The Explanation of Behaviour.* London: Routledge and Kegan Paul.

Taylor, Michael. 1995. "Battering RAMs." *Critical Review* 9:223–34.

Tetlock, Philip E. 1983. "Accountability and Complexity of Thought." *Journal of Personality and Social Psychology* 45:74–83.

Tetlock, Philip E. 1985a. "Accountability: The Neglected Social Context of Judgment and Choice." *Research in Organizational Behavior* 7:297–332.

Tetlock, Philip E. 1985b. "Accountability: A Social Check on the Fundamental Attribution Error." *Social Psychology Quarterly* 48:227–36.

Tetlock, Philip E., Jane Bernzweig, and Jack L. Gallant. 1985. "Supreme Court Decision Making: Cognitive Style as a Predictor of Ideological Consistency of Voting." *Journal of Personality and Social Psychology* 48:1227–39.

Thaler, Richard H. 1991. *Quasi Rational Economics.* New York: Russell Sage Foundation.

Thomas, Martin. 1985. "Election Proximity and Senatorial Roll Call Voting." *American Journal of Political Science* 29:96–111.

Thomas, Virginia Lamp. 1991. "Breaking Silence." *People Weekly,* November 11, 108–16.

Thurstone, L. L., and J. W. Degan. 1951. "A Factorial Study of the Supreme Court." *Proceedings of the National Academy of Sciences* 37:628–35.

Tillman, Robert, and Henry N. Pontell. 1992. "Is Justice 'Collar-Blind'? Punishing Medicaid Provider Fraud." *Criminology* 50:547–71.

Toma, Eugenia Froedge. 1991. "Congressional Influence and the Supreme Court: The Budget as a Signaling Device." *Journal of Legal Studies* 20:131–46.

Tonry, Michael H. 1996. *Sentencing Matters.* New York: Oxford University Press.

Truelove, Scott. 1996. "A Condorcet Perspective on the Certiorari Process in the United States Supreme Court." Paper presented at the annual meeting of the Midwest Political Science Association, April 18–20, Chicago.

Tushnet, Mark. 1992. "Thurgood Marshall and the Brethren." *Georgetown Law Journal* 80:2109–30.

Uhlman, Thomas M. 1978. "Black Elite Decision Making: The Case of Trial Judges." *American Journal of Political Science* 22:884–904.

Uhlman, Thomas M., and Darlene N. Walker. 1980. "'He Takes Some of My Time; I Take Some of His': An Analysis of Judicial Sentencing Patterns in Jury Cases." *Law and Society Review* 14:323–41.

Ulmer, Jeffery T., and John H. Kramer. 1996. "Court Communities Under Sentencing Guidelines: Dilemmas of Formal Rationality and Sentencing Disparity." *Criminology* 34:383–408.

Ulmer, S. Sidney. 1965. "Toward a Theory of Sub-Group Formation in the United States Supreme Court." *Journal of Politics* 27:133–52.

Ulmer, S. Sidney. 1970a. "Dissent Behavior and the Social Background of Supreme Court Justices." *Journal of Politics* 32:580–98.

Ulmer, S. Sidney. 1970b. "The Use of Power in the Supreme Court: The Opinion Assignments of Earl Warren, 1953–1970." *Journal of Public Law* 19:49–67.

Ulmer, S. Sidney. 1972. "The Decision to Grant Certiorari as an Indicator to Decision 'On the Merits'." *Polity* 4:429–47.

Ulmer, S. Sidney. 1973a. "The Longitudinal Behavior of Hugo Lafayette Black: Parabolic Support for Civil Liberties, 1937–1971." *Florida State University Law Review* 1:131–53.

Ulmer, S. Sidney. 1973b. "Social Background as an Indicator to the Votes of Supreme Court Justices in Criminal Cases: 1947–1956 Terms." *American Journal of Political Science* 17:622–30.

Ulmer, S. Sidney. 1984. "The Supreme Court's Certiorari Decisions: Conflict as a Predictive Variable." *American Political Science Review* 78:901–11.

Ulmer, S. Sidney. 1986. "Are Social Background Models Time-Bound?" *American Political Science Review* 80:957–67.

Ungs, Thomas D., and Larry R. Baas. 1972. "Judicial Role Perceptions: A Q-Technique Study of Ohio Judges." *Law and Society Review* 6:343–66.

United States General Accounting Office. 1992. *Sentencing Guidelines: Central Questions Remain Unanswered.* Washington, D.C.: U.S. Government Printing Office.

United States Sentencing Commission. 1991. *Mandatory Minimum Penalties in the Federal Criminal Justice System.* Washington, D.C.: U.S. Government Printing Office.

United States Sentencing Commission. 1992. *Annual Report 1991.* Washington, D.C.: Self-published.

Van Raaij, W. Fred, Gery M. Van Veldhoven, and Karl-Erik Wärneryd, eds. 1988. *Handbook of Economic Psychology.* Dordrecht, The Netherlands: Kluwer Academic Publishers.

Van Winkle, Steven R. 1996. "Three-Judge Panels and Strategic Behavior on the United States Courts of Appeals." Paper presented at the Conference on the Scientific Study of Judicial Politics, St. Louis, November 15–16.

Vaughan, Diane. 1996. *The Decision to Launch the Challenger.* Chicago: University of Chicago Press.

Vines, Kenneth N. 1964. "Federal District Judges and Race Relations Cases in the South." *Journal of Politics* 26:337–57.

Vines, Kenneth N. 1965. "Southern State Supreme Courts and Race Relations." *Western Political Quarterly* 18:5–18.

Vines, Kenneth N. 1969. "The Judicial Role in the American States: An Exploration." In *Frontiers of Judicial Research,* ed. Joel B. Grossman and Joseph Tanenhaus, 461–85. New York: John Wiley and Sons.

Von Hirsch, Andrew, Kay A. Knapp, and Michael Tonry, eds. 1987. *The Sentencing Commission and Its Guidelines.* Boston: Northeastern University Press.

Von Weizsäcker, Carl Christian. 1971. "Notes on Endogenous Change of Tastes." *Journal of Economic Theory* 3:345–72.

Vose, Clement E. 1972. *Constitutional Change: Amendment Politics and Supreme Court Litigation Since 1900.* Lexington, Mass.: Lexington Books.

Voss, James F., Christopher R. Wolfe, Jeanette A. Lawrence, and Randi A. Engle. 1991. "From Representation to Decision: An Analysis of Problem Solving in International Relations." In *Complex Problem Solving: Principles and Mechanisms,* ed. Robert J. Sternberg and Peter A. Frensch, 119–58. Hillsdale, N.J.: Lawrence Erlbaum Associates.

Wahlbeck, Paul J. 1997. "The Life of the Law: Judicial Politics and Legal Change." *Journal of Politics* 59:778–802.

Wahlbeck, Paul J., Forrest Maltzman, and James F. Spriggs, II. 1996. "Strategic Choices and the Deliberative Process on the U.S. Supreme Court." Paper presented at the annual meeting of the American Political Science Association, San Francisco, August 29–September 1.

Wahlbeck, Paul J., James F. Spriggs, II, and Forrest Maltzman. 1996. "Marshalling the Court: Bargaining and Accommodation on the U.S.

Supreme Court." Paper presented at the annual meeting of the Western Political Science Association, San Francisco, March 14–16.

Wald, Patricia M. 1992. "Some Real-Life Observations About Judging." *Indiana Law Review* 26:173–86.

Walker, Thomas G. 1976. "Leader Selection and Behavior in Small Political Groups." *Small Group Behavior* 7:363–68.

Walker, Thomas G., and Deborah J. Barrow. 1985. "The Diversification of the Federal Bench: Policy and Process Ramifications." *Journal of Politics* 47:596–617.

Walker, Thomas G., Lee Epstein, and William J. Dixon. 1988. "On the Mysterious Demise of Consensual Norms in the U.S. Supreme Court." *Journal of Politics* 50:361–89.

Walker, Thomas G., and Eleanor C. Main. 1973. "Choice Shifts in Political Decisionmaking: Federal Judges and Civil Liberties Cases." *Journal of Applied Social Psychology* 3:39–48.

Waller, Niels G., Verónica Benet, and Darrell L. Farney. 1994. "Modeling Person-Situation Correspondence Over Time: A Study of 103 Evangelical Disciple-Makers." *Journal of Personality* 62:177–97.

Wasby, Stephen L. 1970. *The Impact of the United States Supreme Court: Some Perspectives.* Homewood, Ill.: Dorsey Press.

Wasby, Stephen L. 1991. "Justice Harry A. Blackmun: Transformation from 'Minnesota Twin' to Independent Voice." In *The Burger Court: Political and Judicial Profiles,* ed. Charles M. Lamb and Stephen C. Halpern, 63–99. Urbana: University of Illinois Press.

Wasby, Stephen L. 1995. *Race Relations Litigation in an Age of Complexity.* Charlottesville: University of Virginia Press.

Washington Post. 1995. "Justices, Judges Took Favors From Publisher with Pending Cases." March 6, A7.

Watson, Richard A., and Rondal G. Downing. 1969. *The Politics of the Bench and the Bar: Judicial Selection Under the Missouri Nonpartisan Court Plan.* New York: John Wiley.

Weaver, R. Kent. 1988. *Automatic Government: The Politics of Indexation.* Washington, D.C.: Brookings Institution.

Weiss, Janet A. 1982. "Coping with Complexity: An Experimental Study of Public Policy Decision-Making." *Journal of Policy Analysis and Management* 2:66–87.

Weissberg, Robert. 1976. *Public Opinion and Popular Government.* Englewood Cliffs, N.J.: Prentice-Hall.

Welch, Susan, Michael Combs, and John Gruhl. 1988. "Do Black Judges Make a Difference?" *American Journal of Political Science* 32:126–36.

Wice, Paul B. 1985. *Chaos in the Courthouse: The Inner Workings of the Urban Criminal Courts.* New York: Praeger.

Wildavsky, Aaron. 1994. "Why Self-Interest Means Less Outside of a Social Context: Cultural Contributions to a Theory of Rational Choices." *Journal of Theoretical Politics* 6:131–59.

Wilkerson, John D. 1990. "Reelection and Representation in Conflict: The Case of Agenda Manipulation." *Legislative Studies Quarterly* 15:263–82.

Williams, Armstrong. 1995. "Two Wrongs Don't Make Right for Thomas." *Charleston (S.C.) Post and Courier,* August 17, A13.

Williams, Shirley, and Edward L. Lascher, Jr., eds. 1993. *Ambition and Beyond: Career Paths of American Politicians.* Berkeley, Calif.: Institute of Governmental Studies Press.

Winter, David G. 1973. *The Power Motive.* New York: Free Press.

Winter, David G. 1987. "Leader Appeal, Leader Performance, and the Motive Profiles of Leaders and Followers: A Study of American Presidents and Elections." *Journal of Personality and Political Psychology* 52:196–202.

Winter, David G., and Leslie A. Carlson. 1988. "Using Motive Scores in the Psychobiographical Study of an Individual: The Case of Richard Nixon." *Journal of Personality* 56:75–103.

Winter, David G., Margaret G. Hermann, Walter Weintraub, and Stephen G. Walker. 1991. "The Personalities of Bush and Gorbachev Measured at a Distance: Procedures, Portraits, and Policy." *Political Psychology* 12: 215–45.

Wittman, Donald. 1985. "Is the Selection of Cases for Trial Biased?" *Journal of Legal Studies* 19:185–214.

Wold, John T. 1974. "Political Orientations, Social Backgrounds, and Role Perceptions of State Supreme Court Judges." *Western Political Quarterly* 27:239–48.

Wold, John T. 1978. "Going Through the Motions: The Monotony of Appellate Court Decisionmaking." *Judicature* 62:58–65.

Wolfe, Christopher. 1991. *Judicial Activism: Bulwark of Freedom or Precarious Security?* Pacific Grove, Calif.: Brooks/Cole.

Wolpert, Robin M. 1991. "Explaining and Predicting Supreme Court Decision-Making: The Gender Discrimination Cases, 1971–1987." Paper presented at the annual meeting of the Midwest Political Science Association, Chicago, April 18–20.

Wood, Sandra L. 1996. "Bargaining and Negotiation on the Burger Court." Paper presented at the annual meeting of the American Political Science Association, San Francisco, August 29–September 1.

Wood, Sandra L., and Gary Gansle. 1995. "Mustering the Minority: The Dissent Assignments of William J. Brennan Jr." Paper presented at the annual meeting of the Midwest Political Science Association, Chicago, April 6–8.

Woodward, Bob, and Scott Armstrong. 1979. *The Brethren: Inside the Supreme Court.* New York: Simon and Schuster.

Wright, John R. 1990. "Contributions, Lobbying, and Committee Voting in the U.S. House of Representatives." *American Political Science Review* 84:417–38.

Wyzanski, Charles E., Jr. 1979. "The Importance of the Trial Judge." In *Courts, Judges, and Politics: An Introduction to the Judicial Process,* 3d ed., ed. Walter F. Murphy and C. Herman Pritchett, 456–58. New York: Random House.

Yarbrough, Tinsley E. 1992. *John Marshall Harlan: Great Dissenter of the Warren Court.* New York: Oxford University Press.

Zeckhauser, Richard. 1987. "Comments: Behavioral Versus Rational Economics: What You See Is What You Conquer." In *Rational Choice: The Contrast Between Economics and Psychology,* ed. Robin M. Hogarth and Melvin W. Reder, 251–65. Chicago: University of Chicago Press.

Zorn, Christopher J., and Gregory A. Caldeira. 1995. "Separation of Powers: Congress, the Supreme Court, and Interest Groups." Paper presented at the annual meeting of the Public Choice Society and Economic Science Association, Long Beach, Calif., March 24–26.

Court Cases

Bank One Chicago v. Midwest Bank and Trust Company. 1996. 133 L. Ed. 2d 635.

Board of Education v. Barnette. 1943. 319 U.S. 624.

Brewer v. Lewis. 1993. 997 F.2d 530 (9th Cir.).

Brown v. Board of Education. 1954. 347 U.S. 483.

Callins v. Collins. 1994. 510 U.S. 1141.

Carnival Cruise Lines, Inc. v. Shute. 1991. 499 U.S. 585.

Chevron, U.S.A. v. Natural Resources Defense Council. 1984. 467 U.S. 837.

Conroy v. Aniskoff. 1993. 507 U.S. 511.

Continental Eagle Corp. v. Tanner and Co. Ginning. 1995. 663 So.2d 204 (La. App. 3d Cir.).

Department of Defense v. Federal Labor Relations Authority. 1994. 510 U.S. 487.

Furman v. Georgia. 1972. 408 U.S. 238.

Gomez v. United States District Court. 1992. 503 U.S. 653.

Grove City College v. Bell. 1984. 465 U.S. 555.

Hammond-Knowlton v. United States. 1941. 121 F.2d 192 (2d Cir.).

Jaffree v. Board of School Commissioners. 1983. 554 F. Supp. 1104 (S.D. Alab.).

Kilpatrick v. Alliance Casualty and Insurance Company. 1995. 663 So.2d 62 (La. App. 3d Cir.).

Lawrence v. Chater. 1996. 133 L. Ed. 2d 545.

Louisiana v. Mississippi. 1995. 133 L. Ed. 2d 265.

Marbury v. Madison. 1803. 1 Cranch 137.

McCarty v. McCarty. 1981. 453 U.S. 210.

Miranda v. Arizona. 1966. 384 U.S. 436.

Motor Vehicle Manufacturers Assn. v. State Farm Mutual. 1983. 463 U.S. 29.

Nationsbank of North Carolina v. Variable Annuity Life Insurance Co. 1995. 513 U.S. 251.

New York Times v. United States. 1971. 403 U.S. 713.

Osborn v. U.S. Bank. 1824. 9 Wheaton 738.

Paris Adult Theatre I v. Slaton. 1973. 413 U.S. 49.

Petition of Doe. 1994. 638 N.E. 2d 181 (Ill. Sup. Ct.).

Planned Parenthood v. Casey. 1992. 505 U.S. 833.

Roe v. Wade. 1973. 410 U.S. 113.

United States v. Concepcion. 1992. 795 F. Supp. 1262 (E.D.N.Y.).

United States v. Dixon. 1993. 509 U.S. 688.

United States v. Nixon. 1974. 418 U.S. 683.

Vasquez v. Harris. 1992. 503 U.S. 1000.

Webster v. Reproductive Health Services. 1989. 492 U.S. 490.

Whren v. United States. 1996. 135 L. Ed. 2d 89.

Name Index

Dodd, Lawrence C., 15n, 27n, 147
Dolbeare, Kenneth M., 24, 148
Donley, Richard E., 100n
Dorff, Robert H., 108–9
Dorsen, Norman, 74
Douglas, William O., 1, 25, 41,
    43–44, 113
Downing, James W., 139
Downing, Rondal G., 31, 33, 145
Downs, Anthony, 103
Dubois, Philip L., 31, 77, 115n, 145n
Ducat, Craig R., 39, 59, 115n
Dudley, Robert L., 39
Dworkin, Ronald, 66

Eagly, Alice H., 136, 139
Easterbrook, Frank H., 66
Eckstein, Harry, 12
Edwards, Harry T., 67
Eisenberg, Theodore, 68
Eisenstein, James, 7, 24, 129
Eisler, Kim Isaac, 1, 43, 111, 113
Elder, Harold W., 134
Ellsberg, Daniel, 142n
Elster, Jon, 5, 100–101
Emmert, Craig F., 28, 31, 63
Enelow, James M., 91, 111
Engle, Randi A., 140
Epstein, Lee, 15, 18, 26, 42, 43n,
    50–51, 53, 64, 75, 82n, 93–94, 106,
    109–10, 122, 132, 139, 142n, 146
Epstein, Richard A., 14–15, 27,
    120n, 134
Erikson, Robert S., 49
Eskridge, William N., Jr., 27, 71n,
    90n, 97, 103, 119n, 120, 122, 132,
    134
Esler, Michael, 76, 142n
Etheredge, Lloyd S., 139n

Fararo, Thomas J., 131, 133
Farber, Daniel A., 131n
Farney, Darrell L., 31
Farquharson, Robin, 90
Farr, James, 142n
Fazio, Russell H., 139
Feeley, Malcolm M., 45, 145
Feige, Edgar L., 9n
Feldman, Stanley, 140

Felitti, Eve M., 65
Fenno, Richard F., 12, 27n, 90n,
    112, 149
Ferejohn, John A., 6, 12, 60, 94n,
    132–34, 143n
Fiorina, Morris P., 27n, 34, 99,
    132–33
Fishbein, Martin, 139
Fisher, Marc, 54
Fisher, William W., III, 64
Fiske, Susan T., 12, 14n, 136,
    138–40
Flango, Victor Eugene, 59, 84, 115n
Flemming, Roy B., 7, 24, 49–50, 129
Foley, James P., 87
Fortas, Abe, 2, 43–45
Fowler, Linda L., 144
Frank, Jerome, 68, 118n
Frank, John P., 43, 48
Frank, Robert H., 15, 100
Frankfurter, Felix, 1, 20n, 25, 57,
    59, 103, 129, 137
Franklin, Kurt A., 97n
Frase, Richard S., 86
Freedman, David A., 9n
Frese, Michael, 12
Frickey, Philip P., 90n, 119–20, 131n
Fried, Charles, 117
Friedman, Jeffrey, 132–33, 142
Friedman, Milton, 5
Fuld, Stanley H., 54
Funder, David C., 139
Furnham, Adrian, 12

Galanter, Marc, 24, 114
Gallant, Jack L., 137
Gansle, Gary, 111n
Gardner, Roy, 91n
Gates, John B., 11n, 74–75
Gely, Rafael, 27n, 97, 119–21, 132
George, Tracey E., 53, 75
Gerber, Elisabeth R., 139n
Gerhart, Eugene C., 43
Gertner, Robert H., 132n
Gibson, James L., 11, 18, 24, 38,
    84–85, 138, 146–47
Giesen, Bernhard, 7
Giles, Micheal W., 29, 93, 105
Gillman, Howard, 70

Ginsburg, Ruth Bader, 107
Glazer, Amihai, 98
Glendon, Mary Ann, 47
Glennon, Robert Jerome, 119n
Glick, Henry R., 19, 24, 28–29, 31,
    63, 69n, 84–85, 145n, 147
Goldberg, Arthur, 43
Goldman, Sheldon, 28, 31, 38, 40, 63
Gordon, Jeffrey N., 134
Gorton, Peter A., 148
Goshko, John M., 1
Gould, Stephen Jay, 5
Goulden, Joseph C., 33
Graham, Jean Ann, 12
Green, Donald P., 133, 143
Green, Justin, 77
Greenberg, Jeff, 65
Greenberg, Paul E., 30
Greenhouse, Joel B., 10
Greenwald, Anthony G., 9n
Gressman, Eugene, 46, 67
Griset, Pamala, 86
Grofman, Bernard, 135
Gross, Samuel R., 68
Grossman, Joel B., 11n, 59, 84, 114
Gruenfeld, Deborah H., 137
Gruhl, John, 24, 116
Gryski, Gerard S., 28

Haar, Charles M., 23n
Hagan, John, 86
Hagle, Timothy M., 39, 42, 93, 108
Haines, Charles Grove, 61
Haire, Susan, 28, 83, 116
Haley, James A., 30
Hall, Melinda Gann, 28–29, 44, 83,
    115, 132, 145, 147
Halpern, Stephen C., 27, 59, 146
Handberg, Roger, 26, 82n
Hansen, John Mark, 12
Hansen, Wendy L., 146
Hanson, Roger A., 68n
Harsanyi, John C., 48
Hastie, Reid, 140, 149
Hausegger, Lori, 122
Hawkes, Paul, 117
Hayes, Allison L., 28, 84
Haynie, Stacia L., 82n
Heckman, James J., 82n

Hedges, Larry V., 10
Heinzelmann, Fred, 87
Heiple, James, 1
Hempel, Carl G., 5
Hendry, David F., 9n
Henschen, Beth M., 97, 122
Hensley, Thomas R., 11n
Hermann, Margaret G., 16, 100n,
    138n
Heumann, Milton, 24, 85, 129
Hibbing, John R., 144
Higgins, E. Tory, 135
Higgins, Richard S., 61, 134
Hirsch, H. N., 1, 19, 103, 129,
    137–38
Hoekstra, Valerie, 139, 142n
Hogarth, Robin M., 133, 135–36
Holding, Reynolds, 99n
Horwitz, Morton J., 64
Howard, J. Woodford, Jr., 19,
    28–29, 62, 85, 105, 115n, 119,
    129
Huckfeldt, Robert, 142n
Hughes, Charles Evans, 43, 149

Ickes, William, 139
Ignagni, Joseph A., 49, 75, 97n, 122
Iyengar, Satish, 10

Jackson, Donald Dale, 25n
Jackson, Donald W., 34
Jackson, John E., 139n
Jackson, Robert, 43
Jacob, Herbert, 6, 11n, 24, 145
Jahnige, Thomas P., 38, 40
James, Dorothy B., 84
Jaros, Dean, 28
Jefferson, Thomas, 23n
Jeffries, John C., Jr., 47
Johnson, Charles A., 11n, 20n, 28,
    105n, 115–16, 118
Johnson, Lyndon, 2, 43, 45
Johnson, Renée J., 146
Johnston, David, 12
Judd, Charles M., 139

Kahn, Ronald, 26
Kahneman, Daniel, 98, 141
Kalman, Laura, 2, 44–45

Subject and Case Index